DAILY LIFE IN

THE OTTOMAN EMPIRE

Recent Titles in
The Greenwood Press Daily Life Through History Series

Chaucer's England, Second Edition
Jeffrey L. Forgeng and Will McLean

The Holocaust, Second Edition
Eve Nussbaum Soumerai and Carol D. Schulz

Civil War in America, Second Edition
Dorothy Denneen Volo and James M. Volo

Elizabethan England, Second Edition
Jeffrey L. Forgeng

The New Americans: Immigration since 1965
Christoph Strobel

The New Inuit
Pamela R. Stern

The Indian Wars
Clarissa W. Confer

The Reformation
James M. Anderson

The Aztecs, Second Edition
David Carrasco and Scott Sessions

The Progressive Era
Steven L. Piott

Women during the Civil Rights Era
Danelle Moon

Colonial Latin America
Ann Jefferson and Paul Lokken

DAILY LIFE IN

THE OTTOMAN EMPIRE

MEHRDAD KIA

The Greenwood Press Daily Life Through History Series

 GREENWOOD

AN IMPRINT OF ABC-CLIO, LLC
Santa Barbara, California • Denver, Colorado • Oxford, England

Library of Congress Cataloging-in-Publication Data

Kia, Mehrdad.
  Daily life in the Ottoman Empire / Mehrdad Kia.
      p. cm. — (The Greenwood Press daily life through history series)
  Includes bibliographical references and index.
ISBN 978-0-313-33692-8 (hardcopy : alk. paper) —
ISBN 978-0-313-06402-9 (ebook)
  1. Turkey—Civilization—1288–1918. 2. Turkey—Social
conditions—1288–1918. 3. Turkey—History—Ottoman Empire,
1288–1918. I. Title.
  DR432.K43 2011
  956'.015—dc23   2011016662

ISBN: 978-0-313-33692-8
EISBN: 978-0-313-06402-9

15 14 13 12 11   1 2 3 4 5

This book is also available on the World Wide Web as an eBook.
Visit www.abc-clio.com for details.

Greenwood
An Imprint of ABC-CLIO, LLC

ABC-CLIO, LLC
130 Cremona Drive, P.O. Box 1911
Santa Barbara, California 93116-1911

This book is printed on acid-free paper ∞

Manufactured in the United States of America

To
my mother, Kiadokht Kia

It is certain that Europeans . . . resident in Turkey [are] as ignorant of all that relates to her political economy, her system of government, and her moral ethics, as [if] they had never left their own country . . . If you succeed in prevailing on them to speak on the subject, they never progress beyond exanimate and crude details of mere external effects . . . It is a well-attested fact that the entrée of native houses, and intimacy with native families, are not only extremely difficult, but in most cases impossible to Europeans; hence the cause of the tissue of fables which, like those of Scheherazade, have created genii and enchanters . . . in every account of the East. The European mind has become so imbued with ideas of Oriental mysteriousness, mysticism, and magnificence, and it has been so long accustomed to pillow its faith on the marvels and metaphors of tourists, that it [is] to be doubted whether it will willingly cast off its old associations, and suffer itself to be undeceived.

Julia Pardoe, *The City of the Sultan*

CONTENTS

NOTE ON PRONUNCIATION, TRANSLITERATION, AND SPELLING

The multiplicity of languages used in the Ottoman Empire and the varieties of spelling that were adopted throughout centuries present a number of problems, making complete consistency impossible. With a few exceptions, I have used the modern Turkish spelling system. I have not, however, applied Turkish spellings and pronunciations to non-Turkish words. Thus, Sharif (Arabic) has not been spelled as Şerif (Turkish); and Shah (Persian), not Şah (Turkish).

c (Turkish)	j (English)
ç (Turkish)	ch (English)
ö (Turkish)	ö (German)
ş (Turkish)	sh (English)
ü (Turkish)	ü (German)

INTRODUCTION

Much has been written about the rise, decline, and fall of the Ottoman Empire and the achievements of its greatest and most charismatic rulers, Mehmed II (1444–1446, 1451–1481), the conqueror of Constantinople; Selim I (1512–1520), who brought the Arab Middle East and Egypt under Ottoman rule; and Süleyman the Magnificent (1520–1566), who led his armies to the gates of Vienna after conquering Belgrade and Budapest. Historians have also written extensively about the causes for the decline of the Ottoman state, which began at the end of the 16th century, and the military defeats that the empire suffered at the hands of European powers, forcing Ottoman sultans and statesmen to introduce administrative, political, social, economic, and educational reforms throughout the 19th century.

For nearly six centuries, the Ottoman dynasty ruled a vast empire that at the height of its power stretched from Budapest on the Danube to Basra at the mouth of the Persian Gulf, and from Crimea on the northern shores of the Black Sea to Tunis on the southern shores of the Mediterranean. In Europe, the empire comprised Crimea, Hungary, Podolia, Transylvania, Moldavia, Wallachia, Serbia, Montenegro, Bosnia, Herzegovina, Albania, Macedonia, Bulgaria, Greece, as well as the Aegean Isles, Crete, and Cyprus, while in Asia it ruled Anatolia, the Arab Middle East as far south as the

Persian Gulf and the Gulf of Aden, as well as parts of southern Caucasus. Finally, in North Africa, the Ottomans controlled Egypt, Libya (Tripoli and Benghazi), Tunisia, and Algeria.

The population of the empire included Turks, Tatars, Hungarians, Serbs, Montenegrins, Bosnians, Albanians, Romanians, Bulgarians, Greeks, Georgians, Circassians, Abkhazians, Armenians, Arabs, Berbers, Kurds, Jews, and many others. Each group possessed its own unique customs and traditions that distinguished it from others. The majority of the population in Anatolia, the Middle East, North Africa, and parts of the Balkans, such as Bosnia and Albania, was Muslim, while the majority of the population in the Balkans was Christian. The Jews lived predominantly in the urban centers of the empire. Thus, ethnic, linguistic, and religious diversity and heterogeneity constituted the most basic characteristic of the state. To write a comprehensive book on everyday life in the Ottoman Empire requires an in-depth study of the traditions, customs, and beliefs of all the communities that lived under Ottoman political and administrative control and whose cultures, habits, and manners, differed so widely. The present monograph, however, is a far more humble effort; it makes no pretense of using original documents or offering bold new interpretations. It is designed to provide the general reader with a series of selective representations of daily life in the Ottoman Empire.

The everyday life of the people of the Ottoman Empire changed significantly during the six centuries that extended from the formation of the state in the last decade of the 13th century to the collapse of the empire in the aftermath of the First World War. As the Ottoman dominion expanded from a small principality in western Anatolia to one of the largest and most powerful empires in the world, its increasingly diverse population grew, and patterns of social, economic, and cultural interaction underwent a dramatic transformation. This transformation was further intensified in the 18th and 19th centuries as Ottoman society was impacted by the rise of capitalism and a world economic system that battered down the walls of traditional and precapitalist social formations. The daily life of an Ottoman subject was greatly affected by the rise of market economy and the arrival of European ideas, goods, and customs.

It is beyond the scope of this book to include the social and cultural history of all the ethnic and linguistic communities who lived and worked as the subjects of the sultan and analyze the profound changes that the Ottoman society experienced throughout the six hundred years of its existence. After providing the reader with a brief historical overview of the Ottoman Empire in chapter 1, in chapter 2, I have discussed the role of the sultan and the imperial palace in the daily life of the empire. In chapter 3, I have made a short presentation on the Ottoman ruling elite, which managed the empire and ensured the smooth functioning of the highly complex and stratified Ottoman society that assigned exact functions to members of each social strata. From a discussion of the Ottoman ruling elite, the book moves to a brief presentation on three important social classes in the Ottoman society, namely the merchants, the craftsmen, and the peasant farmers. Throughout chapter 4, the reader gets a glimpse of everyday life in the rural and agricultural communities of the empire as well as the internal structure of the urban economy, including the central role played by the guilds. In chapter 5, I have analyzed the *millet* system, which divided the subjects of the sultan into religious communities, including the Orthodox Christians, the Armenians, and the Jews. From the non-Muslim communities, we move to a discussion in chapter 6 on the teachings and the role of Islam in the Ottoman Empire. As a religion that legislated and regulated all aspects of a Muslim's daily life, Islam had a profound and immediate impact on the social, economic, and cultural institutions of the empire. Building on our discussion of Islam in chapter 6, we move to a short presentation on Islamic education and law in chapter 7. Islam was not, however, the only cultural and spiritual force in the Ottoman Empire. Chapter 8 focuses on the Sufi or mystical orders, which enjoyed enormous popularity and influence in the Ottoman Empire, and, at times, challenged the cultural and ideological monopoly enjoyed by the Islamic religious establishment. From this discussion of religious and spiritual life, chapter 9 focuses on courtship and marriage, particularly among the Muslim communities of the empire, and chapter 10 deals with sex, family, childbirth, childrearing, circumcision, and divorce. In chapter 11, I have presented an overview of the rich and diverse Ottoman cuisine. Although each ethnic and religious community had its own rich culinary traditions, after several centuries of living together and interacting with neighbors who had also developed their own unique cuisine, a distinctive Ottoman cooking tradition emerged. From food and popular drinks, the book moves in chapter 12 to a discussion of popular sports that enjoyed an enormous following among all communities living in the Ottoman Empire. Finally, chapter 13 focuses on sickness, dying, and death in the Ottoman Empire, introducing the popular fears, superstitions, and healing methods prevalent among the empire's diverse communities.

CHRONOLOGY

1260–1310	The establishment of Turcoman principalities in western Anatolia.
1326	Ottomans capture Bursa.
1327	The first Ottoman silver coin (*akçe*) is minted.
1331	Ottoman conquest of Iznik (Nicaea).
1337	Ottoman conquest of Izmit (Nicomedia).
1354	Ottomans take Ankara and Gallipoli.
1361	Ottoman conquest of Edirne (Adrianople).
1363–1365	Ottoman conquest of southern Bulgaria and Thrace.
1371	Ottoman victory over the Serbs at Chermanon.
1385	Ottoman conquest of Sofia.
1387	Ottoman conquest of Thessaloniki (Salonika/Salonica).
1388	A coalition of Serbs, Bosnians, and Bulgarians defeat the Ottomans at Plošnik (Ploshnik).
1389	Battle of Kosovo Polje. Ottoman sultan Murad I is killed.
1389–1392	Ottoman conquest of Turcoman principalities of western Anatolia.

1394	Ottoman conquest of Thessaly.
1396	Bayezid I defeats a Crusader army at the Battle of Nicopolis.
1397	Bayezid I annexes Karaman.
1398	Ottoman conquest of the principality of Vidin.
1399	Ottoman conquest of the Mamluk-held cities of Malatya and Elbistan in the Euphrates valley.
1402	Timur defeats Bayezid I at the Battle of Ankara.
1402–1413	Interregnum. Sons of Bayezid fight for Ottoman throne.
1413	Mehmed I unifies Ottoman territories under his rule.
1413–1416	Revolt of Şeyh Bedreddin.
1423–1430	Ottoman-Venetian war.
1430	Ottomans capture Salonika.
1437	Ottoman conquest of the Turcoman principality of Hamidili.
1441–1442	John Hunyadi defeats the Ottomans in Transylvania.
1443–1468	Rebellion of George Kastrioti (Gjergi Kastrioti) also known as Iskender Beg (Skanderbeg) in northern Albania.
1444	Ottomans defeat a Crusader army at Varna.
1453	Ottoman conquest of Constantinople.
1459	Mehmed II orders the construction of Topkapi Palace.
1460–1461	Mehmed II orders the construction of the Covered Bazaar in Istanbul.
1460	Ottoman conquest of Morea.
1463	Ottomans capture Bosnia.
1469–1474	Ottoman pacification of Karaman.
1473	Mehmed II defeats Uzun Hasan, the chief of Aq Qoyunlu.
1478	Crimean Tatars accept Ottoman suzerainty.
1480	Ottoman conquest of Herzegovina.
1481	Death of Mehmed II.
1481–1483	War of Succession between Prince Bayezid and Prince Cem ends with Bayezid's victory.
1484	Bayezid II attacks Moldavia and captures Kilia and Akkerman.

1484–1491	Ottoman-Mamluk War.
1496	Ottomans enter Montenegro.
1497–1499	War with Poland.
1501	Shah Ismail seizes the throne of Iran and establishes the Safavid dynasty.
1504	Shah Ismail captures Baghdad.
1512	Selim I forces his father to abdicate.
1514	Selim I defeats Shah Ismail at the Battle of Chaldiran.
1516	Ottoman conquest of eastern Anatolia.
1516–1517	Selim I defeats the Mamluks and captures Syria and Egypt. The holy cities of Mecca and Medina fall under Ottoman rule.
1520–1566	Reign of Süleyman I.
1521	Ottomans capture Belgrade.
1522	Ottoman conquest of Rhodes.
1526	Süleyman I defeats the Hungarians at the Battle of Mohács.
1529	Süleyman I captures Buda.
1529	First Ottoman siege of Vienna.
1534–1555	War with Safavid Iran, culminating with the Treaty of Amasya.
1556	Construction of Süleymaniye mosque-complex begins.
1570	Ottomans capture Tunis and Nicosia.
1571	Ottomans are defeated at the Battle of Lepanto by the Holy League.
1571	Ottoman conquest of Cyprus.
1575	Selimiye mosque-complex completed in Edirne.
1578–1590	War with Safavid Iran.
1590s	Celali revolts against the Ottoman central government in Anatolia.
1593–1606	War with Habsburgs.
1596	Ottoman victory at Mezőkeresztes.
1603–1618	War with Safavid Iran.

1603	Iran re-conquers Tabriz.
1604	Iran captures Yerevan (Erivan), Kars, and Shirvan.
1606	Peace treaty between the Ottomans and Austrians at Zsitva-Torok.
1617	Sultan Ahmed Mosque in Istanbul is completed.
1623	Iranian forces capture Baghdad.
1624–1639	War with Safavid Iran.
1638	Murad IV captures Baghdad.
1644–1669	Ottoman war with Venice over Crete.
1656–1661	Mehmed Köprülü serves as grand vizier.
1660–1664	War with Habsburgs.
1661–1676	Fazil Ahmed Köprülü serves as grand vizier.
1663	Ottoman forces are defeated near St. Gotthard.
1671–1672	War against Poland.
1683	Second Ottoman siege of Vienna.
1686	Habsburg forces capture Buda.
1687	Venetian forces invade Greece.
1688	Habsburg forces capture Belgrade.
1690	Ottoman forces recapture Belgrade.
1697	Ottomans are defeated near Zenta.
1699	Treaty of Karlowitz.
1709–1714	Charles XII of Sweden seeks refuge at the Ottoman court after his defeat at the hands of the Russians at Poltava.
1710–1711	War against Russia.
1715–1718	War against the Habsburgs and Venice.
1720s	Tulip Period.
1722	Fall of the Safavid dynasty in Iran.
1724	Ottoman Empire and Russia agree to partition northern and western Iran.
1724–1746	Ottoman military campaigns in Iran.
1730	Patrona Halil uprising.

1739	Treaty of Belgrade.
1755	Nuruosmaniye Mosque is completed in Istanbul.
1768–1774	War with Russia culminates in the treaty of Küçük Kaynarca
1783	Russia annexes the Crimea.
1787–1792	War with Russia.
1788–1791	War with Austria.
1791	Selim III establishes the Nizam-i Cedid (New Army).
1798	French forces under Napoleon Bonaparte invade Egypt.
1799	Napoleon returns to France.
1805	Mohammad Ali (Mehmed Ali) is appointed governor of Egypt.
1807	Selim III is deposed.
1808	Selim III is murdered. Mustafa IV is deposed.
1808–1839	Reign of Mahmud II.
1820–1823	War against Qajar Iran.
1821–1830	Greek revolt.
1826	Mahmud II destroys the janissaries.
1828–1829	War against Russia.
1830–1831	First Ottoman census.
1830	France invades Algiers.
1830	Serbia is recognized as an autonomous principality.
1831	Mohammad Ali of Egypt invades Syria.
1833	Egyptian army arrives in Kütahya in western Anatolia after defeating Ottoman forces.
1833	Treaty of Hünkar Iskelesi with Russia.
1839	Ottoman troops are defeated by Egyptian forces at Nizip.
1839	Hatt-i Şerif-i Gülhane, the Noble Rescript of the Rose Garden, signals the beginning of the Tanzimat era.
1846	Istanbul's slave market is closed.
1853–1856	Crimean War.
1856	Hatt-i Hümayun (the Imperial Rescript of Reform) is issued.

1856	Treaty of Paris.
1863	Imperial Ottoman Bank is established.
1869	Opening of Suez Canal.
1876	First Ottoman constitution.
1877–1878	War against Russia.
1878	Treaty of San Stefano with Russia.
1878	Congress of Berlin.
1881	France establishes a protectorate over Tunisia.
1882	British forces invade and occupy Egypt.
1891	Hamidiye regiments are created to police eastern Anatolia.
1894	Violent clashes between Hamidiye regiments and local Armenians in Bitlis.
1896	Armenian Dashnak organization attacks Ottoman Bank headquarters in Istanbul.
1897	Ottoman-Greek war.
1897	Crete gains its autonomy.
1908	Young Turk revolution forces Abdülhamid II to restore the constitution.
1908	Austro-Hungarian Empire annexes Bosnia. Greece seizes the Island of Crete. Bulgaria unifies with Eastern Rumelia.
1909	Abdülhamid II is deposed.
1911	Italy occupies Tripoli.
1912–1913	First Balkan War: Greece, Serbia, Montenegro, and Bulgaria invade Ottoman treaty. Edirne is captured by Bulgarian forces.
1913	Second Balkan War: Ottoman forces recapture Edirne.
1914–1918	First World War: Ottoman Empire is allied with Germany and Austro-Hungarian Empire.
1915	Deportation of Armenians from eastern Anatolia.
1915	Ottoman victory at Gallipoli.
1915	Sykes-Picot Agreement partitions the Ottoman Empire between British and French spheres of influence.
1916	Arab Revolt backed by the British starts in Hejaz.

1918	Moudros Armistice.
1918	Allied forces occupy Istanbul.
1919	Mustafa Kemal arrives in Samsun and commences the Turkish national liberation movement.
1920	Grand National Assembly is convened in Ankara.
1920	Treaty of Sèvres partitions the Ottoman Empire.
1921–1922	Turkish national movement fights and defeats Greek forces in western Anatolia.
1922	Mudanya Armistice.
1922	Grand National Assembly abolishes Ottoman sultanate.
1923	Treaty of Lausanne.
1923	Republic of Turkey is established.
1924	Institution of caliphate is abolished, and the members of the Ottoman royal family are exiled.

1

HISTORICAL OVERVIEW

The Ottoman state was born as a small principality in western Anatolia during the last two decades of the 13th century. As with other Turkish chieftains who had settled in the region, the family of Osman (1281?–1324/1326), the founder of the Ottoman Empire, arrived as nomadic tribesmen from Central Asia. Turcoman tribes had been settling in Anatolia since 1071, when the Seljuk Turks defeated the Greek Byzantine Empire at the battle of Manzikert (Malazgird). The victory at Manzikert destroyed Byzantine defenses and allowed Turcoman tribesmen from Central Asia and Iran to push westward and settle in Anatolia. In 1087, a branch of the Seljuk dynasty established itself in central and eastern Anatolia. The Turcoman chiefs, who settled in the region, swore their allegiance and paid annual tribute to the Rum Seljuks, who ruled from their capital, the town of Konya, in central Anatolia. When the Mongols defeated the Seljuks at the battle of Köse Dagh in 1243, Turcoman principalities such as Menteşe, Aydin, Saruhan, and Ottoman, emerged as autonomous fiefdoms that paid tribute to a new master, the Il Khanid Mongols of Iran. Toward the end of the 13th century, as Mongol power began to decline, the Turcoman chiefs assumed greater independence.

FOUNDERS OF THE OTTOMAN STATE

The founder of the Ottoman state, Osman, began his career as a *gazi,* or a warrior for Islam, who waged holy war on the Byzantine state from his small principality in the district of Sögüt in western Anatolia. Osman's son and successor, Orhan (1324/1326–1362) attacked and conquered the important urban center of Bursa in 1326, proclaiming it as the Ottoman capital. He used his newly acquired territory to capture the towns of Nicaea (Iznik) in 1331 and Nicomedia (Izmit) in 1337. In 1354, the Ottomans crossed into Europe and established a foothold on the Gallipoli Peninsula while at the same time pushing east and taking Ankara on the dry Anatolian plain. In 1355, Stephen Dušan (Dushan), the ruler of Serbia, died, and his empire disintegrated, allowing the Ottomans to push farther into the Balkans and capture the important town of Adrianople (Edirne) in 1361. Shortly after ascending the throne, the third Ottoman sultan, Murad I (1362–1389), moved against Thrace and southern Bulgaria. In response, the Pope declared a crusade. The Serbs also called for a united front of all Orthodox Christian rulers. Despite growing resistance against the Ottomans, Murad I's armies scored an impressive victory at Chermanon on the Maritsa River in 1371, seizing significant territory in Bulgaria, Macedonia, and southern Serbia. To neutralize the threat posed by rival Turcoman principalities in Anatolia, Murad I also attacked and annexed Germiyan and Hamidili. Meanwhile, the Ottomans pushed farther into Bulgaria and took Sofia in 1385. In the same year, they annexed Nish, and in 1387, they took Thessaloniki (Salonika) in modern-day northern Greece.

Once again, the Christian powers of southeast Europe tried to set aside their rivalries and organize an anti-Ottoman coalition. A joint force of Serbs, Bosnians, and Bulgarians defeated the Ottomans at Plošnik (Ploshnik) in 1388, but the defeat did not slow down the pace of Ottoman expansion. After occupying northern Bulgaria, Murad I moved against the Balkan states that had unified under the leadership of the Serbian prince, Lazar (1371–1389). In June 1389, the Ottoman forces defeated the Christian coalition at Kosovo-Polje (Field of the Blackbirds). Both Murad I and Lazar died on the battlefield.

The victory at Kosovo-Polje allowed the new Ottoman sultan, Bayezid I (1389–1402), to continue with the conquest of the Balkans. Skopje, in Macedonia, was taken in 1391, and Ottoman forces entered Thessaly in 1394. With the conquest of northern Bulgaria, the ruler of Wallachia, Mircea the Old (1386–1418), was forced to accept Ottoman sovereignty in 1395. Bayezid's forces were now in a position to raid Hungary and Albania. Meanwhile, in the east, the sultan annexed Karaman in southwestern Anatolia in 1396–1397.

The emergence of an Ottoman-dominated Balkans posed a direct threat to the Hungarian state, which viewed Serbia as a buffer. Thus, when Pope Boniface IX (1389–1404) called for a Christian crusade against the Ottomans, the Hungarian monarch Sigismund (1387–1437) assumed leadership of the Christian army. Bayezid rushed back from Anatolia to confront the large crusader force that was approaching the shores of the Danube. The two armies clashed at Nicopolis in September 1396, where the Ottomans scored an impressive victory. Thousands of Christian knights died, either on the battlefield or as they tried to cross the Danube. Bayezid built on this victory by annexing the principality of Vidin in 1398. Confident of his power in the west, the sultan shifted his focus to Anatolia and the threat posed by the Mamluk state that ruled Egypt and parts of the Arab Middle East from its capital in Cairo. In 1399, he captured the towns of Malatya and Albistan in the Euphrates valley.

Bayezid's drive to expand Ottoman territories in the east coincided with the rise of the world conqueror, Timur, who had created a vast empire extending from Central Asia to India and Iran. In 1400–1401, Timur moved his forces toward Anatolia, sacking Sivas and challenging the Ottoman sultan to a confrontation. Enraged by Timur's condescending attitude and insulting language, and confident of his ability to defeat the Central Asian adventurer, Bayezid moved his forces eastward. The critical battle took place in July 1402 at Ankara, where Timur's army routed the Ottoman forces and captured Bayezid and his sons. The defeat at Ankara brought the Ottoman state to the brink of extinction. Timur pushed his conquests to Smyrna (Izmir) on the eastern shores of the Aegean Sea and restored the independence of the Turcoman principalities conquered by the Ottomans. He also granted Bayezid's sons small principalities in Anatolia and the Balkans so that they would fight among themselves for control of what was left of their father's empire. Thus began the period known as *Fetret,* or Interregnum, which lasted from 1402 to 1413. After a series of campaigns against his brothers, Mehmed, who ruled Amasya in northern Anatolia, emerged as the new ruler of the Ottoman state.

Mehmed I (1413–1421) and his successor Murad II (1421–1444; 1446–1451) spent much of their reigns suppressing internal revolts staged by members of the Ottoman dynasty and restoring the power of the central government by subduing the Turcoman principalities, which had regained their independence under Timur. The Ottoman rulers also resumed their westward march into the heartland of the Balkans. Once again, a crusade was organized, this time under the leadership of Vladislav (1434–1444), the ruler of Poland and Hungary. Serbia, led by George Branković, also joined, but the true leader of the anti-Ottoman coalition was the governor of Transylvania, John Hunyadi, who fought for the Hungarian king. Initially, Hunyadi was successful in his campaigns against the Ottoman forces and pushed them out of Bulgaria. When the Turks struck back, however, the Christian forces suffered a devastating defeat at Varna in 1444. King Vladislav died on the battlefield, and the Christian effort to halt Ottoman occupation of the Balkans came to a sudden end.

ZENITH OF OTTOMAN POWER

Building on the victory at Varna, Murad I's son and successor, Mehmed II (1444–1446; 1451–1481), embarked on an ambitious campaign to complete the Ottoman conquest of the Balkans. The first target of the new sultan was, however, the city of Constantinople, which fell after a two-month siege on 29 May 1453. The conquest of the capital of eastern Christianity allowed the Ottomans to establish their control over maritime trade routes that connected the Black Sea to the Mediterranean, one of the most important avenues of international commerce in the world.

Mehmed II's ambitious campaign to impose Ottoman rule over the entire Balkan Peninsula began with the capture of Morea (Peloponnese Peninsula or Peloponnesus) in southern Greece in 1458, and the conquest of Bosnia in 1463. In sharp contrast to other Christian-populated regions of the Balkans, there was a large-scale conversion to Islam in Bosnia. As the local landowning nobility converted to Islam, many urban and rural communities followed suit.

The conquest of Greece and Bosnia set the stage for an invasion of Albania. To the northeast, the Tatars of Crimea accepted the suzerainty of the sultan in 1475, allowing the Ottomans to extend their authority to the northern shores of the Black Sea. In 1480, Herzegovina was conquered. Despite his best efforts, however, Mehmed II could not capture the strategic fortress of Belgrade, which would have paved the path to the conquest of Hungary. He also faced fierce resistance in Albania, where a local hero, George Kastrioti (Gjergi Kastrioti), also known as Iskender Beg (Skanderbeg), fought heroically against Ottoman forces from 1443 until his death in 1468.

To the east, the Ottomans scored a decisive victory over the Aq Qoyunlu Turcomans and their chief, Uzun Hasan, who ruled Iran and southern Caucasus, at the battle of Başkent in 1473. When the Venetian allies of Aq Qoyunlu attacked the Aegean coast and the island of Lesbos, the Ottomans struck back and laid siege to Venetian fortresses in northwestern Albania, including Shkodër (Scutari), which was captured in 1479. By 1481, when Mehmed II died, the Ottoman forces had landed at Otranto in anticipation of a full-fledged invasion of Italy.

Prince Bayezid, after defeating his brother Cem (who was the favorite of their father), ascended the Ottoman throne as Bayezid II (1481–1512) and embarked on a campaign to extend Ottoman rule to the western and northern shores of the Black Sea by attacking Moldavia and conquering the fortresses of Kilia and Akkerman in 1484. The invasion brought the Poles into confrontation with the Ottomans. The wars with Hungary and Venice also continued until the end of Bayezid II's reign. In the east, the conflict between the Ottomans and the Mamluks, who ruled Egypt and Syria, was concluded in 1491 when the two powers agreed to sign a peace treaty.

Meanwhile, a new and far more threatening menace was emerging in the east. The rise of the Shia Safavid dynasty in Iran forced the Ottomans to shift their focus to eastern Anatolia where the power and popularity of the Iranian dynast Shah Ismail (1501–1524) posed a direct threat to the authority of the sultan. Under the charismatic leadership of their shah, the Safavid forces occupied Baghdad in 1504 and pushed into southeastern Anatolia. The failure of the aging and ailing Bayezid II to organize an effective response to the threat posed by the Safavids allowed one of his sons, Selim, to seize power in 1512.

It was during the reign of Selim I (1512–1520) that the Ottoman Empire emerged as the most powerful state in the Middle East and North Africa. First, Selim I defeated the Safavids at the battle of Chaldiran in August 1514 and occupied the strategically important province of Azerbaijan. He then attacked and defeated the Mamluk armies, first in Syria in 1516, and then in Egypt in 1517, thus bringing the Arab lands of the Middle East, including the two holy cities of Mecca and Medina, under Ottoman rule.

Egypt emerged as the largest and the most lucrative province of the Ottoman Empire, sending the largest amount of taxes to the central treasury in Istanbul. The conquest of Egypt allowed the Ottomans "to participate in the traffic in African gold, which passed through Ethiopia and the Sudan, and in the spice trade with Christian countries."[1] The Ottomans also used their military and naval presence in Egypt to impose their hegemony over the greater Red Sea region and annex Abyssinia that "extended from the southern border of Egypt all the way to the Horn of Africa, encompassing most of present-day Sudan, Djibouti on the horn of Africa, and coastal Ethiopia."[2]

When Selim I's son, Süleyman (1520–1566), succeeded his father, the territorial expansion of the empire continued. The new sultan attacked and captured Belgrade in 1521, using the conflict and personal jealousies between the Habsburg King, Charles V, and the French monarch, Francis I, to his advantage. A year later, the Ottomans occupied Rhodes despite fierce resistance from the Knights of St. John, who had ruled the island since the 13th century. Using Belgrade as a territorial base, Süleyman invaded and occupied Hungary after defeating King Louis II at the battle of Mohács in 1526. With the disappearance of the Hungarian state, the Habsburgs emerged as the northern neighbors of the Ottoman Empire and the power most threatened by Turkish expansionism. The expected attack on the Habsburg capital, Vienna, came in September 1529, but the arrival of the rainy season made the roads impassable for the Ottomans, forcing Süleyman to abandon the siege.

Meanwhile, to the east, the sultan pushed the frontiers of his empire by attacking Iran in 1535 and occupying Iraq and the Iranian cities of Tabriz and Hamedan. After several successful campaigns against Iran, the Ottomans forced the Safavid dynasty to sign the Treaty of Amasya in May 1555, ceding much of Azerbaijan and the southern Caucasus to the Ottoman Empire. Meanwhile, Süleyman ordered the construction of a naval force and appointed the legendary Hayreddin Paşa as his chief admiral (*kapudan-i derya*). Hayreddin Paşa captured Tunis in 1533 and established Ottoman hegemony on the southern shores of the Mediterranean. Finally, to the south, the Ottomans extended their rule in the Arab world by occupying Sana'a, the capital of Yemen in 1547.

Some historians have identified the reign of Süleyman's son, Selim II (1566–1574), as the beginning of the long process of decline, which culminated with the defeat of Ottoman forces outside Vienna in 1683 and the gradual retreat of the Ottoman state from southeast Europe. The decline of the empire did not, however, happen overnight. The process was already under way during the reign of

Süleyman the Magnificent, but it did not manifest itself to outsiders until a century later.

MILITARY CHALLENGE FROM IRAN

The first signs of Ottoman military weakness appeared at the beginning of the 17th century on the battlefields of eastern Anatolia as a rejuvenated Iranian state under the charismatic Shah Abbas (1587–1629) attacked and defeated Ottoman forces in Azerbaijan and the south Caucasus. The Iranians moved at blazing speed, catching Ottoman garrisons in Azerbaijan and the Caucasus by surprise and capturing the city of Tabriz in 1603 and Nakhchivan in 1604.[3] Shortly after, Yerevan (Erivan) and Kars were sacked.[4] Using Armenia as his base, Shah Abbas invaded and occupied the entire eastern Caucasus as far north as Shirvan.[5]

The crisis caused by the campaigns of Shah Abbas coincided with the death of Mehmed III (1595–1603) and the accession of Ahmed I (1603–1617), who mobilized a large force against Iran.[6] When the two armies clashed in September 1605, however, the Iranians scored an impressive victory against the larger Ottoman force.[7] In addition to Azerbaijan and the Caucasus, the Safavids captured southeastern Anatolia and Iraq. The defeat undermined the Ottoman rule in Anatolia and the Arab world. Kurdish and Turcoman tribal chiefs defected, and a series of revolts erupted, particularly in Syria, where the Kurds staged an uprising against the Ottoman state.[8]

During the reign of Murad IV (1623–1640), the Ottomans tried to restore peace and order in Anatolia and remove Iranian forces from Iraq. After several long campaigns against Iran, the Ottoman army captured the city of Baghdad and re-established Ottoman control over the Arab Middle East that lasted until the end of the First World War. In May 1639, on the plain of Zahab near the town of Qasr-i Shirin/Kasr-i Şirin (in present-day western Iran), the Ottoman Empire and Iran signed a peace treaty that ended nearly one hundred forty years of hostility between the two Islamic states.[9] The treaty established the Ottoman sultan as the master of Iraq while the Safavids maintained control over Azerbaijan and southern Caucasus.[10]

KÖPRÜLÜ VIZIERS

When Murad IV died in February 1640, he was succeeded by his brother Ibrahim (1640–1648), who had lived his entire life in the royal harem and had no training or experience in ruling an empire. While Ibrahim became increasingly infatuated with the pleasures of the inner palace, his mother, his tutor, the grand vizier, the chief eunuch, and janissary commanders, vied for power and influence. When Ibrahim was murdered and his son, Mehmed IV (1648–1687), ascended the Ottoman throne, the new ruler remained a pawn at the hands of those who surrounded him—his grandmother, mother, the grand vizier, and the chief eunuch.

In 1656, the financial crisis, political chaos, and the failure of the Ottoman navy to lift the Venetian siege of the capital, finally forced the sultan to appoint Mehmed Köprülü as grand vizier, thus inaugurating the rise to power of a family of Köprülü ministers, who tried to restore the authority of the Ottoman state by imposing peace and order and introducing badly needed reforms.

The son of an Albanian father, the first Köprülü grand vizier, Mehmed Köprülü, had served many masters and patrons both within the palace and in various provinces, acquiring a reputation for competence and honesty. He and his son, Köprülüzade Fazil Ahmed, who succeeded his father in 1661 and dominated Ottoman politics until 1676, crushed antigovernment revolts in Anatolia and re-established the authority of the central government in the provinces. Both father and son pursued a foreign policy aimed at checking the Habsburg intervention in Transylvania and defeating the alliance of Catholic forces known as the Holy League, which had been organized under the leadership of the Pope.[11] When Christian and Ottoman forces clashed near the village of St. Gotthard in August 1664, the Ottomans were defeated and lost many more men and much more equipment than the troops of the Holy League, which included Habsburg, Spanish, and French units. When the peace treaty was negotiated at Vasvár, however, the Habsburgs agreed to evacuate their troops, and Ottoman rule over Transylvania was once again secured.

When Köprülüzade Fazil Ahmed died in 1676, his brother-in-law, Merzifonlu Kara Mustafa Paşa, succeeded him. The new grand vizier pursued the policy of the two previous Köprülüs, focusing his energies on checking Russian advances on the northern shores of the Black Sea and crushing the Habsburg's military machine. Convinced that the Habsburg military was on the verge of collapse and encouraged by the French, who viewed an Ottoman invasion as essential to their victory in the west, Kara Mustafa Paşa moved with a large army against Vienna in June 1683. By July, the Habsburg capital was under Ottoman siege. The Habsburg emperor had, however, organized a coalition that included Jan Sobieski of Poland, the Pope, the Spanish, and the Portuguese. In a fierce battle on September 12, the Ottoman forces were routed and 10,000 men were killed on the battlefield.[12] The Ottoman army disintegrated and lost any semblance of organization and discipline, leaving behind its heavy cannon and badly needed supplies.[13] The shocked Kara Mustafa Paşa tried to rally his army in Belgrade, but it was already too late. His enemies in Istanbul had convinced the sultan that his chief minister was solely responsible for the humiliating debacle at the gates of Vienna. On 25 December 1683, the grand vizier was executed by the order of his royal master.[14]

MILITARY DEFEATS IN EUROPE AND LOSS OF CONFIDENCE

The execution of Kara Mustafa Paşa only exacerbated the political and military crisis. Without a commander capable of rallying the troops and facing a shortage of equipments and supplies, the Ottoman forces fell into disarray. Worse, a new Holy League was formed in 1684 that included the Habsburgs, Venice, Poland, the Pope, Malta, Tuscany, and later Muscovy (Russia). After repeated attempts to regain the territories they had lost, in November 1698 an Ottoman delegation began to negotiate a peace treaty with representatives of the Holy League powers.[15] According to the Treaty of Karlowitz, signed in January 1699, the Habsburgs remained in control of Hungary and Transylvania while the Ottomans maintained their rule over the Banat of Temeşvár. Poland received Podolia (Podole), and Russia established its rule over Azov and the territory north of the Dniester. Venice emerged as the master of Dalmatia, the Morea, and several strategic islands in the Aegean.[16] According to the terms of the treaty, the sultan was also forced to guarantee freedom of religion for his Catholic subjects. Thus, the Ottoman Empire entered the 18th century in turmoil and decline. The past glory of its able and charismatic sultans had become, by 1700, a distant memory. Long wars against the Habsburgs, Venice, Poland, and Russia had drained the resources of the state, which could not even pay the salaries of its officials and troops. Consequently, corruption and nepotism became rampant. Against this background, the Ottoman elite once again appealed to a member of the Köprülü family to save the empire. Amcazade Hüseyin Paşa became the grand vizier in September 1697 and embarked on another series of reforms aimed at reducing the financial burdens of the state without imposing heavier taxes on the peasantry. But, as would happen again and again over the next two hundred years, the new chief minister ran into formidable opposition from the traditional elite, who forced him to step down in September 1702.[17]

CONFRONTING THE HABSBURG MONARCHY AND RUSSIA

Once again, the process of decline accelerated. Taxes remained uncollected, and government officials and troops were not paid their wages. The treasury was drained, and corruption spread to all levels of the civil administration. The reigning sultan, Mustafa II (1695–1703), spent much of his time in Edirne and did not even realize the severity of the political and economic crisis in the capital, where the troops, who were being sent on a military campaign to the southern Caucasus, refused to obey orders unless they were paid. With the army taking the lead, artisans, shopkeepers, merchants, and students from various religious schools joined in a rebellion in July 1703. Mustafa II responded by dismissing his grand vizier, but the rebels, emboldened by the concessions from the sultan, began a march from Istanbul to Edirne. The sultan himself led his army against the rebels, but the fatal clash was avoided when the troops marching with the sultan defected and joined the rebels, forcing Mustafa II to abdicate in favor of his brother, Ahmed III (1703–1730).

The Ottomans tried to buy time and reorganize their army by keeping the empire out of war. Every effort was made to increase the revenue generated by the central government and reduce state expenditures. The memory of recent defeats and the humiliating Treaty of Karlowitz were still fresh in the minds of many Ottoman officials who wished to avoid another military debacle. The Ottoman refusal to initiate a military campaign, however, emboldened the Russian tsar, Peter the Great, who attacked and defeated a European ally of the sultan, Charles XII of Sweden, at Poltava in the summer of 1709. The Russians then moved their forces against the Ottoman Empire.

Fortunately for the Ottomans, the Habsburgs did not provide any support to Peter. With princes of Wallachia and Moldavia reneging on their promise to provide support for his troops, Peter, who had crossed the Pruth into Moldavia in July 1711, was forced to retreat. As the Russian army was about to cross the Pruth on its return journey, however, the Ottoman forces struck and surrounded the tsar and his troops. The founder of modern Russia and his army were at the mercy of the Ottoman grand vizier, who could have annihilated them in one blow. Recognizing the severity of his situation, Peter promised to surrender his cannonry, return the Ottoman-held territories he had occupied, and remove the forts he had built along the frontier with the Ottoman Empire. In return, the Ottomans allowed Russian merchants to trade freely in their territory and agreed to mediate a peace treaty between Russia and Sweden.[18]

One of the most important implications of the Russo-Ottoman war was the change in the political structure of the principalities. The secret negotiations between the princes of Wallachia and Moldavia and the Russian government convinced the sultan that he should remove the native princes and replace them with governors (*hospodars*) appointed directly by the sultan.[19] New governors were selected from among the Greek Phanariote families of Istanbul, who played an important role within the Ottoman state as dragomans (interpreters and translators) because of their diplomatic and linguistic abilities, which included a knowledge of Turkish and several European languages.[20] As these new governors rose to power, the native populations in Wallachia and Moldavia began to develop a deep resentment toward the ascendancy of the Greek language and culture within their administrative system.[21]

Despite the Ottoman peace with Russia, the internal court intrigues continued. The advocates of peace between Russia and the Ottoman Empire triumphed when a new treaty was signed between the two powers in June 1713. The tsar promised to abandon the territories he had occupied on the northern shores of the Black Sea, withdraw his forces from Poland, and allow Charles XII of Sweden to return to his country.[22] The Russian retreat only emboldened the anti-Venice war party, which began to advocate fresh military campaigns to recapture the Morea in southern Greece. While the Ottoman forces attacked Venetian positions and regained control over the Morea in 1715, their advances against Croatia forced the Habsburgs to ally with the Venetians and declare war on the sultan.

Once again, confrontation with the Habsburg army proved to be disastrous for the Ottomans, whose forces were routed at Petrovaradin in August 1716. The Ottoman defenses collapsed, and they lost Temeşvár in September 1716, followed by Belgrade, which was taken by the Habsburgs in August 1717. These demoralizing defeats undermined the position of the war party in the court and allowed the sultan to appoint his closest advisor, Nevşehirli Damad Ibrahim Paşa, as his new grand vizier in May 1718.

Peace negotiations resulted in the signing of the Treaty of Passarowitz in July 1718. The Habsburgs received the Banat of Temeşvár and northern Serbia, including Belgrade and Oltenia (Wallachia west of the river Olt).[23] They also received assurances that their merchants could operate freely in the sultan's domains. Moreover, Catholic priests regained old privileges that allowed the Habsburg emperor to interfere in the internal affairs of the Ottoman Empire by acting as the champion and protector of the Catholic community.[24]

THE TULIP PERIOD

The new grand vizier, Ibrahim Paşa, purged the sultan's inner circle and installed his own men in key positions within the royal harem. To focus the sultan's attention on sexual desires and personal fantasies, he ordered the construction of a palace named Saadabad (Place of Joy), which was to serve as the center for various royal entertainments. Designed after the Palace of Fontainebleau (Château de Fontainebleau) outside Paris, Saadabad emerged as the model for other palaces later built by the wealthy members of the ruling elite along the banks of the Bosphorus. Ibrahim Paşa himself built a palace on the Anatolian side of the strait. It contained gardens and fountains in the French style.

The tulip emerged as the popular flower of the time, which later came to be known as Lale Devri (the Tulip Period).[25] During late night garden parties, turtles with candles on their backs moved through the tulip beds, while entertainers, including poets and musicians, performed their latest lyrics and songs for a dazzled audience that included foreign dignitaries and diplomats.[26] If the lower classes could not afford to build palaces with gardens and fountains, they could still enjoy the increasing number of coffeehouses that served as centers of public entertainment.[27]

The grand vizier, Ibrahim Paşa, understood that the empire needed to use diplomacy as the principal means of resolving conflict, reserving warfare as the last resort. He dispatched Ottoman ambassadors to European capitals, where they served not only as diplomats but also as informants who visited factories, hospitals, and zoos, reporting back to him on the latest European fort building techniques and other innovations.[28] One of these innovations was the first printing press, which was introduced to the Ottoman

Empire in 1727, and was immediately opposed by the religious establishment and the scribes who feared that it would put an end to their relevance in society. The grand vizier silenced the opposition by promising that the printing press would only be used for nonreligious publications, particularly in the arts and sciences.[29]

A crisis in Iran and Ottoman intervention in that country's internal affairs brought the Tulip Period to a sudden end. Ottoman–Iranian relations had remained peaceful following the campaigns of Murad IV and the signing of the Treaty of Qasr-i Shirin in 1639. In October 1722, however, an Afghan army, which had rebelled against the Safavid monarchy in Iran, sacked the Iranian capital, Isfahan, and deposed the reigning shah, Sultan Husayn.[30] The sudden collapse of the Safavid state created opportunities as well as anxieties for the Ottomans. The sultan and his grand vizier could use the vacuum created by the disintegration of the Safavid state to occupy Iran's western provinces and increase the revenue collected by the central government. But Ahmed III was not the only sovereign determined to conquer this valuable territory. Having triumphed over Sweden, the Russian tsar Peter the Great was determined to profit from the sudden disappearance of the Safavid dynasty in Iran, a country that could serve Russia as a land bridge to the warm waters of the Persian Gulf and the riches of India.

Despite early victories in Iran, the Ottomans soon ran into trouble after the Iranian leader, Nader Qoli (soon to become Nader Shah), struck back and pushed Ottoman forces out of western Iran in 1730. The decision to start a new campaign against Iran ignited an urban rebellion in Istanbul. The leader of the revolt was Patrona Halil, a member of the janissary corps, who denounced the sultan and his grand vizier as incompetent and corrupt. The rebels succeeded in forcing the sultan to dismiss his chief minister and eventually order his execution. The revolt, however, did not subside. Emboldened by their initial success, the rebels demanded the abdication of the sultan in favor of another member of the Ottoman ruling family. Without any power to resist the rebels, the palace deposed Ahmed III and replaced him with Mahmud I (1730–1754). A few weeks later, the new sultan invited Patrona Halil to the palace, where he was murdered by the royal guards. His followers and supporters were also put to death. Meanwhile, the war with Iran continued with attacks and counter attacks from both sides until 1746, when the two Muslim states agreed to sign a peace treaty that restored the borders that had been stipulated by the Treaty of Qasr-i Shirin in 1639.

THREAT FROM RUSSIA

In the last years of Mahmud I's reign, as well as the reigns of the next two sultans, Osman III (1754–1757) and Mustafa III (1757–1774), the Ottomans declined to play a role in the War of Austrian Succession (1740–1748) and the Seven Years' War (1756–1763).[31] Even the murder of the Iranian monarch, Nader Shah, in 1747, could not entice them to invade their old Shia nemesis to the east. Instead of using the long period of peace to reorganize the central administration and the army, however, the Ottomans fell into a deep sleep again. They were awakened from it in 1768, when Russia, under Catherine the Great (1762–1796), embarked on an aggressive campaign to establish her rule on the northern shores of the Black Sea.

After several initial successes against the Russians, the Ottoman forces suffered a devastating defeat in the summer of 1769. The victory allowed the tsarist forces to occupy Wallachia and Moldavia. A Russian naval force also attacked from the west and sank the Ottoman fleet, which had anchored at Çeşme, in 1770. After six years of war and intermittent negotiations, the Ottomans signed the peace treaty of Küçük Kaynarca with Russia in 1774. The treaty forced the new Ottoman sultan, Abdülhamid I (1774–1789), who came to the throne on the death of Mustafa III, to accept the independence of Crimea. In 1783, the Russians annexed the Crimea and established themselves as the dominant naval force in the Black Sea.

The devastating loss of the Crimea did not end the confrontation with Russia. Conflict between the two powers erupted again in 1787. A year later, the Austrians also declared war on the Ottoman Empire. Once again the war dragged on for several years, with the Ottomans receiving support from Sweden and Prussia. By 1791, when the sultan signed the peace treaty of Sistova with the Austrians, the Ottoman forces were exhausted. The defeat at the hands of the Russians in 1792 forced the sultan to sign the peace treaty of Jassy (Iaşi/Yassy), which allowed Russia to expand its territories along the northern shores of the Black Sea.

GOVERNMENTAL REFORMS

The new sultan, Selim III (1789–1807), who had watched the abysmal performance of his armies, embarked on a new campaign to reform the Ottoman military organization. He introduced the *Nizam-i Cedid* (New Army) units, which were organized and trained in accordance with European military techniques. The first modern military hospital was also completed a year later and, in 1795, the first military engineering school was established. Meanwhile, the events unfolding in Europe began to cause anxieties for the sultan. The French Revolution, which began in 1789, and the subsequent execution of Louis XVI in 1791 shocked the Ottomans, who viewed the French monarch as a friend and an ally. Even more worrisome was the occupation of Egypt by a French expeditionary force headed by Napoleon Bonaparte in the summer of 1798. The French invasion forced the sultan to seek the support of Russia and England. After defeating the French at Acre and suffering a defeat at the hands of the French at Abukir, the Ottoman-English alliance forced Bonaparte out of Egypt in 1799. Ottoman-French ties were restored in 1806, when Russia moved its forces against Wallachia and Moldavia.

Meanwhile, in 1807, the growing opposition to Selim III's reforms brought the religious establishment, the janissaries, and the anti-reform elements within the government together in a united front. When the revolt broke out, Selim hesitated and did not use his new army to crush the rebellion. Emboldened by their initial success, the rebels demanded the deposition of Selim III and the accession of Mustafa IV (1807–1808) as his successor. The pro-Selim III provincial notables (*ayans*), however, refused to accept defeat and mobilized their forces against the new sultan and his supporters in Istanbul. The powerful *ayan* Bayrakdar Mustafa Paşa of Rüsçuk (modern-day Ruse in northeastern Bulgaria), who supported Selim III, attacked Istanbul to remove Mustafa IV and reinstate the deposed sultan. Mustafa IV responded by ordering the execution of Selim III and his cousin, Mahmud II, the two male members of the Ottoman royal house who could replace him. The executioners succeeded in their mission to murder Selim III, but Mahmud II managed to escape and find refuge in Bayrakdar Mustafa Paşa's camp, where he remained until Mustafa IV was deposed and he could assume the throne.

RISE OF NATIONALISM IN THE BALKANS

Starting with Serbia in 1804 and Greece in 1821, nationalist revolutions erupted among the Christian subjects of the sultan. In each case, the nationalists were supported by one or more European imperial powers that intended to use the eruption of antigovernment uprisings as a justification to intervene and undermine Ottoman power and authority in the Balkans. As a multiethnic, multilinguistic, and multireligious empire that recognized the supremacy of religious identity, the Ottoman state failed to develop an antibiotic for the bacteria called nationalism. The Ottoman system was built on the principle of dividing the population of the empire into separate and distinct religious communities, or *millets*. The *millet* system had worked well in an era when religious identity reigned supreme. Ironically, the preservation of national cultures within the framework of religious communities allowed distinct ethnic and linguistic feelings and identities to survive. By the end of the 18th century, under the influence of the French Revolution, a modern intelligentsia imbued with nationalistic ideas began to challenge the ideological hegemony of the traditional religious hierarchies that had historically collaborated with the Ottoman regime.

Despite the Serbian revolt that forced the Ottomans to grant autonomy to a small Serbian principality in 1814–1815 and the Greek Revolution, which succeeded in establishing an independent Greece in 1832, Mahmud II was determined to reassert the authority of the central government by building a modern army. As long as the janissaries survived, however, the antireform forces could always rely on their support to challenge the authority of the central government. Thus, the sultan abolished the janissary corps in June 1826, but he could not create a new and strong army overnight. The absence of a well-trained army undermined Ottoman attempts to maintain their rule over Greece. But if the loss of Greece struck a devastating blow to Ottoman prestige and power, it was the revolt of Muhammad Ali (Mehmed Ali), the governor of Egypt, that brought the empire to the verge of extinction.

CHALLENGE FROM EGYPT

Muhammad Ali, originally an Albanian from northern Greece, had emerged as the master of Egypt after building a strong and modern army with direct assistance and support from France. Mahmud II, who was fully aware of Muhammad Ali's successes and his newly acquired military capability, asked for his support when the Greek Revolution erupted. The defeat in Greece, however, forced the governor of Egypt to withdraw his troops. Moreover, he lost his fleet during the Greek campaign, and he could not receive any satisfactory compensation from the sultan in Istanbul.[32] The battles of the Greek Revolution had demonstrated that the Ottoman army was in a sorry state. Initially, Muhammad Ali had thought of building his own kingdom in North Africa by attacking

Algeria and Tunisia, but the French had acted faster by attacking and occupying Algiers in July 1830.

With North Africa falling into the hands of the French, Muhammad Ali and his son Ibrahim Paşa, who acted as his father's army commander, turned their attention eastward and attacked Palestine and Syria in October 1831.[33] In May 1832, the town of Acre fell, followed by Damascus in June. By July, Ibrahim Paşa had routed Ottoman forces twice and established his rule over the entire country.[34] As in the case of the Greek Revolution, the sultan refused an offer for a negotiated settlement, which allowed the Egyptian army to push into Anatolia and defeat the Ottoman troops who had been sent from Istanbul. By February 1833, the Egyptians had reached Kütahya in western Anatolia. Mahmud II responded to the military reverses by opening negotiations with European powers with the aim of securing their support against his rebellious subject. When the British and Austrians turned down the request, the sultan asked for military intervention from Russia, which agreed to provide it. While the arrival of the Russian fleet, in February 1833, prevented Muhammad Ali from marching his troops to Istanbul, it could not dislodge the Egyptian forces from their newly conquered territories in Anatolia. To end the crisis, the sultan agreed to sign the Treaty of Kütahya in April, and appointed Muhammad Ali the governor of Syria. In July of the same year, he also signed the Treaty of Hünkar Iskelesi with Russia, an eight-year defense pact that obligated the Ottoman government to close the straits to all ships at time of war between Russia and a foreign power.

Despite the peace with Muhammad Ali, the sultan was anxious to strengthen his army and strike back at the disloyal governor of Egypt. The British, greatly alarmed by the growing power and influence of Russia, viewed Muhammad Ali as an ally of France, whose policies toward the Ottoman Empire had forced the sultan to depend on the Russians for his survival. Meanwhile, the sultan hoped to utilize British anxiety over Muhammad Ali to gain their support for a campaign against him.

In 1838, the tension between the sultan and Muhammad Ali erupted again when the latter stated his intention to declare his independence from the Ottoman Empire. When his closest ally, France, opposed this provocative move, Muhammad Ali backed down. The sultan was determined to secure the support of Great Britain in a campaign to destroy Muhammad Ali. Using this opportunity to expand its economic interests in the region, the British government signed a commercial treaty with the Ottoman state in August 1838 that confirmed British capitulatory privileges and opened the Ottoman markets to British investment and trade.[35] Despite warnings from the British, Mahmud II mobilized a force against Muhammad Ali's army in Syria. Once again, however, Egyptian forces under the command of Ibrahim Paşa defeated the Ottoman army, which had attacked Syria in June 1839. Less than a week later, Mahmud II died in Istanbul after a long battle with tuberculosis.

TANZIMAT

To halt the disintegration of the Ottoman state, a small group of Ottoman officials used the death of Mahmud II to embark on a new program of governmental reforms, which came to be known as *Tanzimat* (Reorganization). On 3 November 1839, the new Ottoman sultan, Abdülmecid (1839–1861), ordered his ministers and dignitaries as well as representatives of foreign powers, to gather in the rose garden of the Topkapi Palace, where his foreign minister, Mustafa Reşid Paşa, read a decree entitled *Hatt-i Şerif-i Gülhane,* the Noble Rescript of the Rose Garden.[36] The document guaranteed the subjects of the sultan security of life, honor, and property.[37] It also promised a regular system for assessing and levying taxes, as well as a just system of conscription and military service.[38] The royal rescript also committed the central government to a number of essential reforms such as establishing a new penal code, eradicating bribery, and creating a regular and just tax system that would eliminate inequities and special privileges, such as tax farming. Thus, the imperial decree demonstrated a new commitment by the sultan and his advisors to the rule of law, the equality and fair treatment of all Ottoman subjects regardless of their religion and ethnicity, and the establishment of a new justice system that protected their life and property against arbitrary attacks and confiscation.[39]

In addition to the modernization of the empire's infrastructure, the Tanzimat period also witnessed a significant transformation in the Ottoman educational system. Mahmud II had introduced the *Ruşdiye* (adolescent) schools, which provided a secular education for male students who had completed the *mekteps* (the traditional schools devoted to the study of the Quran).[40] The principal objective for the creation of modern schools was to train a new educated elite capable of administering an empire. The fear of opposition from conservatives, however, slowed down educational reform and forced the reformers to attach modern schools to various governmental ministries and bureaus. Thus, the first medical and engineering schools in the Ottoman Empire were introduced as academic units within a military school.[41] The introduction of modern educational institutions also suffered from a lack of adequate funding and the absence of well-trained teachers and instructors. Despite these difficulties, a new bureaucracy, which was four to five times larger than the imperial administration and relied heavily on graduates from the modern schools, was created.[42]

Finally, the men of Tanzimat tried to create a modern financial structure and an efficient tax collection system that would provide the central treasury with sufficient funds to support governmental reforms. The "main thrust" of their financial reforms was "to simplify the collection of revenues" by delegating "the responsibility of tax collection to the salaried agents of the government, rather than governors, holders of prebendal grants, or other intermediaries of the classical system."[43]

Despite their best efforts to focus on reform, the men of the Tanzimat faced serious challenges both from internal rebellions and foreign aggression that ultimately undermined their efforts and resulted in the disintegration of the empire. In October 1840, the Ottomans and the British began to exert military pressure on Muhammad Ali, forcing his troops to evacuate Palestine and Syria in February 1841. The sultan, however, issued a decree granting Muhammad Ali and his family the right to rule Egypt. The second important foreign policy crisis of the Tanzimat era was the Crimean War, which forced the Ottoman Empire to declare war on Russia in October 1853.[44] By acting as the big brother and protector of Serbia, the Danubian Principalities, and the sultan's Orthodox Christian subjects, Russia intended to replace both the Ottoman Empire and Austria as the dominant power in the Balkans. The ultimate goal of Russian foreign policy was to create a series of satellite states that depended on Russian protection and support for their political survival. During this time, Catholic and Orthodox churches debated over their right to various holy sites in Jerusalem, with Russia championing the Orthodox position and France that of Rome. In 1852, the Ottoman government announced its decision on the question of Christian Holy Places in Palestine and sided with the French position. The Russian government was outraged, and Tsar Nicholas I ordered a partial mobilization of his army to back a new series of demands, including the Russian right to protect the sultan's Orthodox Christian subjects. Confident that it would receive support from Great Britain, France, and Austria, the Ottoman government rejected the Russian demands. When the tsarist forces invaded the Danubian Principalities, the Ottoman Empire declared war on Russia.

As the British and the French naval forces crossed the Turkish Straits on their way to the Black Sea, the Ottomans fought the Russian navy at Sinop, where the Ottoman fleet was destroyed and thousands of sailors were killed. After negotiations collapsed in March 1854, France and Great Britain declared war on Russia. Fearing an attack from Austria, the Russian forces withdrew from Wallachia and Moldavia.[45] The military campaigns that followed, particularly the attack on Sevastopol, which was occupied in October 1855, forced Russia to sue for peace.

While the representatives of European powers were arriving at the peace conference in Paris in February 1856, the sultan, under pressure from France and Great Britain, issued a second major reform decree, the *Hatt-i Hümayun,* or the Imperial Rescript, committing his government to the principle of equality of all Ottoman subjects. The Treaty of Paris, signed in March 1856, forced Russia to withdraw from Wallachia and Moldavia, which, along with Serbia, were to regain their autonomy under Ottoman rule. Russia's access to the Danube was blocked by its surrender of southern Bessarabia to Moldavia. That famous river, as well as the Turkish Straits, was declared open to ships of all countries and the Black Sea was demilitarized. Russia was also obliged to withdraw its forces from eastern Anatolia, including the city of Kars, which it had occupied during the war. The Crimean War and the Treaty of Paris resulted in the de facto inclusion of the Ottoman Empire in the "Concert of Europe" that had tried to maintain the balance of power on the continent since the defeat of Napoleon and the convening of the Congress of Vienna in 1814.[46] The territorial integrity of the Ottoman Empire was, thus, theoretically preserved and Russia's expansion into southeast Europe contained.

With Russian aggression checked, the leaders of Tanzimat could once again focus on the implementation of their reform agenda. The Crimean War had been very costly and forced the Ottoman government to apply for high interest loans that eventually undermined the economic independence of the state. The accumulation of significant debt to European banks and the continuous struggle to generate sufficient revenue to repay them undermined efforts to reform the government for the remainder of the 19th century.

OTTOMAN CONSTITUTION

After the death of Âli Paşa, the last great statesman of the Tanzimat era in September 1871, several grand viziers came and went, while Sultan Abdülaziz (1861–1876) became increasingly involved in running the everyday affairs of the empire, thus introducing an element of chaos. Then, in the early hours of Tuesday, 30 May 1876, a small group of officials and army commanders led by the reform-minded statesman Midhat Paşa, who had served as governor of Nish (1861–1868) and Baghdad (1869–1872), carried out a peaceful military coup.[47] A nephew of Abdülaziz, Prince Murad, was brought out of his residence to the ministry of war and declared the new sultan.

Before the new monarch could establish himself, however, news of Abdülaziz's sudden death was announced to a shocked populace. The body of the deposed sultan had been discovered in his private bedroom, his wrists slashed with a pair of scissors, leading many to conclude that he had been murdered. To diffuse the rumors of assassination, the government called on doctors from several foreign embassies in Istanbul to examine the body and offer their medical opinion on the cause of death, which was officially declared a suicide. The events profoundly affected the new sultan, Murad, who suffered a nervous breakdown. Accordingly, Midhat and his colleagues decided to depose Murad in favor of his brother, who ascended the Ottoman throne in August as Abdülhamid II. Meanwhile, Midhat Paşa was appointed grand vizier in December, and shortly after, the first Ottoman constitution was introduced.[48]

These momentous events in Istanbul took place in the context of major developments in European power politics and another crisis in the Balkans that erupted when Serbia and Montenegro attacked the Ottoman Empire in July 1876. With chaos and uncertainty reigning in Istanbul and revolt and instability spreading to the rural communities in Bosnia-Herzegovina, Russia had pushed for military intervention by Serbia and Montenegro. This Pan-Slavic project designed by Russia failed when Ottoman troops struck back, defeating the Serbs and forcing them to sue for peace. Russia then instigated a nationalist uprising in Bulgaria, which was crushed by Ottoman forces with heavy casualties and massacres of the civilian population. This allowed the tsar to demand that the Ottoman Empire introduce reforms and grant autonomy to the Bulgarian people. Recognizing the threat of Russian intervention in the Balkans, the British government intervened and called for the convening of an international conference to meet in Istanbul with the intention of diffusing the possibility of another war between Russia and the Ottoman Empire. On the first day of the conference, 23 December 1876, however, the Ottoman delegation shocked the European participants by announcing that a constitution had been promulgated and that any attempt by foreign powers to press the Ottoman state into introducing reforms in its European provinces was unnecessary since, under the new political regime, all Ottoman subjects would be treated as equals with their rights protected and guaranteed by the government.[49]

The Ottoman constitution did not prevent another military confrontation with Russia. Continuous palace intrigues convinced Abdülhamid II to dismiss Midhat Paşa, who was sent into exile in February 1877, an event that was soon followed by a Russian declaration of war in April. The Ottoman forces delayed the Russian southward incursion for several months at Plevna (Pleven) in Bulgaria, but by December, the tsarist army was encamped a mere 12 kilometers outside Istanbul.[50] On 3 March 1878, the Treaty of San Stefano was signed between Russia and the Ottoman Empire. Among other things, it called for the establishment of an autonomous Bulgarian state, stretching from the Black Sea to the Aegean, which Russia would occupy for two years. Serbia, Romania, and Montenegro were also to be recognized as independent states, while Russia received Batumi in southern Caucasus, as well as the districts of Kars and Ardahan in eastern Anatolia. Additionally, the Ottoman government was obliged to introduce fundamental reforms in Thessaly and Armenia. Other European powers could not tolerate the rapid growth of Russian influence in the Balkans and the Caucasus. They agreed to meet in Berlin at a new peace conference designed to partition the European provinces of the Ottoman Empire in such a way as to prevent the emergence of Russia as the dominant power in the region.

DISINTEGRATION OF THE EMPIRE
IN THE BALKANS

The Congress of Berlin, which began in June 1878, was a turning point in the history of the Ottoman Empire and southeast Europe. When the congress ended a month later, the Ottoman Empire was no longer a political and military power in the Balkans.[51] The Ottomans lost eight percent of their territory and four and a half million of their population.[52] The majority of those who left the empire were Christians, while tens of thousands of Muslim refugees from the Balkans and the Caucasus fled into the interior of the empire. The large Bulgarian state that had been created three months earlier at the Treaty of San Stefano was divided into three separate entities.[53] The region north of the Balkan Mountains and the area around Sofia were combined into a new autonomous Bulgarian principality that would recognize the suzerainty of the sultan, but for all practical purposes act as a Russian satellite. The region lying between the Rhodope and Balkan mountains, which corresponded with Eastern Rumelia, was established as a semiautonomous region under its own Christian governor, who was to be appointed by the sultan and supervised by European powers.[54] The third area of Thrace and Macedonia remained under Ottoman rule.[55]

The Berlin Congress did not provide Greece with any new territory. Instead, the powers asked that Greece and the Ottoman Empire enter into negotiations on establishing the future of their boundaries, including the status of Thessaly and Epirus. Austria was granted the right to occupy and administer Bosnia-Herzegovina as well as the *sancak* of Novi Pazar, a strip of land that separated Serbia from Montenegro.[56] Further, while the Congress recognized Serbia, Romania, and Montenegro as independent states, the Romanian state was forced to hand southern Bessarabia to Russia and, in return, receive Dobrudja and the Danube Delta.[57] Russia also received the districts of Batumi, Kars, and Ardahan, thereby establishing military control over the eastern shores of the Black Sea and a strategically important land bridge to Anatolia.[58]

The British received the island of Cyprus, which contained a Greek majority and a Turkish minority population. By handing Albanian-populated areas and towns to Montenegro and Greece, the European powers ignited a new nationalist movement among a proud people who had faithfully served the Ottoman state on many occasions in the past.[59] Thus, Albania, with its emerging national movement, would replicate the model set by the Serbs, the Romanians, and the Bulgarians and demand independence.

Although Serbia, Montenegro, Romania, and Bulgaria gained their independence or autonomy in 1878, the Congress of Berlin left the newly independent states dissatisfied and hungry for more territory. The Romanians were angry because they were forced to cede the rich and productive Bessarabia in return for gaining the poor and less productive Dobrudja. The Bulgarians were outraged because they lost the greater Bulgarian state, which had been created by the Treaty of San Stefano. Serbia gained limited territory, but it did not satisfy the voracious appetite of Serbian nationalists who dreamed of a greater Serbia with access to the sea. Montenegro received a port on the Adriatic, but, as in the case of Serbia, it did not acquire the towns and the districts it had demanded. Of all the participants in the Congress, Russia was perhaps the most frustrated. In return for its massive human and financial investment in the war against the Ottoman Empire, it had received only southern Bessarabia in the Balkans, while the Austrians, who had opportunistically sat on the sidelines, had been awarded Bosnia-Herzegovina.

These frustrated dreams turned the Balkan Peninsula into a ticking bomb. By carving the Ottoman Empire into small and hungry independent states, the European powers laid the foundation for intense rivalries. Thirty-six years after the conclusion of the Berlin Congress, the Balkan tinderbox exploded on 28 June 1914, when Serbian nationalists assassinated the Austrian crown prince, Archduke Franz Ferdinand, in Sarajevo, sparking the First World War.

ABDÜLHAMID II

With the removal of Midhat Paşa in 1877, the center of power began to shift back from the office of the grand vizier to the sultan. Despite the defeat at the hands of the Russians and the territorial losses imposed by the Congress of Berlin, the new sultan, Abdülhamid II (1876–1909), remained committed to the reforms introduced during the Tanzimat period. Indeed, it was during his reign that a new and Western-educated officer corps emerged. Ironically, the same officers would play an important role in deposing the sultan in April 1909. In addition to emphasizing military training, the sultan expanded elementary and secondary education (including the opening of a new school for girls in 1884), introduced a modern medical school, and established the University of Istanbul. To create a modern communication system for the empire, he developed telegraph services and the Ottoman railway system, connecting Istanbul to the heartland of the Arab world as far south as the holy city of Medina in Hejaz.[60] The Hejaz railroad, which was completed in July 1908, allowed the sultan to dispatch his troops to the Arab provinces in case of a rebellion.

As with the reforms introduced by the men of Tanzimat, the principal objective of Abdülhamid II's modernization schemes was to establish a strong and centralized government capable of maintaining the territorial integrity of the empire. In practical terms, this meant suppressing uprisings among the sultan's subjects and defending the state against the expansionist policies of European powers. Despite the sultan's best efforts, however, the empire continued to lose territory.

Building on their occupation of Algeria in 1830, the French imposed their rule on Tunisia in May 1881. A year later, the British invaded and occupied Egypt. In addition to these losses, the Ottoman Empire also continued to lose territory in the Balkans. After the Congress of Berlin, the only area left under Ottoman rule was a relatively narrow corridor south of the Balkan Mountains that stretched from the Black Sea in the east to the Adriatic in the west, incorporating Thrace, Thessaly, Macedonia, and Albania.[61] Greece, Serbia, Montenegro, and Bulgaria coveted the remaining territory of the dying Ottoman Empire. In accordance with the promises made at the Congress of Berlin, the Ottomans handed much of Thessaly and a district in Epirus to Greece in July 1881. Despite these gains, Greece continued to push for additional territorial concessions including the island of Crete, where several uprisings, encouraged by Athens, forced the sultan in 1898 to agree to the creation of an autonomous Cretan state under Ottoman suzerainty. The island finally became part of Greece in December 1913.

Aside from the military disasters and territorial losses that the empire suffered, the reign of Abdülhamid II proved to be a period of significant social, economic, and cultural transformation. The autocratic sultan continued with the reforms that had been introduced by the men of Tanzimat. There was, however, a fundamental difference. The statesmen of the Tanzimat had begun their governmental careers as translators and diplomats attached to Ottoman embassies in Europe, and thus wished to emulate European customs and institutions. Abdülhamid II, in contrast, may have been a modernizer, but one who believed strongly in preserving the Islamic identity of the Ottoman state. With the loss of its European provinces, the number of Christian subjects of the sultan decreased and Muslims began to emerge as the empire's majority population.[62] The Muslim population was not only loyal to the sultan but also felt a deep anger toward the sultan's Christian subjects for allying themselves with the imperial powers of Europe in order to gain their independence. Abdülhamid II understood the new mood among his Muslim subjects and countered European imperial designs by appealing to Pan-Islamism, or the unity of all Muslims, under his leadership as the caliph, or the religious and spiritual leader of the Islamic world.

A view of Istanbul between 1880 and 1890. (Library of Congress)

YOUNG TURKS SEIZE POWER

Despite Abdülhamid II's best efforts to preserve the territorial integrity of the empire and to modernize the Ottoman society, the government failed to neutralize the opposition of the young, educated, and secular minded elements in the society. As early as 1889, small groups of patriotic students, civil servants, and army officers had organized secret societies. Princes of the royal family, government officials, teachers, artists, and army officers educated and trained in modern schools and military academies, had concluded that the restoration of the 1876 constitution and the establishment of a new government based on a parliament were the only means through which the Ottoman Empire could be saved from further disintegration. As the police began to crack down on the opposition, some chose exile over imprisonment and settled in European capitals, where they published newspapers that denounced the autocratic policies of the sultan. Others recruited young cadets and organized secret cells among army units stationed in the Balkans and the Middle East. This diverse group of antigovernment Ottoman intellectuals and activists, who were known in Europe as

Jeunes Turcs, or the Young Turks, organized themselves as the Committee of Union and Progress (CUP).

Revolution came, unexpectedly, from Macedonia in July 1908, when army officers loyal to CUP revolted and demanded the restoration of the 1876 constitution.[63] After a faint effort to suppress the rebellion, Abdülhamid II concluded that resistance was futile. On 23 July, he restored constitutional rule and ordered parliamentary elections throughout the empire.[64] As the news of the revolution spread, massive celebrations erupted, particularly in Istanbul, where Turks, Jews, Armenians, and Arabs joined hands and embraced in the streets of the capital.[65] Among the deputies to the new parliament, which opened on 17 December, there were 142 Turks, 60 Arabs, 25 Albanians, 23 Greeks, 12 Armenians, 5 Jews, 4 Bulgarians, 3 Serbs, and 1 Romanian.[66]

The Young Turks had convinced themselves that the restoration of the parliamentary system of government would secure the support of European powers for the preservation of the territorial integrity of the Ottoman Empire.[67] They were mistaken. Shortly after the victory of the revolution, the Austro-Hungarian Empire formally annexed Bosnia-Herzegovina, while Greece seized the island of Crete, and Bulgaria unified with Eastern Rumelia, which had remained an autonomous province under the nominal rule of the Ottoman sultan.[68]

Meanwhile, an attempted counter coup by supporters of Abdülhamid II in April 1909 provided an excuse for the two chambers of parliament to depose the sultan and replace him with his younger brother, who ascended the throne as Mehmed V (1909–1918).[69] The center of power had shifted once again, this time from the palace to the army, the bureaucracy, and the parliament. The central government, however, continued to be plagued by internal factionalism and growing opposition from both conservative and liberal groups and parties. The weakness of the government was demonstrated by its failure to respond effectively to the unrest in Albania, the uprising of Imam Yahya in Yemen, and the Italian invasion of Tripoli and Benghazi in Libya.[70] The Italian attack on the Dardanelles and the occupation of the Dodecanese Islands in May 1912 forced the Ottoman government to accept the loss of Libya and sue for peace.[71]

The Italian victory emboldened the neighboring Balkan states, which had been waiting for an opportunity to invade and occupy the remaining Ottoman provinces in Europe. After a series of negotiations, Serbia and Bulgaria formed an alliance in March 1912.[72]

Shortly after, in May, Bulgaria signed a similar agreement with Greece.[73] Finally, in October, Serbia and Montenegro formed an alliance.[74] Shortly after, the Balkan states declared war on the Ottoman Empire. The Bulgarians soon defeated the Ottomans at the battles of Kirklareli/Kirkkilise (22–24 October) and Lüleburgaz (22 October–2 November), followed by a Serbian victory at the battle of Kumanovo (23–24 October).[75] Meanwhile, the Greeks captured Salonika on 8 November.

Without a coordinated plan and in the absence of a unified command, the Ottomans were forced either to retreat or to take defensive positions. The major urban centers of the empire in Europe were surrounded by the invading Balkan armies. In December, the Ottoman government sued for peace. As the discussions dragged on in London, Bulgaria demanded the city of Edirne. This was too much for a group of young officers in Istanbul, who staged a military coup on 23 January 1913, killing the minister of war and forcing the government to resign. When the news of the coup in Istanbul reached London, the Balkan states resumed their military campaigns. Despite a promise to take the offensive, the new government in Istanbul failed to repulse the Bulgarian forces, who captured Edirne on 28 March, and the Serbs, who seized Shkodër on 22 April. On 30 May, the Ottoman government was forced to sign the Treaty of London, which resulted in the loss of much of its territory in Europe, including the city of Edirne.

Fortunately for the Ottomans, intense rivalries and jealousies among the Balkan states erupted shortly after the signing of the Treaty of London. Romania, which had not participated in the war, demanded territory from Bulgaria. The Greeks and Serbs also expressed dissatisfaction with the division of territory in Macedonia. As the negotiations for the creation of an anti-Bulgarian alliance began, Bulgaria attacked Serbia, igniting a new Balkan war between the victors of the first. The Ottomans used the opportunity to recapture Edirne and forced Bulgaria to sign the Treaty of Istanbul in September 1913.[76]

DEFEAT IN THE FIRST WORLD WAR AND THE FALL OF THE EMPIRE

The military coup of January 1913 brought the Ottoman government under the control of the CUP. As the CUP began to consolidate its power over the organs of the state, a triumvirate of army officers comprised of Cemal Paşa, Enver Paşa, and Talat Paşa began to rule the empire with the support of an inner circle that represented the various factions within the CUP. With the clouds of war gathering over Europe, the beleaguered Ottoman government appraised its various options, none of which looked very promising given the predatory nature of the European powers. The decision to enter the war on the side of Germany and the Austro-Hungarian Empire brought the Ottoman state into open military confrontation with France, Russia, and Great Britain. In the Constantinople Agreement of 1915, these three Entente powers agreed to the complete partition of the Ottoman Empire after the end of the war.[77]

The Allied expectation that the empire they had dubbed the "sick man of Europe" would be destroyed with one single military blow proved to be wishful thinking. The British attempt to force the Ottoman Empire out of the war called for a massive landing of Allied troops at the foothills of Gallipoli on the European shores of the Dardanelles. After establishing a beachhead in April 1915, the troops planned to climb the hills and destroy the Ottoman forces that defended the heights. To the dismay of the British, the Ottomans, supported by German officers, fought back heroically, inflicting an impressive defeat on the enemy, who retreated with heavy casualties in January 1916. Another advancing British force in southern Iraq also met unexpected resistance and suffered heavy losses. With their military efforts coming to a sudden halt, the British resorted to the strategy of fomenting an internal rebellion among the sultan's Arab subjects. They cast their lot with Sharif Husayn of Mecca and his sons, who were promised an independent and united Arab kingdom if they organized a revolt against the Ottoman Empire.

Unknown to Sharif Husayn, the British were also negotiating about the fate of the Arab provinces of the Ottoman Empire with their principal ally in Europe, the French. In negotiations between Mark Sykes, who represented the British government, and his French counterpart, Georges Picot, the two European powers carved the Arab provinces of the Ottoman Empire into British and French zones of influence. According to the Sykes-Picot Agreement (16 May 1916), the British promised Greater Syria, which included the present-day country of Lebanon, and the Ottoman province of Mosul in present-day northern Iraq, to France. In return, the British gained control over the provinces of Baghdad and Basra, with an adjacent territory that stretched to the Mediterranean towns of Acre and Jaffa, including the imprecisely defined Holy Land, or Palestine.[78]

In November 1917, the British government made a third critical promise that would have a long lasting impact on the Middle East. In a letter addressed to Lord Rothschild, one of the leaders of the Zionist movement in Europe, Arthur James Balfour, the British Foreign Secretary, expressed the support of his government for the Zionist movement's aim to establish a Jewish National Home in Palestine. This declaration would prove to be one of the most significant stepping-stones toward the establishment of the state of Israel. The map of the Middle East would be redrawn as the British government attempted to fulfill the conflicting promises it had made to the Arabs, the French, and the Zionist movement in the aftermath of the First World War.

For the Ottomans, the First World War came to an end when British troops, supported by Arab fighters under the leadership of Prince Faisal, the son of Sharif Husayn of Mecca, entered Damascus in August 1918. The Ottoman Empire sued for peace in October 1918. With Russia out of the picture, the British were the only power with troops in the Middle East who could dictate the terms of an armistice to the Ottomans. On 31 October 1918, after a week of negotiations, the terms of the Armistice of Mudros were presented to the Ottoman government.[79] They included Allied occupation of Istanbul and the forts on the Bosphorus and Dardanelles. Two days later, the three Young Turk leaders, Enver Paşa, Talat Paşa, and Cemal Paşa, fled the country for Berlin. On 15 May 1919, with support from the British, the French, and the Americans, the Greek government, which had joined the Allies at the end of the First World War, landed troops in Izmir.[80]

In the midst of this chaos and humiliation, Mustafa Kemal Paşa (1881–1938) was appointed "Inspector General of Ottoman forces in northern and northeastern Anatolia" and dispatched by the sultan to disarm and disband the remaining Ottoman army units and pacify the local population.[81] Having enrolled in the Ottoman military academy, Mustafa Kemal had joined the Young Turks before the 1908 revolution but had refused to assume political office. An Ottoman army officer who had fought with distinction at Gallipoli (1915), the Caucasus (1916), and Palestine (1917), Mustafa Kemal had emerged as a hero of the First World War and was considered to be the ideal officer capable of diffusing a rebellion against the sultan and the allies.

By the time Mustafa Kemal arrived in Samsun on the northern coast of Anatolia on 19 May, he had already decided to disobey his orders and organize a national resistance movement.[82] Support came from other Ottoman commanders and officers who shared his determination to remove all foreign forces from Anatolia. After creating a national congress and launching a series of successful military campaigns against the newly established Armenian state in eastern Anatolia and the Greek forces in western Anatolia, the Turkish nationalists forced foreign troops to evacuate the "Turkish homeland" in the summer of 1922.

The military victories of the nationalist movement resulted in a shift of attitude by the European powers, which recognized the new reality on the ground. Having witnessed the decisive defeat of Greek forces in August 1922 and realizing that their allies, particularly the French, did not intend to fight the Turkish nationalists, the British convinced the Greek government to withdraw from eastern Thrace and sign the Armistice of Mudanya with the Turks on 11 October 1922. On 1 November, the Grand National Assembly in Ankara abolished the Ottoman sultanate.[83] Shortly after, a Turkish delegation led by the hero of the war of independence, Ismet Paşa, arrived in Lausanne, Switzerland, to negotiate a peace treaty with the allies, which was concluded on 24 July 1923.

Following the signing of the Treaty of Lausanne, British troops evacuated Istanbul in October 1923, and Mustafa Kemal and his victorious army entered the city. The time had come to deal with the Ottoman royal family, who had collaborated with foreign occupation forces throughout the war of national liberation and had condemned Mustafa Kemal to death in absentia. On 29 October 1923, the Grand National Assembly proclaimed the establishment of the Republic of Turkey, with Mustafa Kemal as its first president, while a member of the Ottoman ruling family, Abdülmecid, remained the caliph. Determined to cut the country's ties with its Ottoman past and to create a secular republic, the new government moved the capital from Istanbul to Ankara and on 3 March 1924, the Grand National Assembly abolished the caliphate and the last member of the Ottoman royal family was sent into exile. The 600-year Ottoman Empire had ceased to exist, replaced by the Republic of Turkey.

NOTES

1. Fernand Braudel, *The Mediterranean and the Mediterranean World in the Age of Philip II*, 2 vols. (New York: Harper & Row Publishers, 1973), 2:668.

2. Jane Hathaway, *Beshir Agha: Chief Eunuch of the Ottoman Imperial Harem* (Oxford: Oneworld Publications, 2005), 17.

3. Eskandar Beg Monshi, *History of Shah Abbas the Great* (*Tarikh-e Alamara-ye Abbasi*), trans. Roger M. Savory, 2 vols. (Boulder, CO: Westview Press, 1978), 2:830–33; Mustafa Naima (Mustafa Naim), *Annals of the Turkish Empire from 1591 to 1659 of the Christian Era*, trans. Charles Fraser (New York: Arno Press, 1973), 243–46, 263–64.

4. Eskandar Beg Monshi, *History of Shah Abbas the Great*, 833–36; Naima, *Annals of the Turkish Empire*, 248–49; Sir Percy Sykes, *A History of Persia* (London: Macmillan and Co, 1951), 2:178.

5. See Naima, *Annals of the Turkish Empire*, 264–65.

6. Ibid., 249–51.

7. Sykes, *A History of Persia*, 2:178; Stanford J. Shaw, *History of the Ottoman Empire and Modern Turkey*, 2 vols. (Cambridge: Cambridge University Press, 1976), 1:188.

8. Shaw, *History of the Ottoman Empire*, 1:188.

9. Mohammad Ma'sum ibn Khajegi Isfahani, *Khulasat us-Siyar* (Tehran: 1990), 268–75.

10. J. C. Hurewitz, *Diplomacy in the Near and Middle East: A Documentary Record 1535–1956*, 2 vols. (Princeton: D. Van Norstand Company, 1956), 1:21–23.

11. A. N. Kurat, "The Reign of Mehmed IV, 1648–87," in *A History of the Ottoman Empire to 1730*, ed. M. A. Cook (Cambridge: Cambridge University Press, 1976), 169–70.

12. Caroline Finkel, *Osman's Dream: The Story of the Ottoman Empire 1300–1923* (New York: Basic Books, 2005), 286.

13. Shaw, *History of the Ottoman Empire*, 1:214–15.

14. Finkel, *Osman's Dream*, 287.

15. Rifa'at Ali Abou-El-Haj, "Ottoman Diplomacy at Karlowitz," in *Ottoman Diplomacy: Conventional or Unconventional*, ed. A. Nuri Yurdusev (New York: Palgrave Macmillan, 2004), 89.

16. Peter F. Sugar, *Southeastern Europe under Ottoman Rule: 1354–1804* (Seattle: University of Washington Press, 1996), 200.

17. Shaw, *History of the Ottoman Empire*, 1:226.

18. Ibid., 1:231. See Hurewitz, *Diplomacy in the Near and Middle East*, 1:39–40.

19. Barbara Jelavich, *History of the Balkans: Eighteenth and Nineteenth Centuries* (Cambridge: Cambridge University Press, 1983), 101–2.

20. Ibid., 102; See Charles and Barbara Jelavich, *The Establishment of the Balkan National States, 1804–1920* (Seattle: University of Washington Press, 1977), 10, 84; Donald Quataert, *The Ottoman Empire, 1700–1922* (Cambridge: Cambridge University Press, 2005), 47–48.

21. Shaw, *History of the Ottoman Empire*, 1:231.

22. Ibid.

23. Jelavich, *History of the Balkans*, 68.

24. Shaw, *History of the Ottoman Empire*, 1:232–33.

25. Quataert, *Ottoman Empire*, 43–44.

26. Shaw, *History of the Ottoman Empire*, 1:234.

27. Ibid.

28. Ibid., 1:235.

29. Ibid., 1:236–37.

30. H. R. Roemer, "The Safavid Period," in *Cambridge History of Iran*, 6 vols. (Cambridge: Cambridge University Press, 1986), 6:324.

31. Jelavich, *History of the Balkans*, 68.

32. Erik-Jan Zürcher, *Turkey: A Modern History* (London: I. B. Tauris, 2004), 36.

33. Ibid.

34. Ibid.

35. Ibid., 38, Shaw, *History of the Ottoman Empire*, 2:50.

36. Roderic H. Davison, *Reform in the Ottoman Empire, 1856–1876* (New York: Gordian Press, 1973), 36; Zürcher, *Turkey*, 50–51.

37. Davison, *Reform in the Ottoman Empire*, 36–38.

38. Justin McCarthy, *The Ottoman Turks: An Introductory History to 1923* (London, New York: Wesley Longman Limited, 1997), 297.

39. Ibid., 296–97; Shaw, *History of the Ottoman Empire*, 2:59–61. Zürcher, *Turkey*, 50–51.

40. Zürcher, *Turkey*, 62.

41. McCarthy, *The Ottoman Turks*, 299.

42. See Carter V. Findley, *Bureaucratic Reform in the Ottoman Empire: The Sublime Porte 1789–1922* (Princeton: Princeton University Press, 1980); Kemal H. Karpat, "Comments on Contributions and the Borderlands," in *Ottoman Borderlands: Issues, Personalities and Political Change*, eds. Kemal H. Karpat with Robert W. Zens (Madison: University of Wisconsin Press, 2003), 11.

43. Reşat Kasaba, *The Ottoman Empire and the World Economy: The Nineteenth Century* (Albany: State University of New York Press, 1988), 50.

44. Finkel, *Osman's Dream*, 456–58.

45. Jelavich, *The Establishment of the Balkan National States*, 107.

46. Zürcher, *Turkey*, 54; Shaw, *History of the Ottoman Empire*, 2:140–41.

47. Davison, *Reform in the Ottoman Empire*, 335–38; Roderic H. Davison, *Nineteenth Century Ottoman Diplomacy and Reforms* (Istanbul: Isis Press, 1999), 99–100.

48. McCarthy, *The Ottoman Turks*, 304.

49. Zürcher, *Turkey*, 74.

50. Ibid.

51. See Hurewitz, *Diplomacy in the Near and Middle East*, 1:189–91.

52. Kemal H. Karpat, *Ottoman Population 1830–1914: Demographic and Social Characteristics* (Madison: University of Wisconsin Press, 1985), 28; Finkel, *Osman's Dream*, 491; Shaw, *History of the Ottoman Empire*, 2:191. Shaw writes that "the Ottoman Empire was forced to give up two-fifths of its entire territory and one-fifth of its population, about 5.5 million people, of whom almost half were Muslims."

53. Shaw, *History of the Ottoman Empire*, 2:190–91.

54. Ibid., 2:191.

55. Jelavich, *History of the Balkans*, 360.

56. Ibid.

57. Ibid., 360; Zürcher, *Turkey*, 75.

58. Hurewitz, *Diplomacy in the Near and Middle East*, 1:190.

59. Jelavich, *History of the Balkans*, 361–66.

60. Zürcher, *Turkey*, 77; Shaw, *History of the Ottoman Empire*, 2:226–30.

61. Shaw, *History of the Ottoman Empire*, 2:195.

62. Donald Quataert, "Age of Reforms, 1812–1914," in *An Economic and Social History of the Ottoman Empire*, eds. Halil Inalcik with Donald Quataert, 2 vols. (Cambridge: Cambridge University Press, 1994), 1:782–84.

63. Shaw, *History of the Ottoman Empire*, 2:266–67.

64. Feroz Ahmad, *The Young Turks* (Oxford: Clarenden Press, 1969), 12; Andrew Mango, *Atatürk: The Biography of the Founder of Modern Turkey* (New York: Overlook Press, 1999), 77–78.

65. Shaw, *History of the Ottoman Empire*, 2:273.

66. Mango, *Atatürk*, 85.

67. Ibid.

68. Zürcher, *Turkey*, 104.

69. Ibid., 98.

70. Ibid., 105–6.

71. Ibid.

72. Jelavich, *The Establishment of the Balkan National States*, 216–17.

73. Zürcher, *Turkey*, 106.

74. Ibid.

75. Ibid., 107.

76. Ibid., 108.

77. Hurewitz, *Diplomacy in the Near and Middle East*, 2:7–11.

78. Zürcher, *Turkey*, 143.

79. Hurewitz, *Diplomacy in the Near and Middle East*, 2:36–37.

80. Mango, *Atatürk*, 217.

81. McCarthy, *The Ottoman Turks*, 377.

82. Mango, *Atatürk*, 218–21.

83. Hurewitz, *Diplomacy in the Near and Middle East*, 2:119–20.

2

SULTAN AND THE PALACE

The Ottomans divided their society into two distinct classes; the rulers (*askeri* or the military) and the ruled (*reaya* or the flock). Because "the state was organized as a war machine" geared toward conquest, "the ruling classes were deemed to be part of the military organization."[1] The three major strata within the Ottoman ruling class were "the men of sword or the military, the men of the religious sciences (*ilm*) known as the ulema (or the religious establishment), and the men of the pen or bureaucrats."[2] High officials in the Christian communities such as the patriarchs of the Orthodox Church were also included as members of the ruling class.[3] The *reaya* consisted of merchants, craftsmen, peasant farmers, and nomads. They produced the goods and paid the taxes that sustained the state. The guild tradesmen or craftsmen constituted an important segment of the urban *reaya*.[4] Other urban *reaya* included the *saraf* (money changers) and the merchants who organized the caravan and overseas trade.[5] The peasant farmers constituted the overwhelming majority of the population in the empire. The "Ottoman state preferred peasants to nomads" because those who cultivated the land "were settled, paid taxes and could be recruited for the army, whereas nomads, who were not settled, disliked and avoided both."[6] As "an armed and mobile group, the nomads were unruly and difficult to bring into line, and the Ottomans struggled throughout their history to settle them and turn them into peasants."[7]

At the top of the power pyramid stood the sultan, an absolute divine-right monarch.[8] Since in theory the sultan enjoyed ultimate god-given authority to rule, his subjects considered him the sole source of legitimate power; he could, therefore, demand absolute obedience from them, including complete control over their lives and possessions. He owned all state lands and could dispose of them as he saw fit. Despite his absolute power, the sultan could not violate the Islamic law or custom; the opinion of the Muslim community, expressed through the ulema, could strongly influence his decisions and actions. God had entrusted his people to him and the sultan was responsible for their care and protection.[9]

As the Ottoman state transformed from a small principality into a full-fledged imperial power, the political, social, and military institutions that had given rise to the early Ottoman fiefdom underwent a profound transformation. The principality founded by Osman and his son Orhan was based on the active participation of charismatic rulers or *gazis*, religiously driven warriors who fought in the name of Islam. Under this system, power and authority derived from military units organized and led by the *gazis* who fought with the Ottoman ruler. The Ottoman army was not only the backbone of the state but was the state itself. The seat of power was the saddle of the sultan, who organized and led raids during time of war. His leadership required him to visit and inspect the territory under his rule.

The early Ottoman sultans relied heavily on fortresses they had seized as defense against enemy attack and as a territorial base for further expansion. The North African traveler Ibn Battuta wrote that the Ottoman ruler Orhan visited these fortresses frequently to put them in good order and examine their condition but never stayed for more than a month.[10] The sultan rode from one fortress to the next and fought the Byzantine Greeks and other Christian powers of southeast Europe, attacking them continually and keeping their towns under siege.[11] Thus, the everyday life of the early Ottoman sultan did not differ greatly from the commanders and soldiers who fought in his armies. Their wealth and power depended on the taxes they collected and the booty they accumulated from various raids into enemy territory.

PALACE

As their territory expanded, new urban centers were added to the emerging empire, allowing Ottoman sultans to build palaces, mosques, bazaars, *bedestans* (covered markets for the sale of valuable goods), schools, bathhouses, *hans* (inns), and fountains. Only after the conquest of Constantinople in May 1453 did the Ottoman sultan Mehmed II, known as the Conqueror (*Fatih*), introduce the idea of a permanent residence for the sultan. The construction of Istanbul's world-renowned Topkapi (Canon Gate) Palace, built on "Seraglio Point between the Golden Horn and the Sea of Marmara," began in 1465 and ended 13 years later in 1478.[12] Built on a hill looking down at the Bosphorus, the location of the new palace offered both defensibility and stunning views. A high wall with several towers and seven gates surrounded the palace.[13] At the height of Ottoman power, the palace housed 4,000 residents.

The palace was a complex of many buildings centered on four main squares or sections: "an area for service and safety also known as the Birun, or outer section"; an "administrative center where the Imperial Council met"; an "area used for education, known as Enderun, or inner section"; and "a private living area, dominated by the Harem or women's section."[14] Three monumental

Principal square in Grand Cairo, with Murad Bey's Palace, Egypt, c. 1801. A column of soldiers crossing a large square surrounded by buildings with domes and minarets. Other people are in the square in the distance. From *Views in Egypt, Palestine, and Other Parts of the Ottoman Empire.* Thomas Milton (London, 1801–1804). (HIP / Art Resource, NY)

gates marked the passages of the palace. These began with the first or Imperial Gate (Bab-i Hümayun); followed by the second or Middle Gate, known also as the Gate of Salutation (Bab-üs Selam); and finally the third gate, known as the Gate of Felicity (Bab-üs Saadet).

The first palace courtyard was the largest of the four, and functioned as an outer park that contained fountains and buildings such as the imperial mint. At the end of this courtyard, all those riding a horse had to dismount and enter the second court, or the Divan Square, through the Gate of Salutation, or the Middle Gate. With exception of the highest officials of the state and foreign ambassadors and dignitaries, no one could enter the second courtyard, which housed a hospital, a bakery, army quarters, stables, the imperial council, and the kitchens. This courtyard served principally as the site where the sultan held audience. At the end of this courtyard stood the Gate of Felicity, which served as the entrance to the third courtyard, also known as the inner court, or the *enderun*. It was in front of this gate that the sultan sat on his throne during the main religious festivals and his accession, while his ministers and court dignitaries paid him homage, standing in front of their royal master. It was also here that, before every campaign, the sultan handed the banner of the prophet Muhammad to the grand vizier before he departed for a military campaign.

Beyond the Gate of Felicity lay the inner court and the residential apartments of the palace. No one could enter this court without special permission from the sultan. In this inner section of the palace, the sultan spent his days outside the royal harem surrounded by a lush garden and the privy chamber (*has oda*), which contained the royal treasury and the sacred relics of the prophet Muhammad, including a cloak, two swords, a bow, one tooth, a hair from his beard, his battle sabers, a letter, and other relics.

The audience chamber, or chamber of petitions (*arz odasi*), was located a short distance behind the Gate of Felicity in the center of the third courtyard. The chamber served as an inner audience hall where the government ministers and court dignitaries presented their reports after they had kissed the hem of the sultan's sleeve. The mosque of the eunuchs and the apartments of the palace pages, the young boys who attended to the sultan's everyday needs, were also located here. Another "important building found in the third courtyard was the Palace School," where Ottoman princes and the promising boys of the child levy (*devşirme*) "studied law, linguistics, religion, music, art, and fighting."[15] From its inception in the

Reception at the court of Sultan Selim III at the Topkapi Palace, Istanbul. Anonymous, 18th century. (Bridgeman-Giraudon / Art Resource, NY)

15th century, the palace school prepared numerous state dignitaries who played a prominent role in Ottoman society. Only in the second half of the 19th century did the ruling elite cease using the palace school. The fourth and the last courtyard included the royal harem, which comprised nearly four hundred rooms and served as the residence for the mother, the wives, and children of the sultan and their servants and attendants.

In 1856, a new palace called Dolmabahçe replaced Topkapi as the principal residence of the sultan and his harem. Dolmabahçe "embraced a European architectural style" and "was designed with two stories and three sections, with the basement and attic serving as service floors."[16] The "three sections of the palace were the official part . . ., the ceremonial hall . . ., and the residential area (HAREM)."[17] The "official section was used for affairs of state and formal receptions," while the second section "was used for formal ceremonies."[18] The harem or the "private residential area of the palace" occupied "the largest area of the palace" and included "the sultan's personal rooms: a study, a relaxing room, a bedroom, and a reception room."[19]

The mother of the sultan also had her own rooms "for receiving, relaxing, and sleeping."[20] Each of "the princes, princesses, and wives of the sultan (*kadinefendiler*) also had his or her own three-or-four room apartments in the palace, living separately with their own servants."[21]

In 1880, the Ottoman sultan Abdülhamid II moved the royal residence to the Yildiz (Star) Palace, where an Italian architect Riamondo D'Aronco was commissioned to build new additions to the old palace complex. The new structures, built of white marble, were European in style and contained the sultan's residence, a theater and opera house, an imperial carpentry workshop, an imperial porcelain factory to meet the demands of upper-class Ottomans for European-style ceramics, and numerous governmental offices for state officials who served their royal master. The only section of the Yildiz Palace accessible to foreign visitors was the *selamlik,* or the large square reception hall, where the sultan received foreign ambassadors.[22] In the royal harem, which was hidden within a lush and richly wooded park and was known for its rare marbles and superb Italian furniture, Abdülhamid II received his wives and children. At times he spent the evening there with a favorite wife and children and played piano for them.[23] Within the park, there also lay an artificial lake, on which the sultan and his intimates cruised in a small but elegant boat.[24]

HAREM

In Europe, the "oriental harem" conjured up images of exotic orgies and violent assassinations, in which a turban-clad monarch acted as a bloodthirsty tyrant, forced by his "oriental" instincts to murder his real and imagined enemies while sleeping with as many concubines as he fancied every night. According to this wild and romantic image, the sultan's power over all his subjects was unfettered and his control over the women of the harem unlimited.[25] Thus, in the European imagination, the harem not only symbolized free sex but also a masculine despotism that allowed men, especially the sultan, to imprison and use women as sexual slaves. The meaning of women's lives was defined by their relationship to the male master they served. They dedicated their entire lives to fulfilling the fancies of a tyrant who viewed them as his chattel.[26]

In this imaginary world, constructed by numerous European stories, travelogues, poems, and paintings, Muslim men appeared as tyrannical despots in public and sexual despots in private.[27] In sharp contrast, Muslim women appeared as helpless slaves without any power or rights, who were subjected to the whimsical tyranny of men. Not surprisingly, therefore, the Europeans who travelled to the Ottoman domain were shocked when they realized how different the reality was.[28] First, they quickly recognized that the notion of each Muslim man being married to four wives and enjoying a private harem of his own was absurd and laughable. If Islam allowed Muslim men to marry four wives, it did not follow that the majority of the male population in the Ottoman Empire practiced polygamy. As late as 1830s, the number of men in Cairo who had more than one wife did not exceed five percent of the male population in the city.[29] By 1926, when the newly established Turkish Republic abolished polygamy, the practice had already ceased to exist.[30]

Far from being devoted to wild sexual orgies, the Ottoman palace was the center of power and served as the residence of the sultan. As already mentioned, the palace comprised two principal sections, the *enderun,* or the inner section, and the *birun,* or the outer section.[31] The two sections were built around several large courtyards, which were joined by the Gate of Felicity, where the sultan sat on his throne, received his guests, and attended ceremonies.[32] The harem was the residence of the sultan, his women, and family. A palace in its own right, the harem consisted of several hundred apartments and included baths, kitchens, and even a hospital.

Three separate but interconnected sections formed the harem. The first section housed the eunuchs, while the second section belonged exclusively to the women of the palace. The third and final section was the personal residence of the sultan. The apartments of the imperial harem were reserved for the female members of the royal family, such as the sultan's mother (*valide sultan*), his wives, and his concubines. Many concubines in the royal harem came from the Caucasus. The "sultans were partial to the fair, doe-eyed beauties" from Georgia, Abkhazia, and Circassia.[33] There were also Christian slave girls and female prisoners of war who were sent as gifts to the sultan by his governors. These girls underwent a long process of schooling and training, which prepared them for a new life in the imperial palace. The most powerful woman of the harem was the mother of the sultan, who lived in her own apartment surrounded by servants and attendants. Her apartment included a reception hall, a bedroom, a prayer room, a resting room, a bathroom, and a bath. It was second in size only to the apartment of the sultan.

Topkapi Palace, harem (interior). Hall of the Padisha (Throne Room).
(Vanni / Art Resource, NY)

EUNUCHS

As in other Islamic states, in the Ottoman Empire, the ruler maintained eunuchs or castrated males who were brought as slaves to
guard and serve the female members of the royal household. As
Islam had forbidden self-castration by Muslims or castration of one
Muslim by another, the eunuchs were bought in the slave markets
of Egypt, the Balkans, and southern Caucasus. In the palace, there
were two categories of eunuchs—black and white. Black eunuchs
were Africans, mostly from Sudan, Ethiopia, and the east African
coastal region, who were sent to the Ottoman court by the governor
of Egypt. They served the female members of the royal family who
resided in the sultan's harem. The white eunuchs were mostly white
men imported from the Balkans and the Caucasus and served the
recruits at the palace school. The black eunuchs "underwent the so-
called radical castration, in which both the testicles and the penis
were removed," whereas, in the case of eunuchs from the Balkans
and the Caucasus, "only the testicles were removed."[34]

An important figure in the Ottoman power structure was the
chief black eunuch, who served as the *kızlar ağası* (chief of women)
or *harem ağası* (chief of harem). In charge of the harem and a large

group of eunuchs who worked under his direct supervision, the chief black eunuch enjoyed close proximity to the sultan and his family.

Another important figure was the chief of the white eunuchs, who acted as *kapi ağası* (chief of the Gate of Felicity).[35] Starting with the reigns of Murad III (1574–1595) and Mehmed III (1595–1603), the white eunuchs lost ground, and black eunuchs gained greater control and access to the sultan. Regardless of their race, ethnic origin, or the degree and intensity of castration, the palace eunuchs received privileges—such as lavish clothing, accoutrements, and accommodations—in keeping with their high status. Included among these privileges was access to the best education available. It is not surprising, therefore, that many chief eunuchs were avid readers and book collectors who established impressive libraries.[36]

The *ağa*, or the chief, of the black eunuchs of the harem was not only responsible for the training and supervision of the newly arrived eunuchs but also supervised the daily education and training of the crown prince and "oversaw a massive network of pious endowments that benefited the populations of and Muslim pilgrims to Mecca and Medina."[37] He used his position and access to the throne to gain power and influence over the sultan and government officials. His daily access to the sultan, and close relationship with the mother and favorite concubines of his royal master, made him an influential player in court intrigues. By the beginning of the 17th century, the chief eunuch had emerged as one of the most powerful individuals in the empire, at times second only to the sultan and the grand vizier and, in several instances, second to none.[38]

PALACE PAGES AND ROYAL CHAMBERS

Four principal chambers within the palace served the sultan and his most immediate needs.[39] The privy chamber served his most basic needs such as bathing, clothing, and personal security. The sultan's sword keeper (*silahdar ağa*), the royal valet (*çohadar ağa*), and his personal secretary (*sir katibi*), were the principal officials in charge of the privy chamber.[40] The treasury chamber held the sultan's personal jewelry and other valuable items. The third chamber, the larder, was where the sultan's meals were prepared, and the fourth, or campaign chamber, was staffed by bathhouse attendants, barbers, drumbeaters, and entertainers.[41] Pages with exceptional ability and talent would join the privy chamber after they had served in one of the other three chambers.[42] From the time the sultan woke up to the time he went to bed, the pages of the privy chamber accompanied him and organized the many services that their royal master required.

Surrounded and served as he was by an elaborate hierarchy of pages, eunuchs, and attendants, access to the sultan became increasingly difficult, and the number of individuals who could communicate directly with him decreased significantly. One result was a rapid and significant increase in the power of the royal harem. Starting in the second half of the 16th century, the sultan's mother and wives began to exercise increasing influence on the political life of the palace and the decision making process. They enjoyed direct access to the sultan and were in daily contact with him. With the sultan spending less time on the battlefield and delegating his responsibilities to the grand vizier, the mothers and wives began to emerge as the principal source of information and communication between the harem and the outside world.

The majority of Ottoman sultans, however, were far from simple-minded puppets of their mothers, wives, and chief eunuchs. In the mornings, they attended to the affairs of their subjects, and in the evenings, they busied themselves with a variety of hobbies and activities. According to the Ottoman traveler and writer Evliya Çelebi, who served for a short time as a page in the palace, Murad IV (1623–1640) had a highly structured routine in his daily life, particularly during winter, when it was difficult to enjoy hunting and horseback riding. In the mornings, he attended to the affairs of his subjects. On Friday evenings, he met with scholars of religion and the readers of the holy Quran and discussed various issues relating to religious sciences. On Saturday evenings, he devoted his time to the singers who sang spiritual tunes. On Sunday evenings, he assembled poets and storytellers. On Monday evenings, he invited dancing boys and Egyptian musicians who performed till daybreak. On Tuesday evenings, he invited to the palace old and experienced men, upwards of seventy years, whose opinions he valued. On Wednesday evenings, he gave audience to pious saints and on Thursday evenings, to *dervişes* (members of Sufi or mystical orders).[43]

As the Ottoman Empire entered the modern era, the everyday life of the sultan also underwent a significant change. The slow and easygoing lifestyle that prevailed at the harem of Topkapi and the large ceremonial gatherings, which marked the visit by a foreign ambassador to the imperial palace, gave way to a simple and highly disciplined routine characterized by the informality of interaction between the sultan and his guests. Abdülhamid II, who ruled from 1876 to 1909, awoke at six in the morning and dressed like an ordinary European gentleman, wearing a frock coat, "the breast of which, on great occasions," was "richly embroidered and blazing with decorations."[44] He worked with his secretaries until noon, when he sat for a light lunch. After finishing his meal, the sultan took a short drive in the palace park or a sail on the lake. Back at work, he gave audience to his grand vizier; various court dignitaries; the *şeyhülislam*, or the head of the ulema; and foreign ambassadors. Having abandoned the ceremonial traditions of his predecessors who ruled from Topkapi's inner section, the sultan placed his visitor beside him on a sofa and lighted a cigarette, which he offered to the guest. Since he could speak only Turkish and Arabic, the sultan communicated with foreign ambassadors and dignitaries through interpreters.[45] At eight in the evening, Abdülhamid II dined, sometimes alone and, at times, with a foreign ambassador. According to one source, the dinner was "usually a very silent one" with dishes "served in gorgeous style, *à la française*, on the finest of plate and the most exquisite porcelain."[46] After dinner, the sultan sometimes played duets on the piano with his younger children before he retired to the royal harem. He was fond of light music.[47]

Palace of the Sweet Waters. William H. Bartlett. From Pardoe, Julie, *The Beauties of the Bosphorus* (London 1839). (Library of Congress)

SULTAN IN PUBLIC

The people of the capital could watch their sultan each Friday, leaving his palace for Aya Sofya, the grand mosque, where he prayed. During the classical age of the empire, state dignitaries rode in front of sultan with their proximity to their royal master determined by the position they held at the court and in the government. Behind them rode the sultan's clean-shaven pages, "beardless and clothed in red livery."[48] The sultan was surrounded by foot soldiers armed with bows and arrows, and "among these, certain others again, with the office of courier and letter bearer, and therefore running along most swiftly" and "dressed in scanty clothes, with the hems of their coats in front shortened to the waist, and with their legs half bare: and all of them, wearing livery according to their office, richly attired, and looking charming with feathers decorating their hats."[49] Immediately behind the sultan rode his sword keeper and the royal valet, whose offices were highly esteemed among the Ottomans.[50]

One of the principal functions of the state was waging war, and military parades held before and after a campaign provided a popular spectacle, which was attended by the sultan, his ministers, and thousands of ordinary people. After war had been declared, all army units were assembled and brought to order in an enclosure, where the grand vizier held a divan, or council, that included all the dignitaries and high officials of the government who were to accompany him on the campaign.[51] Once the divan had completed its deliberations, the grand vizier and company met with the sultan, who issued his dispatch and final command.[52] Upon leaving his audience with the sultan, the grand vizier mounted his horse and, accompanied by the entire court and the army units, which had awaited him in various courtyards, set off towards his first encampment.[53] If the campaign was in the east, the army crossed the Bosphorus with galleys and rowboats that transported them to the Asian shore, where the grand vizier waited, allowing his troops to arrive, equip themselves, and prepare for the long journey ahead.[54] Before the troops crossed the straits, however, the people of Istanbul flocked to the windows of their homes or the streets to cheer them on and bid them farewell. The sultan, surrounded by his attendants and the members of the royal family, watched the event from a tower attached to the outside walls of the palace.[55]

The Italian traveler, Pietro della Valle (1586–1652), who was in Istanbul from June 1614 to September 1615, described the military parade organized on the occasion of a new Ottoman campaign against Iran. The parade began with a display of large red and yellow flags held aloft by men on horseback. Behind them, riding two by two came the palace officials and couriers whose duty it was to deliver messages and execute orders (*çavuşes*). Gunners and bombardiers on foot followed, also two by two and armed with scimitars and arquebuses. Behind them came armor-clad soldiers and men carrying a variety of weapons, including "iron clad maces, axes, and swords with double points or blades to each hilt."[56] Next came the *sipahis* (the cavalrymen), armed with bows and arrows and dressed in their special garb, which was tucked up and adorned with diverse skins of wild animals slung across them. The *acemi oğlans* (young recruits to be trained as janissaries or the sultan's elite infantry corps) were led by their *ağa*, or commander, who was a white eunuch. They were followed by the banners of the janissaries and the captains of the janissary corps in pairs and armed with bows and arrows.[57] Behind their flags and captains marched thousands of janissaries packed closely together. They led, by hand, water-bearing horses, adorned with grass and flowers, and festooned with rags, tinsel, little flags, and ribbons.[58] The janissaries were followed by men carrying axes, hatchets, and wooden swords. Then arrived pieces of artillery and galley boats, as well as regular foot soldiers. Finally came their *ağa*, or commander, and the *dervişes* of the Bektaşi Sufi order, singing and shouting prayers for the glorious army.[59]

At the end of the parade came the horses of the grand vizier led by his pages armed with bows and arrows with coats of mail under their trappings or clothes. They were accompanied by the *kadis* (religious judges) of Istanbul and Galata; the two *kadiaskers*, or the army judges of Anatolia and Rumelia (the European provinces of the empire); the *müfti* (the chief Muslim theologian) of Istanbul; and the viziers (ministers) of the imperial council. Finally, the grand vizier himself rode in pomp and ceremony, surrounded by a large number of foot soldiers, with the heron's plume emblem of his office adorning his turban.[60] Behind the grand vizier appeared additional *sipahi* units with their own weapons, which were lances without hilts, bows, arrows, and coats of mail. Behind them rode cavalrymen attached to the chief minister who served as his bodyguards.[61] These men wore antique helmets, buckles, and golden stirrups, and their horses were caparisoned with cloth of gold nearly to the ground.[62]

At times before embarking on a military campaign, the Ottoman government instructed trade and craft guilds in the capital to parade in front of an imperial pavilion where the sultan could review their march.[63] The Ottoman traveler Evliya Çelebi wrote that before invading Iran in 1636, Murad IV ordered all guilds in Istanbul to march in a parade as he and his ministers and pages watched from the procession pavilion at the Topkapi Palace. Members of each guild paraded in their unique attire atop floats or on foot. They displayed their various crafts and trades, trying to outdo one another as they entertained the sultan and the large crowds, which consisted of the entire populace of the city except for those actually marching in the procession. Every guild had its own unique rallying cry, spiritual and religious leader, and patron saint. The parade began with the palace staff, followed by prestigious craftsmen, who were then followed by less prestigious groups such as the manure collectors and the gravediggers. Even "pickpockets, pimps and male prostitutes formed themselves into guilds, although they had to be accompanied by guards."[64] All trade and daily work was interrupted in the city for the three days during which the excitement of the procession filled the capital. These parades reasserted the power and control of the sultan over his subjects and reminded the populace of the existing social hierarchy, providing an outlet for tensions that periodically arose between the ruling elite and the subject classes.[65]

Sultan Mahmud II in procession. Anonymous, 19th century. (V&A Images, London / Art Resource, NY)

Street barbers at work in Istanbul. (Library of Congress)

The tradition of military parades, which included craftsmen and artisans, continued into the 18th century. As late as 1718, the Otto-man troops heading to war against the Habsburgs assembled in Edirne and participated in a parade that lasted eight hours, starting at eight in the morning and ending at four in the afternoon.[66] As the sultan watched from the window of his palace, the procession began with a man of the cloth, mounted on a richly decorated camel, reciting verses from a Quran, which was finely bound and laid on a cushion.[67] He was surrounded by a group of boys dressed in white, reading verses from Islam's holy book. They were followed by a man dressed in green boughs, representing a peasant farmer sow-ing seed, and several reapers with ears of corn and scythes in their hands pretending to mow. After they had passed, a "machine drawn by oxen" appeared with a windmill and several boys grinding the corn; these were followed by another machine drawn by buffaloes carrying an oven, and two more boys, one kneading the bread and the other drawing it out of the oven.[68] These young lads threw little cakes to the cheering crowd and were accompanied by a team of bak-ers marching on foot, two by two, in their best clothes, with cakes, loaves, pastries, and pies on their heads.[69] Once these had passed, "two buffoons" with "their faces and clothes smeared" with food began to entertain the people.[70] Meanwhile, craftsmen from various trades continued the procession with the more respected artisans such as the jewelers and mercers riding horses.[71] An English lady who watched the entire procession selected the furriers, with their large machine "set round with skins of ermines, foxes" and stuffed animals, which "seemed to be alive," followed by music and dancers as one of the best displays.[72] At the end of the procession, the volunteer martyrs who pleaded for permission to die on the battlefield appeared naked down to the waist. In an expression of their zeal for glory and martyrdom, some had their arms and heads pierced through with arrows left sticking in them, with the blood trickling down their faces. Others had slashed their arms with sharp knives, causing blood to spurt out on to the spectators.[73]

When the army returned from a victorious campaign, military parades were organized to display the bound and chained enemy captives, as well as the decapitated heads of their troops. These were flayed and salted, and then stuffed with hay to be carried on poles, pikes, and lances. In his *Book of Travels*, Evliya Çelebi recounted the return of Murad IV (1623–1640) from a successful campaign against Iran:

> On the 19th of Rajab 1045 [29 December 1635] the illustrious emperor made his entry into Istanbul with a splendour and magnificence which no tongue can describe nor pen illustrate. The populace who poured out of the city to meet the emperor had been dissatisfied with the Kaymakam Bayram Paşa [the governor of Istanbul], but, gratified by the sight of their emperor, they became animated by a new spirit. The windows and roofs of the houses in every direction were crowded with people, who exclaimed, "The blessing of God be upon thee, O conqueror! Welcome, Murat! May thy victories be fortunate!" In short, they recovered their spirits, and joy was manifest in every countenance. The sultan was dressed in steel armour, and had a three-fold aigrette in his turban, stuck obliquely on one side in the Persian manner: he was mounted on a Noghai steed, followed by seven led horses of the Arab breed, decked out in embroidered trappings set with jewels. . . . The conqueror looked with dignity on both sides of him, like a lion who seized his prey, and saluted the people as he went on, followed by three thousand pages clad in armour. The people shouted "God be praised!" as he passed, and threw themselves on their faces to the ground . . . During this triumphant procession to the saray all the ships . . . fired salutes, so that the sea seemed in a blaze. The public criers announced that seven days and seven nights were to be devoted to festivity and rejoicing.[74]

Though "the presence of women in public spaces was regarded with considerable misgivings," if the sultan ordered, a large terrace was built to allow women to participate in the festivities organized by the palace.[75] On his return from a campaign against the Habsburgs in 1596, Mehmed III demanded the presence of the women from the royal harem.[76] The sultan's women were also present at a royal circumcision held with pomp and ceremony in 1720.[77]

The conqueror of Constantinople, Mehmed II, began the custom of holding state festivals to mark dynastic events, such as the circumcisions of princes and the weddings of the sultan's daughters and sisters. These celebrations provided an opportunity for the palace to demonstrate its power and for craftsmen to display their goods and encourage increased consumption, while allowing the urban population a few days of rest and distraction before they had to return to the repetition and tension of everyday life. At times of political and economic crisis, particularly after military defeat at the hands of foreign foes, these dynastic festivities were celebrated with special pomp and ceremony. To describe and mark these festivities, poets and writers composed literary works for *surnames* (imperial festival books).

Ottoman sultans organized royal circumcision festivals. Lasting from 10 to 55 days, these imperial feasts marked an "occasion during which royal princes, along with hundreds of the sultan's subjects' boys, were blessed by the ceremony of circumcision."[78] The festivities on such occasions included ceremonial receptions, communal feasts, games and competitions, mock battles, firework displays, and brightly lit ships and watercraft sailing down the Golden Horn. The participation of performers from Iran and Egypt "and various displays of exotic animals like elephants and giraffes gave the ceremonies a more cosmopolitan flavour."[79] Circuses and "musical performances, along with displays of *tableaux vivants* in the shape of dragons" were also "exhibited on the Bosphorus."[80] Aside from illuminating Istanbul "with torches and lamps," the "circumcision feasts included the decoration of public buildings"; "banquets for various foreign and state dignitaries; and public displays of animal sacrifices in the course of rich and spectacular pageantries."[81]

During the first days of the festivities, the princes accompanied their royal father to ceremonies that were held outside the capital where decorations such as *nahils,* or large pyramid-shaped wooden poles "copiously decorated with real or artificial flowers and fruits, often gilded or silver-plated," were displayed.[82] In "its physical form, built with wax and wire, a *nahil* was covered with fresh flowers and sprouting foliage," and it was often "decorated with symbols of birds, plants and animals of various kinds," representing "fertility and the renewal of natural virility embodied in a symbol of erect vitality."[83]

The *nahil* (derived from the Arabic word for date palm) was transported from the imperial palace to the ceremonial ground by a procession that paraded the large wooden pyramid through the streets of Istanbul and included musicians, performers, and "a number of Janissaries who would eventually place it beside the yet to be circumcised prince."[84] After the prince had been circumcised, the *nahil,* which symbolized "birth, the blossoming of life, fertility and regeneration," was returned to the palace.[85] The so-called "*nahil*-processions were usually performed alongside various consumption-related activities like the distribution of sweet pastries, sweet drinks and sherbet, and at times a sacrificial animal would be brought along to be slaughtered on behalf of the circumcised prince and royal family."[86] Sheep were slaughtered to win God's blessing and favor, rice dishes and saffron-colored sweets were prepared, and banquets were arranged by various government officials and court dignitaries, at which musicians played, dancers performed, and numerous guilds paraded in all their splendor.

During the circumcision festivities, weddings, and victory parades, several hundred performers converged and entertained the sultan and the public. Highly talented and famous performers usually received a large sum of money for a night of entertainment.[87] These "lords of misrule," who were, for the most part, Gypsies, Jews, Armenians, and Greeks, and who included dancers, singers, musicians, mimics, comics, tumblers, jugglers, and fire-eaters, competed with each other to produce the most voluptuous dances, the funniest scenes, and the most astounding tricks.[88]

The appointment of a new grand vizier provided another occasion for festive celebration. Astrologers determined the auspicious hour for his arrival in the capital. People rented shops to view the parade that the new minister led.[89] Once the parade had ended, the new grand vizier arrived at the palace. There, sheep were slaughtered, and the meat distributed among the poor. Money and gifts were handed to the troops to secure their support. After arriving in the palace, the sultan dressed his newly appointed chief minister in a sable robe of honor, stuck several royal jeweled aigrettes into his turban with his own hand, and uttered the benediction: "Go, may God the exalted be your Helper."[90]

NOTES

1. Sina Akşin, *Turkey, from Empire to Revolutionary Republic: The Emergence of the Turkish Nation from 1789 to Present* (New York: New York University Press, 2007), 9.

2. Gábor Ágoston, "Administration, Central," in *Encyclopedia of the Ottoman Empire,* eds. Gábor Ágoston and Bruce Masters (New York: Facts On File, 2009), 11.

3. Barbara Jelavich, *History of the Balkans: Eighteenth and Nineteenth Centuries* (Cambridge: Cambridge University Press, 1983), 40.

4. Akşin, *Turkey, From Empire to Revolutionary Republic,* 11.

5. Ibid., 11–12.

6. Ibid., 12.

7. Ibid.

8. Jelavich, *History of the Balkans,* 40.

9. Ibid.

10. Ibn Battuta, *The Travels of Ibn Battuta,* trans. H.A.R. Gibb (Cambridge: Cambridge University Press, 1962), 452.

11. Ibid.

12. Zeynep Tarim Ertuğ, "Topkapi Palace (New Imperial Palace)," in *Encyclopedia of the Ottoman Empire,* 566.

13. Ibn Battuta, *Travels,* 452.

14. Ertuğ, "Topkapi Palace," 566.

15. Ibid.

16. Zeynep Tarim Ertuğ, "Dolmabahçe Palace," in *Encyclopedia of the Ottoman Empire,* 186.

17. Ibid.

18. Ibid.

19. Ibid.

20. Ibid.

21. Ibid.

22. Richard Davey, *The Sultan and His Subjects,* 2 vols. (London: Chapman and Hall LD., 1897), 1:50.

23. Ibid., 1:51.

24. Ibid.

25. Nicholas Tromans, "Harem and Home," in *The Lure of the East: British Oriental Painting* (New Haven: Yale University Press, 2008), 128.

26. Ibid.

27. Ibid.

28. Ibid.

29. Ibid.

30. Ibid.

31. Peter F. Sugar, *Southeastern Europe under Ottoman Rule: 1354–1804* (Seattle: University of Washington Press, 1996), 34–35; Halil Inalcik, *The Ottoman Empire, The Classical Age 1300–1600* (New York: Praeger Publishers, 1973), 76.

32. Sugar, *Southeastern Europe under Ottoman Rule*, 34–35; Inalcik, *The Ottoman Empire*, 77.

33. Alev Lytle Croutier, *Harem: The World Behind the Veil* (New York: Abbeville Press, 1989), 30.

34. Jane Hathaway, *Beshir Agha: Chief Eunuch of the Ottoman Imperial Harem*. (Oxford: Oneworld Publications, 2005), 19.

35. Bernard Lewis, *Istanbul and the Civilization of the Ottoman Empire* (Norman: University of Oklahoma Press, 1963), 77.

36. Hathaway, *Beshir Agha*, xiv.

37. Ibid.

38. Ibid., xiii.

39. Inalcik, *The Ottoman Empire*, 80.

40. Stanford J. Shaw, *History of the Ottoman Empire and Modern Turkey*, 2 vols. (Cambridge: Cambridge University Press, 1976), 1:115.

41. Ibid., 1:117; Inalcik, *The Ottoman Empire*, 80.

42. Inalcik, *The Ottoman Empire*, 80.

43. Evliya Efendi (Çelebi), *Narratives of Travels in Europe, Asia, and Africa in the Seventeenth Century*, trans. Ritter Joseph Von Hammer (London: Parbury, Allen, & Co., 1834), 1:141.

44. Davey, *The Sultan and His Subjects*, 2:34.

45. Ibid.

46. Ibid.

47. Ibid.

48. Pietro Della Valle, *The Pilgrim: The Journeys of Pietro Della Valle*, trans. George Bull (London: The Folio Society, 1989), 21.

49. Ibid.

50. Ibid.

51. Ibid., 26–27.

52. Ibid., 27.

53. Ibid.

54. Ibid., 27–28.

55. Ibid., 28.

56. Ibid.

57. Ibid., 28–29.

58. Ibid., 30.

59. Ibid., 30–31.

60. Ibid., 31–33.

61. Ibid., 33–34.

62. Ibid., 34.

63. Çelebi, *Narratives of Travels*, 1:102.

64. Isabel Böcking, Laura Salm-Reifferscheidt, and Moritz Stipsicz, *The Bazaars of Istanbul* (New York: Thames & Hudson, 2009), 51.

65. Suraiya Faroqhi, *Subjects of the Sultan: Culture and Daily Life in the Ottoman Empire* (New York: I. B. Tauris, 2007), 184.

66. Lady Mary Wortley Montagu, *The Turkish Embassy Letters* (London: Virago Press, 2007), 94.

67. Ibid.

68. Ibid.

69. Ibid.

70. Ibid.

71. Ibid.

72. Ibid., 95.

73. Ibid.

74. Çelebi, *Narratives of Travels*, 1:131.

75. Faroqhi, *Subjects of the Sultan*, 184.

76. Ibid.

77. Ibid., 165, 184.

78. Babak Rahimi, "Nahils, Circumcision Rituals and the Theatre State," in *Ottoman Tulips, Ottoman Coffee Leisure and Lifestyle in the Eighteenth Century*, ed. Dana Sajdi (London: Tauris Academic Studies, 2007), 95.

79. Ibid.

80. Ibid.

81. Ibid.

82. Faroqhi, *Subjects of the Sultan*, 165.

83. Rahimi, "Nahils," 101–2.

84. Ibid., 100–101.

85. Ibid., 101–2.

86. Ibid., 100–101.

87. Çelebi, *Narratives of Travels*, 1:240.

88. Ibid., 240–41.

89. Faroqhi, *Subjects of the Sultan*, 184; Çelebi, *Narratives of Travels*, 1:142.

90. Çelebi, *The Intimate Life of an Ottoman Statesman*, trans. Robert Dankoff (Albany: State University of New York Press, 1991), 238.

3

GOVERNING
AN EMPIRE

The grand vizier administered the daily affairs of the empire from *divan-i hümayun,* or the imperial council, which served as the highest deliberative organ of the Ottoman government. According "to Mehmed II's law code, the grand vizier" (*vezir-i azam* or *sadr-i azam*) was "the head of the viziers and commanders," who in all matters acted as "the Sultan's absolute deputy."[1] He appointed all officials in both the central and provincial administration. Starting in the 17th century, the grand vizier's official residence or Bab-i Ali (High Gate), called the Sublime Porte by Europeans, was synonymous with Ottoman government.

Several times a week, at fixed times, the ministers met to listen to complaints from the subjects of the sultan. The council comprised of the grand vizier, who acted as the personal representative of the sultan, and his cabinet, known as the viziers of the dome, because they met in the domed chamber of the Topkapi Palace.[2] Those attending included the chief of chancellery, or lord privy seal (*nişanci*), who controlled the *tuğra* (the official seal of the Ottoman state) and drew up and certified all official letters and decrees; the chiefs of the Islamic judicial system (*kadiaskers*) who represented the religious establishment or the ulema and assisted the sultan and the grand vizier in legal matters; and the treasurers (*defterdars*) of Anatolia and Rumelia (Ottoman provinces in the Balkans), who oversaw the royal revenues originating from Rumelia, Anatolia, Istanbul, and the northwestern coast of the Black Sea. The *defter-dars* communicated to the grand vizier the daily transactions of the central treasury and had to ensure that the troops stationed in the capital received their pay in a timely fashion.

Prominent military commanders also attended the council. Beginning in the 16th century the *ağa*, or commander of the sultan's elite infantry, the janissaries, took part in the council's meetings. The commander of the *sipahis* also attended. The members of this cavalry corps received revenue from *timars* or fiefs held by them in return for military service. Süleyman I, who recognized the increasing importance of the imperial navy, appointed Grand Admiral Hayreddin Barbarossa to the council. Although the chief admiral of the Ottoman fleet (*kapudan paşa*) attended the meetings of the imperial council, he reported directly to the sultan on the readiness of the imperial arsenal and the Ottoman naval forces.[3] The grand vizier and his cabinet were accompanied by the *çavuş başi* (the head *çavuş*), the chief of the palace officers who maintained order and protocol at imperial council meetings and palace ceremonies, and who were dispatched as couriers to convey messages and execute orders. Clerks and scribes, numbering some 110 in the 1530s, worked under the supervision of the *reisülkütab* or chief of scribes, who acted as the head of the offices attached to the grand vizier. Each Ottoman high official maintained a large household, a kind of imperial palace in miniature, as a manifestation of his prestige and power.[4] His retinue "consisted of several hundred officers, ranging from menial domestics and bodyguards to companions and agents."[5]

At the time of Mehmed II, the imperial divan "met every day of the week, but in ensuing years this changed and the council met four times a week" on Saturdays, Sundays, Mondays, and Tuesdays.[6] The viziers who served in the divan arrived on horseback with pomp and ceremony. They were surrounded by their retinues, including their sword bearer, valet, and seal bearer, and dressed "in solemn dress, according to the offices they held."[7] The grand vizier arrived last riding alone at the end of an imposing cavalcade. Until the reign of Mehmed II, the conqueror of Constantinople, the sultan participated in the deliberations of his ministers. As the power and the territory of the empire grew, the sultan became increasingly detached and stopped participating in the meetings of the divan. Instead, a square window especially cut to overlook the council chamber allowed the sultan to listen in on the deliberations of his ministers whenever he chose.

As the viziers entered the divan, they sat in accordance with their position and status on a low sofa, which was attached to the wall and faced the main door to the audience hall. The *kadiaskers* of Rumelia and Anatolia sat to the left of the grand vizier, while the *defterdars* of Anatolia and Rumelia sat to his right.[8] The scribes sat behind the treasurers on mats, which were spread on the floor. Next to the treasurers sat the *nişanci* with a pen in his hand, accompanied by his assistants. The *reisülkütab* stood close to the grand vizier who frequently requested his opinion and services.

As an executive body, the imperial council conducted all manner of government business. It addressed foreign affairs, granted audiences to ambassadors, and corresponded with foreign monarchs. It oversaw the empire's war efforts by issuing detailed commands regarding the use of manpower, munitions, and provisions. It also supervised the building of public works, notably fortresses and aqueducts in Istanbul and the provinces. In addition, the council dealt with any number of problems brought to its attention through the reports and petitions of governors and judges. Finally, the council both appointed and promoted government officials.

The council also acted as a court of law, hearing cases that involved the members of the ruling class as well as complaints from ordinary folks. As one European observer wrote: "The Pashas" heard first the most important cases, "and then all the others, of the poor as well as of the rich," so that no one departed "without being heard or having" his case settled.[9] Once all the viziers had been seated, the petitioners were allowed to enter the divan and present their case or complaint. There were no attorneys or representatives present, and the authority to make the final judgment on each and every case rested solely with the grand vizier. He was the only government official who spoke during the proceedings unless he sought the opinion of one of his viziers.

The deliberations at the divan continued for seven to eight hours.[10] The members of the imperial council ate three times. First, "at dawn, immediately after their arrival, then 'at the sixth hour,' after the main business, and then after hearing petitions."[11] At noon, the grand vizier asked attendants to serve lunch. Ordinary people who were present at the time were asked to leave so that the cabinet could enjoy their meal free of crowds and noise. Large round copper trays set on four short-leg stools were placed in front of the grand vizier and other members of the divan. The grand vizier shared his food tray with two other officials. Other viziers followed the same pattern. They sat with a colleague or two around the large copper tray, and they shared the meal served by the palace kitchen.

Before they started their meal, all government officials spread a napkin on their knees to keep their garments clean. Then the servers placed freshly baked bread on the trays, followed by dishes of meat. As the viziers tasted from one plate, the servers brought a new dish and removed the plate that had already been tried. The grand vizier and his cabinet dined on mutton, "hens, pigeons, geese, lamb, chickens, broth of rice, and pulse" cooked and covered with a variety of sauces.[12] The leftovers were sent to the retinues of the ministers and dignitaries although they also had their food brought from their own palace kitchen.[13] Unlike the sumptuous meal served to high government officials, however, their lunch was bread and pottage, which was called *çurba*.[14] For drink, sherbets of all kind, as well as water, were served in porcelain dishes.

Meetings "ended in midday in the summer, when daybreak was early, and mid-afternoon in winter."[15] On Sundays and Tuesdays, the grand vizier met with the sultan after the meeting at the divan had ended. At times, other ministers were called to the sultan's audience chamber to provide reports. Aside from the grand vizier, the chief treasurer was the only minister who could speak directly to the sultan, while the other members of the divan merely stood silently with their hands crossed on their chests and their heads bowed as a show of their reverence and obedience. Having listened to these reports and deliberations, the sultan dismissed the members of the divan and the grand vizier, who departed the palace accompanied by a large escort of palace officials. The last to leave the palace was the commander of the janissary corps. On days when they did not meet with the sultan, the imperial council left as soon as their meeting at the divan had concluded.

According to a European diplomat who visited the Ottoman court in the 17th century, the sultan gave audience to foreign dignitaries on Sundays and Tuesdays. There were several specific occasions when the sultan or the grand vizier received foreign envoys. The most common of these was when an envoy arrived at the palace to present his credentials upon first assuming his post or after he had been promoted. Another occasion was the arrival of a foreign envoy who was sent by his government to congratulate the enthronement of a new sultan. The decision about whether the envoy was received by the grand vizier or the sultan depended on the status of the envoy, the ruler and the state he represented, and "the nature and quantity of the gifts" he intended to present.[16] If the foreign envoy "was received by both the sultan and the grand vizier, the audiences took place on different days."[17]

When the sultan agreed to meet with a foreign envoy, the grand vizier dispatched government officials and a group of elite horsemen attached to the palace, comprised of the sons of vassal princes and high government officials, to accompany the ambassador and his men to the royal residence. Once he had arrived at the palace, the ambassador was seated across from the grand vizier on "a stool covered with cloth of gold."[18] After the exchange of customary niceties and formalities, lunch was served with the grand vizier, the ambassador, and one or two court dignitaries, sharing a large, round copper tray covered with a variety of delicately cooked dishes. Coffee and sweetmeats followed the sumptuous meal.

After lunch, the ambassador and his attendants were escorted to a place close to the imperial gate where they waited for the arrival of the chief eunuch, who acted as the master of ceremony. Once he had arrived in the sultan's audience hall, two designated high officials

Dignitari della corte Ottomana (Dignitaries of the Ottoman Court). (Picture Collection, The New York Public Library, Astor, Lenox and Tilden Foundations)

took the ambassador by either arm and led him to kiss his majesty's hand, which in reality was a sash hanging from his sleeve. The same two court officials led the ambassador back to his place at the end of the room, where he stood and watched as the members of his delegation went through the same exact ceremony of being led to the sultan to kiss the royal sleeve. Early Ottoman sultans rose from their seats to recognize envoys who entered the imperial presence. As the Ottoman military power reached its zenith in the 16th century, however, Ottoman sultans, such as Süleyman the Magnificent, neither rose to their feet nor allowed envoys sit in their presence. As late as the 18th century, the sultan continued to be seated, but starting with the reign of Mahmud II (1808–1839), Ottoman monarchs adopted "a more courteous attitude" toward foreign envoys, standing up to greet them.[19] Once the ceremony had finished, the dragoman, or the interpreter, announced the ambassador's diplomatic commission, to which the sultan did not reply because such matters were left to the discretion of the grand vizier.

Until "the 19th-century reforms, the Ottoman government, unlike the governments of modern nation states, was small," and "its tasks were limited to a few key areas: defense of the empire, maintenance of law and order, resource mobilization, and management and supply of the capital and the army."[20] Other important concerns familiar to the governments of modern states such as education, health care, and common welfare were the purview of the empire's religious communities and professional organizations such as pious foundations and guilds.

DEVŞIRME

Those who managed the empire as governors, provincial administrators, and army commanders, received their education and training in the royal palace. They had been recruited as young slaves and brought to the palace, where they were trained as the obedient servants of the sultan. The Ottomans did not recruit these slaves from the native Muslim population. Rather, young Christian boys from the sultan's European provinces provided him with a vast pool from which new slaves could be recruited, converted to Islam, and trained to assume the highest posts in the empire. Known as the *devşirme* (collection), this system also resulted in the creation of the *yeni çeri* (new soldier) or janissary corps, who constituted the sultan's elite infantry and were paid directly from the central government's treasury.

Beginning with the reign of Murad I (1362–1389), Ottoman re-cruiters travelled the newly conquered regions of the Balkans and selected a certain percentage of boys from Christian villages. The Muslim jurists justified the practice by evoking the right of every Muslim conqueror to one-fifth of all movable booty after the end of a military campaign. In this context, "the Christian boys consti-tuted the sultan's fifth."[21] Even when the territorial expansion of the empire slowed down, the idea of recruiting young Christian boys as soldiers and administrators did not stop. As late as the 16th cen-tury, the sultan issued a royal decree ordering his local officials to summon all Christian boys between the ages of 8 and 20 in their rural districts.[22] The government officials selected and registered the most suitable young boys. The recruiters sought unspoiled and unsophisticated non-Muslim lads who did not know any Turkish but possessed strong health, attractive physique, and formidable moral character. The new recruits were sent in groups of a hundred to a hundred and fifty to Istanbul, where they were received by the commander of the janissary corps.[23] The number of boys recruited through this system in the 16th century has been estimated at from one to three thousand a year.[24]

As the future members of the ruling elite, the recruits had to learn Turkish and acquire the customs and etiquette of an Ottoman offi-cial. The best and most talented were retained as pages within the palace system, where they received further education and training in royal palaces in Istanbul and Edirne under the strict supervision of eunuchs and tutors.[25]

Once the pages had completed their education, they were either appointed to positions within the palace or served as the *kapikullari* (the slaves of the sultan) military units. Palace pages were trained by the eunuchs, who organized their daily activities and responsi-bilities. First, the eunuchs taught them silence, followed by proper behavior and posturing.[26] While in the presence of the sultan, they were to have their heads bowed and gaze downward, holding their hands together before them.[27] They then learned how to read and write. They also learned how to speak Turkish and pray in Arabic. Once they had completed this elementary stage, tutors began to teach them Persian and Arabic and encouraged them to read a vari-ety of works in both languages so that they could speak the elegant Turkish of the Ottoman ruling elite, which was very different from the "vulgar" language spoken by the peasant farmers in the villages and small towns of Anatolia.[28] At this stage, they also learned to ride, wrestle, shoot with a bow, throw the mace, toss the pike, and handle a variety of other weapons.[29] Thus, the young boys grew up in the isolation of the palace and with little contact with the outside world. As servants who owed their status and special privileges to the sultan, they remained single until they had reached the age of 30.[30] The system demanded that they devote their loyalty and service to the sultan rather than to a wife and children, who could otherwise occupy their time and energy.

Until the reign of Mehmed II in the middle of the 15th century, the Ottomans, like many previous Muslim dynasties, recruited and trained slaves primarily as soldiers. The majority of non-military functions were reserved for government officials who were recruited from the Muslim Turkish elite. The members of this elite class were, for the most part, educated in traditional bureaucratic and religious institutions where the knowledge of Islamic sciences, as well as Arabic grammar and Persian literature and poetry, was mandatory. Many who served as civil administrators within the Ottoman government were recruited from the ranks of the ulema, or the scholars and practitioners of Islamic law. Beginning in the reign of Mehmed II, however, the sultan began to appoint slaves to the top administrative positions of the empire.[31]

JANISSARIES

As the sultan's elite infantry force, the janissary corps constituted one of the most important pillars of the Ottoman military. The members of the corps were acquired as children from among the non-Muslim populations of the empire through the *devşirme* system. They were kept isolated and received special training in the palace. Their relative isolation from the rest of the population did not, however, prevent some of the janissary battalions from engaging in duties that brought them into contact with the urban populace of Istanbul. They took part in providing security, law and order, or similar municipal tasks. Each janissary battalion was based in one of Istanbul's numerous districts, where it operated out of *kolluk*, which functioned as a modern-day police station.

During the 17th century, the effectiveness of the janissaries began to decline as their discipline and training deteriorated. Worse, their commanders became increasingly involved in court intrigues. Instead of sowing fear in the heart of the enemy, the janissaries emerged as the source of terror and instability for Ottoman sultans. Their physical proximity to the sultan, and his dependence on them

A janissary (Ottoman elite guard). Jacopo Ligozzi (c. 1547–1632). (Nicolo Orsi Battaglini / Art Resource, NY)

for his safety and security, allowed the janissaries to play the role of kingmakers.

In the 18th century, the *devşirme* system finally came to an end as the janissary corps suffered a total "breakdown in discipline and vigour and began to lose its original status."[32] Meanwhile, as inflation set in and the cost of military campaigns increased, the central government faltered in its financial obligations and failed to pay the janissaries their salaries. In response to the sharp decline in their income, the janissaries became involved in activities that increased their real wages. Some opened coffeehouses, while others worked as "butchers, bakers, boatmen, and porters."[33] Some organized protection rackets for shopkeepers and artisans in return for regular payments. As their social and economic interests and activities became intertwined with those of the urban classes, the janissaries ignored the traditional rules, which prohibited them from marrying and living outside their barracks. They also sent their sons to join the janissary corps. In place of recruiting young Christian boys as slave soldiers, the sons of the retiring janissaries began to join the infantry force, thus establishing themselves as the hereditary successors to their fathers. Despite these fundamental changes in their role and function, the janissaries retained a prominent role in the palace and among the ruling elite. Here they exerted a conservative influence, which advocated protectionism in trade and opposed any fundamental reform of the political and military structure of the empire that would replace the corps with a new military force modeled after modern European armies.

In 1826, Mahmud II finally disbanded the janissary corps, shelling their barracks in Istanbul and massacring those who had challenged and threatened his authority. Replacing the janissaries, who had dominated the Ottoman army and political life for centuries, was not easy. It took several decades and numerous humiliating defeats at the hands of European armies before a new and well-trained military force emerged.

PROVINCIAL ADMINISTRATION

Along with the central government, the provincial administration also played an important role in preserving the unity and territorial integrity of the empire. To maintain an efficient provincial administration and a strong military force, the Ottomans had to create a financial organization that would collect taxes effectively and generate revenue. Under Ottoman rule, land constituted the most important source of wealth and income for the government. As in other Islamic states, there were several distinct categories of land ownership. By far the largest category was *miri* (crown land), or land owned and controlled by the state.[34] Theoretically, all lands used for agricultural production in the empire belonged to the sultan. The central government also recognized *vakif* (Arabic: *vaqf*), or land controlled and supervised as a religious endowment with its revenue providing support for charitable objectives.[35] Another category of land ownership was *mülk*, or privately owned land.[36] The *vakif* and *mülk* could be transferred to crown lands by the order of the sultan. Ottoman sultans were always desperate to increase their revenue base by confiscating *vakif* and *mülk* lands, and converting them to *miri*. Under the Ottoman land tenure system, the peasants enjoyed the hereditary right to cultivate the land but could not sell it or transfer the title without permission from the central government.[37] The hereditary right to cultivate the land passed from father to son.[38]

SIPAHIS AND TIMARS

Akçe, a silver coinage, constituted the chief unit of account in the Ottoman state. The Ottoman Empire frequently suffered from a scarcity of this silver coinage, which posed a fundamental challenge to the central government.[39] How could the Ottoman state collect taxes from peasant farmers who could not pay their taxes in cash? And how could the sultan pay his officials and troops their salaries? In response to these challenges, the empire was divided into numerous fiefs. A military fief with an annual value of twenty to one hundred thousand *akçes* was called *kiliç zeamat* (sword fief), or *zeamat* for short. A military fief less than that was called a *timar* (labor).[40] To each *timar*, or military fief, the sultan assigned a *sipahi*, or a cavalryman. The *sipahi* did not exercise the right of ownership over the *timar* he held, but was responsible for collecting taxes and maintaining security in the area under his control, making sure that the cultivation of land would not be disrupted.[41] He provided troops to the army during the time of campaigns, thereby contributing to the central government's cavalry force. Unlike the janissary, who used firearms, the *sipahi* and the men he recruited and organized were armed with medieval weaponry.[42] The revenue generated by his *timar* paid for his military services.

At the time of the conquest of each new territory, the Ottoman government sent agents to the newly acquired territory to identify and quantify taxable sources of income, such as crops, and assess the amount of tax that a particular district was to pay.[43] These calculations were then entered into government registries. Every twenty to thirty years, these tax assessments were revisited and, if necessary, revised.[44] Instead of paying the salaries of military personnel from the sultan's treasury, the troops were thus allowed to directly collect the revenue from agricultural production in lieu of their salary. The *sipahi*, who lived in a village among peasant farmers, collected the taxes in kind and it was his duty to convert it to cash.[45]

Timar holders were grouped together under *sancaks*, or military-administrative units, which were run by a military governor (*sancak bey*).[46] The military governor was called a *sancak bey* because he had received a *sancak*, or a standard/banner, from the sultan as a sign and symbol of his power and authority.[47] The officers positioned between the *sancak bey* and the ordinary *sipahi* were the *alay beys*, who were subordinate to the *sancak bey*, and the *subaşi*, who acted as the district commander responsible for apprehending offenders and keeping the peace.

As the Ottoman Empire grew in size and the number of *sancak beys* increased, the central government created a new position, the *beylerbey,* or *bey* of the *beys,* responsible for the *sancak beys* in his province.[48] Each *beylerbey* ruled from a provincial capital, which had its own janissary garrison, religious judge (*kadi*), and administrators in charge of assessing taxes.[49] This system did not prevail in all provinces and territories controlled by the sultan, however. In many Kurdish- and Arab-populated regions, tribal chiefs were appointed as hereditary *sancak beys.* They were responsible for collecting taxes—much of which they retained—and sending troops to Istanbul at time of war with foreign powers. There were also vassal Christian states, such as Wallachia and Moldavia, which were ruled by their princes, and Muslim principalities, such as the Crimea, that were administered by their khans. The Ottomans required an annual tribute from the vassal prince as a token of his submission.[50] At times, they also demanded that a son of the vassal prince reside as a hostage at the Ottoman court, and his father pay homage to the sultan by visiting the capital once a year and swearing allegiance to the sultan. The vassal prince was also expected to provide military support for the sultan's campaigns against a foreign enemy, and he was to treat the allies and foes of the Ottoman state as his own.

Aside from the *beylerbeys* and the *sancak beys,* who acted as the direct representatives of the Ottoman state, in all legal matters the sultan was represented by a *kadi* (judge), who came from the ranks of the ulema. The governors could not carry out justice without receiving a legal judgment from the *kadi,* but the *kadi* did not have the executive authority to carry out any of his religious rulings.[51] Until the second half of the 16th century, *kadis* were appointed for life, but as the number of prospective judges increased, term limits were imposed by the central government.[52] The *kadi* settled disputes, "drew up civil contracts, did all the notarial work of the district, administered the property of orphans and minors, acted as registrar, and officiated at important weddings."[53] The *kadi* applied the *şeriat,* or the sacred law of Islam, as well as the *kanun,* or the laws issued by the sultan. He could also take into consideration the local customs when issuing his ruling. Applying both the *şeriat* and the *kanun* in criminal cases, the *kadi* punished murder, rape, and highway robbery with execution or mutilation, while adultery, physical assault, wine drinking, and theft were punished by fines or bastinado blows.[54]

NOTES

1. Gábor Ágoston, "Administration, Central," in *Encyclopedia of the Ottoman Empire*, eds. Gábor Ágoston and Bruce Masters (New York: Facts On File, 2009), 11.

2. Çelebi, *The Intimate Life of an Ottoman Statesman*, trans., Robert Dankoff (Albany: State University of New York Press, 1991), 58.

3. Halil Inalcik, *The Ottoman Empire, The Classical Age 1300–1600* (New York: Praeger Publishers, 1973), 92–94, 222, 225; Çelebi, *The Intimate Life of an Ottoman Statesman*, 58. See also André Clot, *Suleiman the Magnificent* (London: Saqi Books, 2005), 344; Selcuk Aksin Somel, *Historical Dictionary of the Ottoman Empire* (Lanham: Scarecrow Press, 2003), 72–73, 145, 215–16, 311; Reuben Levy, *The Social Structure of Islam* (Cambridge: Cambridge University Press, 1969), 401.

4. Çelebi, *The Intimate Life of an Ottoman Statesman*, 10.

5. Ibid., 10–11.

6. Ertuğ, "Topkapi Palace," in *Encyclopedia of the Ottoman Empire*, 567. See also Ottaviano Bon, *The Sultan's Seraglio: An Intimate Portrait of Life at the Ottoman Court* (London: Saqi Books, 1996), 33.

7. Pietro Della Valle, *The Pilgrim: The Journeys of Pietro Della Valle*, trans. George Bull (London: The Folio Society, 1989), 13.

8. Bon, *The Sultan's Seraglio*, 34.

9. Colin Imber, *The Ottoman Empire, 1300–1650: The Structure of Power* (New York: Palgrave Macmillan, 2002), 172.

10. Ibid.

11. Ibid.

12. Bon, *The Sultan's Seraglio*, 35.

13. Hedda Reindl-Kiel, "The Chickens of Paradise, Official Meals in the Mid-Seventeenth Century Ottoman Palace," in *The Illuminated Table, the Prosperous House: Food and Shelter in Ottoman Material Culture*, eds. Suraiya Faroqhi and Christoph K. Neumann (Würzburg: Ergon in Kommission, 2003), 79.

14. Bon, *The Sultan's Seraglio*, 36.

15. Imber, *The Ottoman Empire, 1300–1650*, 172.

16. Hakan T. Karateke, ed., *An Ottoman Protocol Register* (Istanbul: Ottoman Bank Archives and Research Centre, 2007), 16.

17. Ibid.

18. Bon, *The Sultan's Seraglio*, 41.

19. Karateke, *An Ottoman Protocol Register*, 12–13.

20. Ágoston, "Administration, Central," 12.

21. Jane Hathaway, *Beshir Agha: Chief Eunuch of the Ottoman Imperial Harem* (Oxford: Oneworld Publications, 2005), 4.

22. Inalcik, *The Ottoman Empire, The Classical Age 1300–1600*, 78.

23. Ibid.

24. Ibid.

25. Ibid., 78–79.

26. Bernard Lewis, *Istanbul and the Civilization of the Ottoman Empire* (Norman: University of Oklahoma Press, 1963), 79.

27. Ibid.

28. Ibid.

29. Ibid.

30. Inalcik, *The Ottoman Empire*, 79.

31. Justin McCarthy, *The Ottoman Turks: An Introductory History to 1923* (London, New York: Wesley Longman Limited, 1997), 55.

32. Ali Çaksu, "Janissary Coffee Houses in Late Eighteenth-Century Istanbul," in *Ottoman Tulips, Ottoman Coffee Leisure and Lifestyle in the Eighteenth Century*, ed. Dana Sajdi (London: Tauris Academic Studies, 2007), 118.

33. Donald Quataert, *The Ottoman Empire, 1700–1922* (Cambridge: Cambridge University Press, 2005), 45.

34. Inalcik, *The Ottoman Empire*, 109.

35. McCarthy, *The Ottoman Turks*, 116–18.

36. Ibid., 118–19.

37. Inalcik, *The Ottoman Empire*, 109.

38. Ibid.

39. Ibid., 107.

40. Ibid., 217, 226; Levy, *The Social Structure of Islam*, 401.

41. Stanford J. Shaw, *History of the Ottoman Empire and Modern Turkey*, 2 vols. (Cambridge: Cambridge University Press, 1976), 1:26.

42. Inalcik, *The Ottoman Empire*, 108.

43. Ibid.

44. Ibid.

45. Ibid., 107.

46. Shaw, *History of the Ottoman Empire*, 1:26; Gustav Bayerle, *Pashas, Begs and Effendis: A Historical Dictionary of Titles and Terms in the Ottoman Empire* (Istanbul: Isis Press, 1997), 140.

47. Inalcik, *The Ottoman Empire*, 104.

48. Shaw, *History of the Ottoman Empire*, 1:26.

49. McCarthy, *The Ottoman Turks*, 121.

50. Inalcik, *The Ottoman Empire*, 12.

51. Ibid., 104.

52. Bayerle, *Pashas, Begs and Effendis*, 97.

53. Raphaela Lewis, *Everyday Life in Ottoman Turkey* (London: B. T. Batsford Ltd., 1971), 29.

54. Inalcik, *The Ottoman Empire*, 74.

4

CITIES, TOWNS, AND VILLAGES: MERCHANTS, CRAFTSMEN, AND PEASANTS

The Ottoman concept of society divided the productive classes into merchants, craftsmen, and peasant farmers. Until the arrival of the modern industrial era, the major urban centers of the Ottoman Empire were much larger, and far more prosperous, than any urban center in Europe. The rich cultural and historical heritage of these cities was evident in their palaces, mosques, churches, synagogues, mausoleums, tombs, bathhouses, bazaars, schools, and bridges.

Aside from these cities of antiquity, new towns emerged during the long Ottoman rule, many along the main trade and military routes.[1] These urban centers served the Ottoman government as military and administrative centers and connected small towns and villages to the larger cities of the empire.[2] They were originally small, "stretching at most for two or three miles from one end to the other," but "within this compact space" was "a densely packed network of roads, many different kinds of houses, businesses, religious institutions, coffee houses, *hammams* [bathhouses], *waqf* complexes, public fountains and a whole range of other kinds of spaces."[3]

MAHALLES

Each Ottoman urban center was divided into *mahalles*, or city quarters. The *mahalle* constituted a social, cultural, and economic zone, which delineated the cultural life of its residents from other city quarters and neighborhoods.[4] Ottoman towns and cities contained diverse ethnic and religious communities, with each community living in its own *mahalle*. Muslims, Christians, and Jews inhabited their own neighborhoods. They "spent most of their lives in one neighborhood, rarely venturing beyond their local sphere of activity because all their daily needs could be met in their immediate social surroundings."[5] In most *mahalles*, "there was a small market for daily goods, perhaps a small mosque, a butcher shop, fruit vendors, and other institutions providing social services."[6] The residents of a *mahalle* "saw one another regularly, and this fostered a distinctive sense of neighborhood identity, which often took on the characteristics of an extended family."[7] Neighbors in such tightly knit neighborhoods recognized one another and noticed the presence of strangers immediately. Such proximity and familiarity did not always breed good intentions and result in neighborly acts; it also encouraged gossip and speculation.

Mahalles "tended to segregate the urban population" in accordance with "religion and profession."[8] Not surprisingly, many Christian *mahalles* were named after churches, which were located there, while many Muslim quarters traced their names to the main mosque within their boundary. Other *mahalles* took their names from the profession or trade practiced by the majority of residents. Regardless, central to every *mahalle* was the house of worship that served as the religious and cultural heart of the neighborhood. In a Muslim *mahalle*, the small neighborhood mosque, in a Christian quarter, the church, and in a Jewish community, the synagogue, were the focal points of the community. Members of different religious communities lived in their own *mahalles* under the leadership of their religious and administrative heads. A Muslim *mahalle* was represented by an imam, who served as the religious head of his community, and by the *kethüda*, who acted as the representative of the government. Similarly, a Christian or a Jewish *mahalle* was led by a priest or a rabbi. The *mahalle* provided the Ottoman authorities with the means to collect taxes in the urban centers of the empire. At times, the *kethüda* and/or the elder of each *mahalle* functioned as the tax collector for the state.[9]

Though smaller in size and population, Ottoman towns followed the same urban plan as the large cities. Each town had a congregational mosque, neighborhood mosques, inns and caravanserais, bathhouses, schools, lodges of Sufi orders, a bazaar, and shops. The town center was usually reserved for business purposes, administration, and local defense. The majority of residents in the town center were Muslims, who wielded civil and religious authority. They were joined by Greek, Armenian, Jewish, and foreign merchants, who controlled most long-distance commerce. Lying "in a ring around the center were the residential quarters (*mahalles*), where the general urban population lived in low dwellings that faced the meandering and narrow streets, and that were frequently separated from each other by large gardens," making "the towns appear larger than their actual populations would warrant."[10]

Muslim neighborhoods were often "found in the oldest and most prominent sections of the town and close to the center, while those of the Christians," called "*varosh* by the Muslim authorities and inhabitants, were commonly located farther from the center."[11] The homes of the town's Christian residents "tended to be of lower quality than those of Muslims, having few, if any, windows and structurally oriented toward inner courtyards rather than toward the streets."[12] These residential areas were surrounded by a broad circle of land that served as the town's cemetery. In the *varosh* of most towns in the Balkans, the population was highly heterogeneous. In the urban centers of 17th-century Bulgaria, there were Bulgarian, Greek, Armenian, and Albanian communities, as well as "Catholic Croatian merchants" from "the commercial city of Dubrovnik" on the Adriatic coast.[13] The majority of the Muslim and Christian population worked as craftsmen and traders.

Considerable regional differences appeared among Ottoman architectural designs, reflecting the region's climate, geographical and environmental setting, available building material, and distinct architectural traditions.[14] The mansions of the rich and powerful stood in close proximity to the shacks of the poor. Among the wealthy classes, the general plan of a house was an entrance through a blank wall, whose bland appearance was relieved by a beautifully carved wooden door. The house consisted of two courts. The first was the outer court, which served as a reception area for the male visitors and guests. The second court or the inner court was reserved for the women of the family and was in every Muslim household a private place, closed to all outsiders and strangers. The large hall "reserved for the men of the family to socialize with their guests" was called the *selamlik,* and the private section of the house that provided a separate and designated space for female socialization was the *haremlik,* or harem.[15]

In the Balkans, the homes of high government officials were adorned "with beautiful vineyards, gardens, and parks with their pavilions and galleries."[16] They were often two- or three-story high structures made of stone and crowned with red tiled roofs.[17] Each house also had "a source of pure flowing water, a pool and a fountain with water spurting from jets."[18] In most Ottoman towns, the houses of the lower classes did not differ much from those in villages, except that there was sometimes an upper story.

Despite their diverse population, the urban centers of the Ottoman Empire were known for "the absence of capital crimes" and some of "the best conducted people."[19] Janissaries' patrols "ensured that crime was kept to a minimum and the streets were almost deserted after dark, the silence was broken only by the cries of the night watchmen."[20] Those "who had to go out of for any reason were obliged by law to carry a flare."[21] A European observer who visited Istanbul in 1836 noted that the Ottoman capital, "with a population of six hundred thousand souls," had a police force of "one hundred fifty men," which was mostly for show rather than use.[22]

A Turkish apartment in the Fanar (Phanar). William H. Bartlett. From Julie Pardoe, *The Beauties of the Bosphorus* (London: 1839). (Library of Congress)

From dusk the streets were "silent," save when one was "awakened by the footfalls of some individual" who passed, "accompanied by his servant bearing a lantern, on an errand of business or pleasure."[23] Without "these lanterns, no one could stir" as the streets of the Istanbul and other large urban centers of the empire were not lighted and properly paved, making a walk in the dark dangerous.[24] If occasionally "some loud voice of dispute or some ringing of laughter" scared "the silence of the night," it was "sure to be the voice or the laughter of a European," for the "Turk" was "never loud, even in his mirth, a quiet internal chuckle" was "his greatest demonstration of enjoyment."[25]

OTTOMAN CONQUEST AND URBANIZATION

In Istanbul and other major urban centers of the empire, Ottoman conquest introduced a high degree of Islamization to everyday life.[26] Ottoman sultans introduced their faith and decorated the newly conquered cities with palaces, mosques, soup kitchens, schools, bathhouses, and fountains. These buildings and their majestic designs were replicated in provincial capitals around the empire.

Ottoman sultans were great builders, and Ottoman architects left a wide array of monuments, which serve as a testimony to their support for urbanization and economic prosperity. Indeed, architecture was "the most visible manifestation of Ottoman genius," not only in Anatolia, where the majority of the Turkish-speaking population resided but also throughout the Balkans and the Arab lands.[27]

The greatest of all Ottoman architects was Sinan (1489/1490–1578). As the chief architect of Süleyman the Magnificent, Selim II, and Murad III, Sinan designed his first architectural masterpiece in 1543, following the death of Prince Mehmed, one of the Süleyman's sons. The complex, built between 1543 and 1548, was named Şehzade (Prince). Sinan used Aya Sofya, which was built with a central dome supported by two semi-domes, as his model. His plan for the Şehzade complex was centered on a central dome supported by four semi-domes. Sinan's next giant project was the design and construction of the Süleymaniye Mosque. The construction of the mosque began in 1550 and ended in 1557. This magnificent building, set on a hill overlooking the Istanbul harbor, still dominates the city's skyline.[28] The "crowning glory of Ottoman architecture" and Sinan's "architectural paradise," however, was the Selimiye

Mosque in Edirne. This mosque was built between 1568 and 1574.[29] The "four soaring, pencil-thin minarets of the *Selimiye* mosque" surrounds "its lofty central dome, 105 ft wide," and the "honey-colored sandstone" contrasts "with the black lead of the roof and the turrets," which surmounts "the eight buttresses supporting the dome."[30]

The Ottomans also built public fountains for ablutions, which every Muslim was required to perform before praying at a mosque, and for keeping the town supplied with water. These fountains were often located in front of a mosque, or at least in close proximity, so that Muslims could fulfill their obligation of maintaining their cleanliness before they entered a mosque to pray.[31] Mosques and fountains were not, however, the only structures sponsored and built by Ottoman sultans. After the Ottomans conquered an urban center, the sultan ordered the damaged city walls repaired and instructed the new garrison commander to rebuild the fortress. The standard policy was "to return the city to its inhabitants and to restore it just as it had been before."[32] Damaged workshops, bathhouses, caravanserais, and tanneries were repaired. The commer-

Court of the Mosque of Eyoub (Eyub). William H. Bartlett. From Julie Pardoe, *The Beauties of the Bosphorus* (London: 1839). (Library of Congress)

cially oriented people of the empire, particularly the Jews, Greeks, and Armenians, were encouraged to populate the newly conquered towns and cities.

When Mehmed II captured Constantinople, the city lay in ruin and the population had been decimated by naval blockade and warfare. The sultan did not, however, wish to rule over a city of ruins. According to the chronicler Aşikpaşazade, Mehmed II appointed a new city commandant and sent his agents to various provinces, declaring that "whoever wishes, let him come, and let him become owners of houses, vineyards and gardens in Istanbul," and to whomever came, the Ottoman government gave what it had promised, but even this act of generosity was not sufficient to repopulate the city.[33] Thus, the sultan

> gave orders to dispatch families, both rich and poor, from every province. The Sultan's servants were sent with orders to Kadis and commandants of every province, and in accordance with their orders conscribed and brought very many families. Houses were also given to these new arrivals, and this time the city began to be repeopled . . . They began to build mosques. Some of them built

Fountain and market at Tophannè (Tophane). William H. Bartlett. From Julie Pardoe, *The Beauties of the Bosphorus* (London: 1839). (Library of Congress)

dervish convents, some of them private houses, and the city returned to its previous state. . . . The sultan built eight medreses
with a great cathedral mosque in their midst, and facing the mosque
a fine hospice and a hospital, and at the side of the eight medreses,
he built eight more small medreses, to house the students.[34]

The Ottoman state frequently moved Turcoman tribal groups
from Anatolia and settled them in the newly captured towns and
villages of the Balkans. Jews, Greeks, and Armenians also followed
Ottoman armies and opened businesses in the newly conquered
towns. The new settlers injected new blood into the urban econo-
mies, increased the population, and diversified the ethnic, linguistic, and religious composition of the region. In these new Ottoman
administrative centers, government officials, members of the religious classes, commanders of the army, and soldiers of the local
garrison performed the daily work of running a vast empire. These
officials included government agents who supervised tax collection; a *kadi*, or a judge in a religious court; the *sipahis* and their
warden; the janissaries and their commander; the wardens of the
fortress; the market inspector; the toll collector; the poll-tax official; the customs inspector; the chief engineer; the chief architect;
the mayor; as well as the local notables and dignitaries. Always
with the new Muslim populations came the ulema of the Hanafi
School of Islamic law, who acted as the chief muftis, or the officially
appointed interpreters of the Islamic law. The influx of Ottoman
officials, administrators, and army officers, as well as new settlers from Anatolia, created a new Muslim majority in many urban
centers of the Balkans. By 1530, Muslims constituted 90 percent of
the population of Larissa in Thessaly (Greece), 61 percent in Serres
(northern Greece), 75 percent in Monastir and Skopje (Macedonia),
and 66 percent in Sofia (Bulgaria).[35]

VAKIFS

In addition to the sultan, Ottoman officials, dignitaries, and local
notables built and endowed new mosques, schools, bathhouses,
bridges, fountains, and *derviş* convents that came to dominate the
urban landscape. The speed by which these new buildings were
completed, suggested not only plentiful supply of skilled labor
and highly developed architectural traditions, but the sufficient
and ready means necessary to fund such projects through to com-
pletion more reliably and much more quickly than European states
could manage at this time.

The true vehicle of Ottoman urban renewal was the pious foundation, or the *vakif*. By foregoing the revenues from rents on shops and land and instead directing them into a pious foundation, the founder of a *vakif* relinquished his ownership of the property and its resulting income, but in return secured blessings in his own afterlife and in the earthly lives of his children and heirs. Ottoman sultans and their government officials built mosques, schools, hospitals, water installations, roads, and bridges, as well as "institutions, which provided revenue for their upkeep, such as an inn, market, caravanserai, bathhouse, mill, dye house, slaughter house or soup kitchen" supported by *vakifs*.[36] The charitable institutions were "usually grouped around a mosque, while the commercial establishments stood nearby or in some suitably active place."[37] Regardless of their physical location, they played an important role in the civic life of the city by providing essential public services as well as offering goods and services for sale. *Vakifs* also financed Sufi convents, as well as water wells and fountains that kept the city alive and provided water for ablution.[38] They also fostered trade by funding the construction and maintenance of bridges and ferries.

BAZAARS AND BEDESTANS

Outside the imperial palace, urban life focused on the marketplace. Every "Ottoman city had a market district, known in Arabic as *suq* and in Turkish as *çarşi* where both the manufacture and sale of goods were centralized."[39] This was an important public space in any Ottoman city, and it was replicated across the empire. Markets served as the center for the people's social and economic life. The majority of large urban markets also "had an inner market, known as *bedestan,* which could be closed off at night or in times of trouble."[40] To attract merchants and craftsmen to their domain, Ottoman sultans built covered markets with *bedestans* in the cities they conquered. These markets, as well as inns or caravanserais, "served as lodgings for merchants" who "stored their valuable goods in special vaults reserved for them" at "these establishments."[41] At times, *bedestans* were used for storing "grains and other agricultural goods collected as product-tax by the representatives of the central administration."[42] *Bedestans* also "included shops where local and long-distance merchants exchanged their goods."[43] The large covered markets were usually surrounded by wide streets, gardens, and running springs on all sides.[44]

The covered bazaar of Istanbul (*kapali çarşisi*), located in the center of the old city, was a "city within a city, containing arcaded streets, numerous lanes and alleys, squares and fountains, all enclosed within high protecting walls, and covered by a vaulted roof studded with hundreds of cupolas, through which penetrated a subdued light."[45] One 19th-century European visitor explained that the covered bazaar was "composed of a cluster of streets, of such extent and number as to resemble a small covered town, the roof being supported by arches of solid masonry," with "a narrow gallery, slightly fenced by a wooden rail," occasionally connecting "these arches."[46]

The *kapali çarşisi* was designed and developed by Mehmed II, the conqueror of Constantinople, who "built more than 800 shops in the central location that was to become the covered bazaar, mainly shops of cloth merchants and tailors."[47] By the beginning of the 18th century, the bazaar contained three thousand shops, and by the end of the 19th century, four thousand.[48] Aside from shops, the covered bazaar had its own mosque, fountains, public bathhouse,

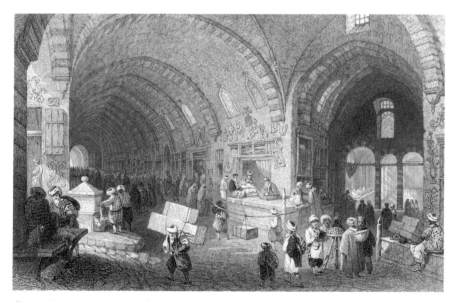

Great Avenue in the *tchartchi* (covered bazaar). William H. Bartlett. From Julie Pardoe, *The Beauties of the Bosphorus* (London: 1839). (Library of Congress)

school, coffeehouses, and warehouses.[49] Shoppers could enter its 61 narrow streets and lanes through 18 gates.[50] Those visiting the covered bazaar for the first time frequently got lost or confused.

Within the covered bazaar, there were distinct quarters and sections for each trade and craft. Manufacturers such as "goldsmiths, shoemakers, carpet merchants, and those who sold coats, furniture, jewelry, furs, cutlery, old clothes, cosmetics, hats, and almost any other kind of goods gathered together in their own sections of the bazaar."[51] The merchants and shopkeepers sat cross-legged on carpets in front of their shops and wore large turbans on their heads. Jewish, Greek, and Armenian traders and shopkeepers dressed and worked like Muslim merchants. Despite the best efforts of several religious sultans to prevent non-Muslim merchants from wearing the same clothes as the Muslim merchants, the Christian and Jewish traders continued to dress and act like their Muslim counterparts.[52]

Outside *kapali çarşisi*, there were also specialized bazaars where particular goods or products were exchanged or sold. Thus, the fish market of Istanbul offered a wide variety of fish taken, with

A scene in the *tchartchi* (covered bazaar). William H. Bartlett. From Julie Pardoe, *The Beauties of the Bosphorus* (London: 1839). (Library of Congress)

net or line, by fishermen of the Black Sea, Sea of Marmara, the Golden Horn, and the Bosphorus, while the Egyptian Market served as the great depot of spices and drugs.[53] Here the merchants sold such goods and products as "cinnamon, gunpowder, rabbit fat, pine gum, peach-pit powder, sesame seeds, sarsaparilla root, aloe, saffron, liquorice root, donkey's milk and parsley seeds, all to be used as folk remedies."[54]

Marketplaces and bazaars served as the centers of the city's commercial life. Men of all nationalities and religious affiliations, along with veiled women, many attended by servants, bargained with merchants and shopkeepers. Although "the markets were largely a part of the male sphere of Ottoman society, women could be found there as well."[55] Indeed, "poor women and peasant women hawked produce they grew themselves or items they made, such as embroidered towels."[56] Other women, "most commonly Jews, acted as peddlers carrying wares in the upper-class neighborhoods, visiting the harems and offering goods to women who were barred by social custom from going to the public markets themselves."[57] Among "the wealthy classes, it was not unusual for women" to own shops.[58] In "such cases, however, social custom did not allow the women to deal directly with men from outside their families," and they were forced to leave "the actual daily running of the business" to "a male relative."[59]

MERCHANTS AND GUILDS

In the Ottoman social hierarchy, the merchants and craftsmen stood below the members of the government and the ruling elite. They were required to dress in their own unique clothes and were prohibited from wearing the garments of the ruling classes.[60] In all Ottoman cities, local manufacturers were organized into guilds that produced consumer goods and handled local trade, while wealthy and well-connected merchants controlled long-distance commerce.

MERCHANTS

There were two categories of merchants in the Ottoman Empire: those who functioned as local traders, buying and selling goods produced by the guilds, and the *tüccar* or *bazirgan*, who were involved in long-distance and overseas trade.[61] The local traders formed a distinct category within the guilds and were, therefore, subject to the same regulations as the handicraftsmen. Those who were involved in long-distance trade were not subject to guild regulations.[62] Though not part of the ruling elite, the wealthy merchants who connected the markets of the Ottoman Empire with those of Europe and "the Orient" enjoyed enormous power and influence among government officials, many of whom invested in international trading ventures.

The *tüccar* performed several important functions in the Ottoman society and economy. The "most important of these was the distribution of raw material, food, and finished goods throughout the empire" and beyond.[63] In addition to trade within the empire, the *tüccar* imported and exported a variety of luxury goods. All these commercial activities resulted in significant contributions of customs and tolls to the imperial treasury. The *tüccar* involved themselves in large-scale exchange of goods or, in the case of luxuries, items of unusually high value.

In the Ottoman society, the few existing industries were controlled either by the state or the guilds, and cash was concentrated

Boutique et marchand turcs (c. 1880–1890). Merchants with an outside shop in Istanbul. Sebah and Joaillier. (Library of Congress)

in the palace and among the small ruling elite. Those who had amassed large fortunes in gold and silver invested in commercial enterprises organized by wealthy merchants. Palace officials, provincial governors and notables, as well as the powerful religious endowments, invested their money through the merchants in *mudaraba*, or in a commercial enterprise or major trading venture suitable for investment by a man of wealth and power.[64]

Wealthy merchants, who mostly operated from a *bedestan*, traded in luxury goods such as "jewels, expensive textiles, spices, dyes, and perfumes."[65] Their fortunes in gold and silver coin, as well as their ownership of slaves and high-quality textiles, were the outer signs of their enormous power and prestige in the urban communities of the Ottoman Empire. While "the merchants were among the most important and influential inhabitants of every city, they were also among the least popular."[66] Given "the profession and the understanding of the market economy" of these businessmen, "it is not amazing that they always aimed to maximize their profit involving speculative ventures of the simplest kind like buying cheap and selling high."[67] Because "this speculative activity included food and raw materials," the merchants "were blamed for all shortages that occurred occasionally."[68] Their reputation and standing "sank even lower in the latter period when their wealth permitted them to go into such professions as tax farming, which was certainly very unpopular with the population at large."[69] Beginning in the second half of the 16th century, the power of the long-distance traders began to decline as European merchant ships came to dominate the overseas trade and as "families descended from kapikulu officers [slaves of the sultan serving as soldiers or administrative at the palace] gained control of tax-farming and began to dominate the towns, both socially and politically."[70]

GUILDS

In the Ottoman Empire, the craftsmen were organized into guilds. The manufacturers, shopkeepers, and small traders who were organized under the guild system were known as *esnaf* (plural of *sinf*). Trade guilds already existed in Constantinople at the time of the Ottoman conquest in 1453. The number of guilds increased significantly as the city was rebuilt and repopulated under Mehmed II and his successors. In the 17th century, the Ottoman writer Evliya Çelebi listed over one thousand guilds in the capital.[71] He also wrote that there were nearly eighty thousand craftsmen in Istanbul alone, "working in more than 23,000 shops and workshops, and divided up into 1,100 different professional groups."[72] Three centuries later, a foreign observer estimated the number of distinct trades and crafts in Istanbul at one thousand six hundred and forty.[73]

Guilds were organized principally to manufacture consumer goods in demand by the population, regulate prices and competition, and facilitate the relationship between various trades and the government. Additionally, guilds provided assistance "to craftsmen to open shops, gave money to the sick, and took on the costs of burial if a member died."[74] They also "paid the wage of guards and firemen, gave alms to beggars in the bazaars, and made sure that the master craftsmen gave proper training to their apprentices, for only by qualifying as masters could the latter open a workshop of their own."[75]

The Ottoman central government frequently intervened in the daily affairs of the guilds. The state "dominated both production and distribution, determining even the range of profits permitted

Metal workers in a factory in Izmir. (Library of Congress)

to a craftsman."[76] With participation and support of guild masters, Ottoman state officials fixed the number of guilds in every city and disallowed the establishment of new shops and workplaces.[77] The guilds were not organized to produce for "a continuously expanding market," and they could not enrich themselves at the expense of the consumer.[78] They manufactured primarily for the population of their city and its neighboring towns and villages, and every effort was made by state officials to protect "both the consumer and the producer" by keeping "the consumption and production balanced."[79]

Given "the weakness of the urban police force," the Ottoman central government also "used the guilds as a means of controlling the urban population."[80] In addition, the guilds procured services needed by the army and navy, and secured payment of taxes and dues. A significant number of craftsmen were drafted into military campaigns. This was done because "to supply the soldiers with boots, coats and tents; the necessary investments had to be made by the relevant guilds."[81] Some guilds, such as those of rowers, oarsmen, waterfront workers, and boatmen who "linked Uskudar, Galata, and the Bosphorus villages to Istanbul," were recruited by the Ottoman navy to work at the dockyards.[82]

The daily activities of urban guilds were inextricably linked to the surrounding villages and rural communities, which supplied the craftsmen with such raw materials as wool, hides, cotton, grain, and other goods.[83] At times, the urban manufacturers purchased these basic materials from peasant farmers. In return, on rare occasions, peasants from nearby villages came to the town's craftsmen to purchase the textiles they used for new clothes at weddings and other important ceremonies. These direct commercial exchanges between the urban guilds and rural communities were rare, however, because peasants "produced most of the goods they needed at home, while many artisans bought through their guilds and/or from tax-farmers, and thus did not do their purchasing directly from villages."[84] In the majority of cases, peasants did not earn sufficient cash to buy finished goods from urban craftsmen. The little cash they earned was paid as tax to government officials. The artisans, on the other hand, did not produce to serve the needs of peasant farmers. Their principal customers were the members of the ruling elite, the merchants, and other craftsmen.[85]

Each guild "had a fixed number of members, and if one died, his place went to his son, or a travelling trader would buy the tools and wares of the deceased, and the money would go to his family."[86] Every guild was distinguished by its own internal structure, code of conduct, and attire. Ottoman guilds were inherently hierarchical, and each possessed its own organization. Customarily, however, its members were divided into the three grades of masters, journeymen, and apprentices. A very old and well-established conduct code obligated the journeymen to treat their masters with utmost respect and obedience, while the apprentices were expected to display reverence and deference to both the journeymen and masters. Within the guild hierarchy, the apprentices constituted the lowest category. Each apprentice had two comrades; one master teacher; and one *pir*, or the leader of his order.[87] The apprentice learned his craft and trade under the close supervision of a master. Members of each guild also met at *derviş* lodges where the masters of the trade taught the apprentices the ethical values and standards of the organization. After several years of hard work, when it was decided that the apprentice was qualified in his craft, a public ceremony was organized where he received an apron from his master.[88] The apron-passing ceremony involved festivities and performances: orators recited poems, singers sang, and dancers danced, while jugglers, rope-dancers, sword swallowers, conjurers, and acrobats performed and showed off their skills.[89]

The *kethüda*, or the senior officer and spokesperson of the guild, collected taxes for the state and represented his craft in all dealings and negotiations with the central government. Moreover, each guild had a *şeyh* who acted as the spiritual and religious head of the craft guild.[90] Among Ottoman guilds, competition and profiteering were viewed as dishonorable. Those who attracted customers by praising and promoting their products, and worked primarily to accumulate money, were expelled from the guild.[91] The craftsman was respected for the beauty and artistic quality of his work and not his ability to market his products and maximize his profit.[92] Not surprisingly, traders did not display signs and advertisements to draw the attention of buyers to their business. They merely displayed the pieces and products, which the buyer requested, and did not bargain over the price.

An important characteristic of the Ottoman guild system was the highly specialized nature of every branch of craft and industry. There were no shops that sold a variety of goods. If one needed to purchase a pair of shoes, he would go to the shoemaker section of the bazaar, and if his wife needed a new saucepan, kettle, or coffeepot, she sent her husband or servant to the street where the coppersmiths were located.

IHTISAB AND MUHTASIB

All Ottoman guilds abided by the traditional rules, which had been set down in the manuals of the semireligious fraternities (*futuwwa*), guild certificates, and various imperial edicts (*fermans*).[93] Specific laws and regulations (*ihtisab*) governed public morals and commercial transactions.[94] All guilds were obligated to follow and respect these rules, which included the right to fix prices and set standards for evaluating the quality of goods that would be sold by tradesmen. Negotiations between the representatives of the central government and the guild masters determined the prices of goods and the criteria for judging the quality of a product.[95] The state involved itself in this process to ensure the collection of taxes from each guild and to support the enforcement of the *ihtisab* laws and regulations.[96]

A market inspector, or a *muhtasib,* and his officers were responsible for enforcing public morals and the established rules. Strolling purposefully through the markets, they apprehended violators and brought them to face the local *kadi* (religious judge). They enforced the sentence handed down from the *kadi* by flogging or fining the violators. According to Islamic traditions and practices, the *muhtasib* dealt primarily with "matters connected with defective weights and measures, fraudulent sales and non-payment of debts."[97] Commercial knavery "was especially within his [the *muhtasib*'s] jurisdiction, and in the markets he had supervision over all traders and artisans."[98] In addition to his police duties, he also performed the duties of a magistrate.[99] He could try cases summarily only if the truth was not in doubt. As soon as a case involved claims and counterclaims and "the evidence had to be sifted and oaths to be administered," disputes were referred to the *kadi.*[100] The *muhtasib* was also the official responsible for stamping certain materials, "such as timber, tile or cloth, according to their standard and [he] prohibited the sale of unstamped materials."[101]

A European observer who visited the Ottoman Empire at the beginning of the 17th century described one form of punishment applied by the *muhtasib*: "Sometimes a cheat is made to carry around a thick plank with a hole cut in the middle, so his head can go through it . . . Whenever he wants to rest, he has to pay out a few aspers [silver coins]. At the front and back of the plank hang cowbells, so that he can be heard from a distance. On top of it lies a sample of the goods with which he has tried to cheat his customers. And as a supposedly special form of mockery, he is made to wear a German hat."[102] As the official responsible for the maintenance and preservation of public morals, the *muhtasib* had to ensure that men did not consort with women in public, and it was his duty to identify and punish bad behavior, particularly stealing, drunkenness, and wine drinking in public. A thief who was caught red-handed would be nailed by his ears and feet to the open shutter of the shop he had tried to rob. He was left in the same state for two days without food or water.[103] The *muhtasib* could take action against violations and offenses only if they had been committed in public. He did not have the right to enter a house and violate the privacy of a family.

BATHHOUSES

A "key resource of any Muslim city was its public baths."[104] A "city was not considered to be a proper city by Muslim travelers in the pre-modern period unless it had a mosque, a market, and a bathhouse."[105] Most "Ottoman cities had a public bathhouse in every neighborhood," which "provided not only an opportunity for cleanliness but also a public space for relaxation and entertainment."[106] This was "especially true for women, as men were allowed to socialize in the coffee houses and public markets."[107]

As early as the 14th century, the North African traveler Ibn Battuta observed that in Bursa, the Ottoman ruler Orhan had built two bathhouses, "one for men and the other for women," which were fed by a river of "exceedingly hot water."[108] At bathhouses, or hammams, men had their "beards trimmed or their hair cut," while women "had their skin scrubbed, their feet briskly massaged, and the whites and yolks of eggs . . . pressed around their eyes to try to erase any wrinkles."[109] In its "steam-filled rooms and private suites, young masseurs pummeled and oiled their clients as they stretched out on the hot stones."[110]

With the conquest of the Balkans, the Ottomans introduced their public baths to the peoples they had conquered. Hammams that received their water from aqueducts were constructed in many towns. Some of these baths were attached to the bazaars, where merchants, artisans, and shopkeepers were attended by serving-boys. Salonika's Bey Hammam, where visitors could still wash themselves until the 1960s, is one of the outstanding examples of early Ottoman culture and architecture.[111]

Having recognized the benefits of cleanliness and to avoid a needless trip to a public bath, the rich and the powerful built their own private baths at home. Many "families allowed their relatives and retainers to use" their private hammam, eliminating any need to use public baths.[112] Despite this development, the public baths remained popular among the masses who could not afford building their own private bathhouse.

Regardless of its size, every public bathhouse consisted of three sections: "the outer hall, in which bathing dress" was arranged; "the cooling room, a well-cushioned and comfortable space, moderately heated and intended for the temporary reception of the bathers"; and "the bath itself, where the atmosphere" was "laden with sulfuric vapor."[113] The public baths were open from eight in the morning to sunset with "men and women frequenting them on alternate days."[114] In "many neighborhoods, there were separate bathhouses for women."[115] For women, the bathhouse served as the best place to meet and "discuss every subject of interest and amusement, whether politics, scandal, or news; to arrange marriages and to prevent them, to ask and to offer advice, to display their domestic supremacy, and to impart their domestic grievances but above all to enjoy the noise, the hurry, and excitement," which stood in sharp contrast to "the calm and monotony of the harem."[116] Social custom strictly prohibited women from patronizing coffeehouses and other venues available to men. For women, the bathhouse became an escape from ordinary routine and offered a space to socialize with friends while drinking coffee and being entertained by female performers. Men "used the baths for many of the same reasons as women, but unlike visits to coffeehouses, there was no hint of impropriety for those who went to the baths to socialize."[117]

Before leaving the reception room and entering the main bath, a large octagon hall with several fountains and numerous small cabinets, the bather was supplied with a pair of wooden sandals, "raised several inches from the floor."[118] Among the upper classes, these sandals were "objects of great cost and luxury, the band by which" they were "secured across the instep being frequently

Cooling room of a hammam. William H. Bartlett. From Julie Pardoe, *The Beauties of the Bosphorus* (London: 1839). (Library of Congress)

inlaid with jewels."[119] Once in the main hall, the bathers gathered around the fountains that were supplied with both hot and cold water. In case of women from wealthy families, each lady was attended by her servants and slaves, "naked from waist upwards," who poured water over the head and body of their matron from a metal basin and gently combed her hair and rubbed her limbs "by a hand covered with a small glove, or rather bag, woven of camel's hair."[120] Once the washing, combing, scrubbing, and massaging had been completed, the female bather changed "her dripping garments for others" that awaited her near the door of the hall and passed into the cooling room.[121] Here, "reclining on mats and carpets," bathers rested for a long time "with their hair concealed beneath heavy" towels and their bodies "wrapped closely in long white" robes.[122] Once they finally ventured back into the reception hall, they lay on sofas where an attendant scattered perfumed water over their face and hands and folded them in warm clothes. As the bather sank "into a luxurious slumber beneath a coverlet of satin," servants and slaves served them sweetmeat, sherbet, and other plates of food.[123]

Khammam, 1812, inside an Otto-
man hammam (bath) for women.
Antoine L. Castellan. (Bildarchiv
Preussischer Kulturbesitz / Art
Resource, NY)

HANS

Khan or *han*, "a word of Persian origin" designated "on the one
hand a staging-post and lodging on the main communication
routes, on the other a warehouse, later a hostelry in the more important urban centers."[124] The highway *han* offered safe lodging
and protection for travelers and their possessions in regions where
nomads and roaming bandits threatened security. The *han* provided services indispensable for safe and successful overland
commerce and was essential in regions where food and water remained elusive.

While the highway *han* was "a staging-post and a relay-station,"
the urban *han* lay "at the end of a journey;" it was "a depot, a place
for commercial transaction and brief stay."[125] Aside from public
baths and coffeehouses, the urban *hans* provided open and free
space for social interaction between a variety of people from diverse ethnic and social backgrounds. Muslims, Christians, and
Jews; travelers, pilgrims, Sufi wanderers, merchants, and traders from various Ottoman provinces and distant lands, such as

Central Asia, India, Iran, and North Africa; all converged at these inns where they interacted without interference from any governmental or religious authority.

Whether built along the main roads or in the midst of cities, most *hans* and caravanserais were similarly designed. Invariably "built of stone, they consisted of a two-story rectangle or square built around an open courtyard in which there was a fountain."[126] Many also "had a small mosque in the corner of the structure facing Mecca."[127] A 17th-century French priest Robert de Dreux described the Ottoman *hans* as large buildings (as large as European churches), built by sultans "to lodge travelers, without care for their station in life or religion, each one being made welcome, without being obliged to pay anything in return."[128] Another European visitor wrote that *hans* were large quadrangular courts "surrounded by stone buildings, solidly massed, and presenting much the appearance of the inner cloisters of a monastery."[129]

Through a high arched doorway that remained chained, the traveler entered the *han*, a quadrangle structure with a fountain in the middle and surrounding stables for horses and camels, as well as storehouses for the goods transported by caravans, and hearths

A public khan (*han*). William H. Bartlett. From Julie Pardoe, *The Beauties of the Bosphorus* (London: 1839). (Library of Congress)

and fires for the convenience of visitors.[130] Storage rooms on the ground floor allowed merchants to store their goods and stable their animals, while themselves occupying apartments on the *han*'s upper floor. The apartments on the lower floor included "counting-houses for the merchants" and a coffeehouse.[131]

The upper story of the *han* was "faced by an open gallery, supported on arches" that stretched "round the entire square," and was "reached by exterior flights of stone steps, situated at two of its angles; and from this gallery" opened "the store-rooms of the merchants," which in the first half of the 19th century, were "generally filled with bags of raw silk, European cottons, bales of rich stuffs, tobacco, spices, arms—and in short, all the most precious articles of Eastern traffic."[132] The articles mentioned here were not found in every *han*; to the contrary, in the large urban centers of the empire such as Istanbul, "the silk merchants" had "their own peculiar rendezvous"; the Persians piled "their gold and silver stuffs apart"; and the tobacco dealers sorted "their various tobaccos in a *caravanserai* of their own; while the mere traveler, pilgrim, and dervish" took up "their abode in common in very inferior" *hans*.[133]

Hans were "closed two hours before midnight by a pair of massive gates; beside one of which stood the little hut" that served as the residence for the *han* keeper, or the *hanci*, who was "answerable for all comers and goers after that time, until day-break; a precaution rendered highly necessary by the immense value of the merchandise" that was "frequently contained in these establishments."[134] The *hancis* were "universally patient and good humored" men, "the very focus of all the news and gossip of the city."[135] Witty, "crafty, and intelligent," they were entrusted with protection of a large volume of precious goods, which had been brought to them by merchants who believed that their goods would never be violated once they were placed in charge of the *hanci*, "who will die at his post rather than suffer even a suspicious eye to rest upon them."[136]

PEASANTS

The most fundamental social and economic unit in the Ottoman society was the peasant family. Owing to the lack of sufficient data, it is impossible to estimate the rural population of the Ottoman Empire, but the vast majority of the empire's population lived and worked as peasant farmers in villages. A typical peasant family consisted of a husband, his wife, and their children, and often included married sons and grandchildren. A highly patriarchal family structure meant that the husband organized the household and served as the ultimate arbiter of its resources and disputes. The state recognized him as the household's taxpayer. In Ottoman survey registers, taxation for each household was listed according to the name of the husband who represented his family.

Under the Ottoman system, "all arable land belonged to the public treasury of the Muslim community" and "in its name to the caliph or the ruler."[137] Because all agricultural land belonged to the sultan and was viewed by the state as crown land (*miri*), the central government enjoyed the inherent right to organize, manage, and supervise all peasant landholdings, along with the entire agrarian society and economy. *Miri* land did not comprise all agricultural land in the empire, but rather areas used as fields and open to the cultivation of grain. Orchards and gardens did not fall into this category. Large masses of people in the Ottoman Empire depended on subsistence economy for their livelihoods, and in particular, on wheat-barley cultivation. To avoid shortages and famines, the state "felt the need to control field agriculture and grain cultivation."[138] Indeed, "Ottoman law codes strictly forbid the conversion of fields into orchards and gardens."[139]

The state defined "landed property," as well as "agricultural force as revenue and subsistence resources," rejecting the definition of land and labor as "commodities privately owned and freely exchangeable in the market for purposes of profit maximization."[140] The two exceptions to *miri*, were *mülk*, or privately owned, and *vakif*, or lands supporting religious endowments where the revenue was used for pious and charitable purposes. The ulema, who were "the principal beneficiaries of *vakif* grants[,] acted in the capacity of administrators, especially of *kadis*."[141]

According to one source, in 1528, about 87 percent of all cultivable land in the empire was *miri*.[142] While the majority of land belonged to the state, the peasant farmer who tilled it had the status of a hereditary tenant, and, in return for his work, he enjoyed a usufructuary right.[143] The peasant's right to cultivate the land passed from father to son, but he could not sell the land, "grant it as a gift, or transfer it without permission."[144] The head of a peasant family could, however, hold a *çift*, or a piece of agricultural land varying in size from 60 to150 dönüms (940 square meters, or 3,084 square feet), large enough to support his family. After the death of the head of the household, his sons worked jointly on the *çift*, since it could not be broken up. Above all, "state rules relating to the organization of agricultural production sought to maintain the integrity of the family farms that constituted the units of subsistence and revenue production."[145] In the Ottoman domains, where labor "was scarce and land was plenty, the need to keep the peasants on the land, to prevent peasant flights," and to ensure the "production of subsistence crops" were the major concerns of the central government.[146]

In the traditional Ottoman land tenure system, the peasant household was required to pay a tithe to the *sipahi* (the cavalryman holding a *timar* in return for military service), who acted as the representative of the central government and resided in the district.[147] Grains "in the form of tithe collected in kind" represented the "primary source of revenue" for the *sipahi*.[148] In addition, the peasant household paid the *sipahi* 22 *akçes* (silver coins) as the annual tax collected from all families holding a *çift*.[149]

The peasant farmer was not allowed to leave the land and relocate to a different village or town. The *sipahi* did everything in his power to keep the peasants working on the land, because their flight reduced his income, as well as the revenue that he was required to send to the central government. If a peasant farmer fled the land, the *sipahi* had 15 years to compel him to return, but he could not force it without a decree from a *kadi* or a religious judge.[150] If the peasant farmer settled in a town and entered a craft, he had to pay the *sipahi* a tax, which was slightly more than one gold ducat a year.[151]

BUILDING HOMES

In most rural communities, houses were built in close proximity to one another. The peasant family did not live in the middle of a large field, but resided inside the village and only went out to the field in the morning.[152] Living together provided security and protection; it allowed the community to organize a united front against threats and attacks from outside forces.[153] Other villagers, particularly one's neighbors, also cooperated in building new homes, adding new sections to existing homes, and harvesting crops.[154]

The material used to build a house was determined by the environmental setting and the availability of basic supplies. In dry climate regions, such as central and eastern Anatolia, Egypt, Syria, and Arabia, where wood was scarce, houses were built of mud brick, which was manufactured by pouring a solution of wet mud and straw into a wooden form that was then left in place while the mud partially dried, usually for one day, then removed as the brick dried completely.[155] The bricks were then left on the ground for another week before they were used in the construction of the house. Aside from environmental factors, the cost of building material made mud brick an attractive material for building homes. Mud brick was made of earth and it was therefore extremely cheap. Mud brick walls also kept village houses cool during summer.[156] On the negative side, mud brick easily broke when earthquakes struck the Anatolian plateau, much of which sat on an earthquake zone. Thus, Ankara, situated in central Anatolia, was significantly damaged, and numerous small towns and villages were destroyed in the earthquake of 1668, while another earthquake in 1688 destroyed Izmir and surrounding rural communities.[157]

A house roof in Anatolia began with poplar poles held firmly in place by mud brick mortar. Woven reeds were then laid to cover the poles, followed by a layer of straw or other material that would produce a flat surface. Onto this surface the villagers poured large quantities of the mud mortar, followed by a layer of clay soil to repel water.[158] They then stamped the roof by foot or rolled a cylindrical stone across it to create a hard, flat surface capable of shedding water and protecting the house from heat.[159]

Peasant families in Anatolia lived in cottages, which contained very little furniture, except "a scanty supply of bedding and a few rugs, stools, and cooking utensils."[160] The "function of today's wooden furniture was taken up by the building itself," with "seats, beds, and storage" built "into the walls of the house, made of the same brick that formed the walls."[161] If the household budget allowed or if the family themselves were weavers, rugs were used to cover the floors. The walls of some peasant homes featured a divan or rug and cushioned-covered outcropping that served as both a seat and, if wide enough, as a bed. More often, however, family members slept on the floor. Bedding was stored away during the day and only brought out at night. Mattresses beneath and quilts above provided the sleeper with warmth and comfort. This form of bedding and sleeping was not confined to the peasant households in the rural communities of the empire. As late as the second half of the 19th century, high government officials and their families who lived in large and spacious homes in the posh neighborhoods of Istanbul also used "Turkish beds," which were "laid out every evening on the carpet and gathered up in the morning and put away."[162] During winter, peasant families in Anatolian villages kept warm with fireplaces built into the walls or with *mangals*, braziers that held hot coals retrieved from the fireplace.[163] Wooden shutters, along with textiles and animal skins, hung over windows and doors to keep out chill drafts. For the most part, however, clothing provided much of the warmth Ottoman villagers enjoyed during the winter months. Household goods consisting of "one poor cooking-pot, wooden spoon, a drinking cup of leather or wood, and a poor mattress of just a single coverlet were sufficient, as the ground served for bedstead, table and stools; nor had the Turks any need of a troop of cooks and scullions to prepare their meals and wash their dishes, as they ate sour curds mixed with bread and water, or fresh curds and cheese and in place of bread they had unleavened cakes baked on cinders."[164]

In the Balkans and the Black Sea region, where the rate of rainfall was greater and the supply of trees more plentiful, wood was widely used in construction of homes. The rainy climate, how-

A neighborhood on the outskirts of Istanbul. (Library of Congress)

ever, forced villagers to use "sloped roofs" that "were covered with wood shingles or ceramic tiles."[165] In many parts of the Balkans, homes were built of stones collected from the beds of rivers. In contrast to peasant houses in Anatolia that were one-story high and a simple structure in which the cattle were also housed, stone houses in the Balkans were usually "two storied, with a stone bottom floor and a wooden top floor, with a sloped roof."[166] The windows were small apertures, high up in the walls, and were sometimes grated with wood. There were no chimneys, but in the center of the roof was an opening to disperse the smoke from a fire pit that burned in the middle of the room. In front of the house was an enclosure, either of thorns or a mud wall, that secured the privacy of the dwelling. If they could afford it, the family built an outer chamber, where the head of household received his visitors and guests.

In Egypt, some of the peasant dwellings comprised two or more apartments, and a few were even two stories high. In the homes of the peasants in Lower Egypt, one of these apartments contained an oven at the farthest point from the entrance, which occupied the whole width of the room.[167] It resembled "a wide bench or seat," was "about breast high," and was "constructed of brick and mud; the roof arched within, and flat on the top."[168] The inhabitants of the house, who seldom had any blankets or quilts during the winter, slept on the top of the oven, having already lighted a fire within it. At times, only the husband and wife enjoyed "this luxury," and the children slept on the floor.[169] The rooms had "small apertures high up in the walls, for the admission of light and air, sometimes furnished with a grating of wood."[170] The roofs of Egyptian peasant dwellings were made out of "palm branches and palm leaves, or of millet stalks, laid upon rafters of the trunk of the palm, and covered with a plaster of mud and chopped straw."[171] The furniture consisted of several mats to sleep on and "a few earthen vessels, and a hand-mill to grind the corn."[172] In many Egyptian villages, large square pigeon houses were built on the roofs of peasant huts "with crude brick, pottery, and mud."[173]

In every Ottoman village, building homes demanded teamwork and cooperation among all members of the family, regardless of age and gender. The team often included members of the extended family who lived in the same village and even neighbors and friends who could lend their labor and architectural expertise. Villagers who had expertise in building particular parts of the house, such as roofs, were in especially high demand, and every effort was made to recruit them for the construction team.[174] While the female members of the family did not usually participate in producing mud bricks and installing roofs, they played a central role in manufacturing the goods essential for household consumption. They wove rugs and carpets, and knitted new beddings and textile products.[175]

In Anatolia, the majority of villages were built at a fair distance from the main road, out of fear of traveling armies, bandits, and antigovernment rebels.[176] Some villages relocated as a direct result of plagues, ongoing warfare, social instability, economic insecurity, and climate change. In times of political uncertainty, the absence of governmental authority forced many to abandon their villages altogether and move to a nearby town or another region.

The mosque or the church, the coffeehouse or the teahouse, and the village store were the most important nonresidential buildings and were usually located in the center of the village. The representatives of the central government did not live in the village and there were no governmental buildings. The principal link between the village and the government was through the village headman, whose most important function was to act as the representative of his community.[177] The headman was not a full employee of the village, but rather one of the most respected members of the community who, like other peasants, worked as a farmer and a herder. Even the barber, who gave haircuts at the village coffeehouse, set off for the fields soon after he had finished cutting the hair of his fellow villagers.[178] Outside every rural community, a small area was designated as the village cemetery.

Family members such as parents, children, uncles, aunts, cousins, nephews, and nieces, lived in the same village and were relied upon to help with work in the field. Marriages within the family, and particularly among cousins, strengthened and consolidated these close-knit social networks. When they were not in the field, men gathered at the village coffeehouse (or teahouse) at one another's houses to discuss the latest news. While doing so they drank tea or coffee, and played chess or backgammon. Women visited each other's homes, where they also partook in refreshments, discussed the latest happenings in the village, and watched each other's children.[179] To sell their agricultural products and to purchase some of the basic goods, which were not available in the village, peasant farmers traveled to the closest market towns.[180]

AGRICULTURAL INSTRUMENTS AND THE PEASANT HOUSEHOLD

In their writings, European travelers praised the Ottoman peasants, and particularly the Turkish peasant in Anatolia, for his "passionate attachment to land," resignation to the will of God, loyalty to the sultan, honesty, sobriety, passive contentment, and cleanliness.[181] Anatolian peasants wore coarse cloaks (*aba*), headgears of varying shapes and forms, and rude sandals on their feet. They began and ended each day with a cup of coffee or tea and a puff on a tobacco pipe.[182] Into their fields, they led yoked bulls, oxen, and buffalo decorated with gilt horns and silken saddlecloths and covers. The most basic means of agricultural production was "a wooden plow pulled by a pair of oxen."[183] Since a pair of oxen acted as the tractor of traditional agriculture, a peasant who lost his animal could become destitute and only be rescued if the government showed mercy and understanding by providing a "tax amnesty."[184]

The instruments of agricultural production and the crops that were grown in Anatolia during the long reign of the Byzantine Empire did not change under Ottoman rule. The plow pulled by a pair of oxen or buffalo was used during cultivation of crops such as wheat, barley, oats, vetch, millet, and rye.[185] These crops were sown and reaped, utilizing the same methods that had been used under Byzantine rule.[186] Vegetables and fruits were also grown in small gardens on the banks of rivers and streams, and on the outskirts of villages and towns.[187]

The foundation of agricultural production was the peasant household, which consisted of a man, his wife, and their children. According to the traditional division of labor in the villages of Anatolia, men were expected to organize "the ploughing, sowing, and harvesting," as well as building homes, going to the market towns, dealing with government officials, and representing the family in its interactions with other families.[188] All other functions such as "child rearing, feeding and sustaining the family and tending the crops and the animals" were "the province of women."[189] This division of work, which assigned "a woman's sphere of control" to "inside of the house" and a man's to outside, "made men and women absolutely dependent on each other."[190] Men "did not cook or care for babies," and they needed wives or daughters to care for them, while women did not deal with the representatives of the government or transport crops to a market town, and they "needed a husband, brother, or son to care" for them.[191] The traditional rural family structure was patriarchal, and, as stated previously, the state recognized the father of the family as the representative of his household and the principal taxpayer. As the head of his family, he was also empowered to organize his household as a production unit, assigning tasks to his sons, both in the field and at the house. The patriarchal nature of the peasant family was best demonstrated by the fact that the central government confiscated the land of a woman whose husband had died and who did not have sons; the state would then transfer it to another peasant household.[192] If the widow had a son who had not reached the proper age for working on the field, the state recognized her as the taxpayer under the title of *bive,* or widow.[193]

RELIGION AND EDUCATION IN THE OTTOMAN VILLAGE

Religion played a central role in bringing the residents of a village together. The most important responsibility of parents in a peasant household was to pass the values, traditions, customs, and practices of their religion to their children. Following the rules and the laws of Islam was essential for Muslim peasant farmers, while obeying the authority of the church and living in accordance with the teachings of Christianity was central to the belief system and the everyday life of Christian peasants. The overwhelming majority of the peasant population was illiterate and an ordinary villager who could not read his holy book for himself often accepted local customs and traditions, including some heterodox beliefs and practices, as integral parts of his religion.[194] The strict application of religious laws and local customs allowed the head of the household to exercise his authority without being challenged by his wife or children. Divine and traditional sanction also provided the father/husband with the authority to supervise relationships between sexes, particularly with respect to selecting a spouse for his children.

In many villages there were schools, but they admitted only boys. The classes were not designed to teach sciences or practical crafts and trades. Instead, young Muslim boys learned how to pray and recite the holy Quran by heart.[195] In exceptional cases, a talented child might be sent by his teacher, who often came from the lower ranks of the religious establishment, to a nearby town where he could attend a school attached to a mosque, but such cases were extremely rare.[196] The majority of the young male population in rural communities of the Ottoman Empire did not receive any formal education and learned how to work the field from their fathers, older brothers, and uncles. As young boys, they started their training by keeping watch over the family's sheep and goats.[197] They then moved with their fathers to the field, where they helped with sowing and harvesting.[198] As they grew older, the nature of their work became increasingly more difficult and they spent longer hours at it. If they displayed a lack of discipline and seriousness, they could be subjected to beating by their fathers or older brothers.

Although they could not attend the village school, young girls received a household education at home. Mothers taught their daughters how to cook, sew, tend to the family's animals, and take care of the younger children in the household. Girls as young as seven or eight carried newly born babies in their arms, changed their diapers, and fed them with little supervision from their parents.[199] This served as a form of apprenticeship, which trained and prepared young girls for the time when they became wives and mothers. As for values, girls were taught proper, modest, and chaste behavior. They had to demonstrate absolute obedience and respect toward their parents and other older members of the family. They also had to preserve their virginity until they were married. Loss of virginity was viewed as a colossal violation that resulted in expulsion from the village, and sometimes in the death of "the violator," who had failed to preserve the honor of her family.

In the Balkans, the Orthodox Christian peasantry was controlled by the Orthodox Church through the *millet* system and the village authorities.[200] These two institutions acted as intermediaries between the Ottoman central government and the rural communities, and were the most essential elements in the everyday life of Balkan Christian peasants.[201] Though aware of the power of the local Ottoman *sipahi,* who was responsible for collecting taxes, the peasant "was most directly affected by the actions of officials of his own religion, including his ecclesiastical authorities."[202] For Christian peasants of the Balkans, Sundays and various Saint's Days broke up the monotony of their everyday lives. On such days, peasants typically took off their plain, dark homespun dress; donned their colorful best; and attended the early mass in a small white-washed church. After returning home, they fed the cattle and chickens and prepared a simple meal. Afterwards, the elders retired to the village's coffeehouse and matrons relaxed in the shade while children played and the young men and women of the village played music and danced.

In the Ottoman Empire, "villages were connected to the outer world through market towns," which served as the centers "of both commerce and government."[203] The governor of the district, a religious judge, responsible for enforcement of Islamic law, tax collectors, and a small unit of janissaries, usually resided in these towns.[204] Since many villages were located within a day's walk of a market town, peasant farmers could sell their surplus at the local town market; purchase "agricultural implements, farm animals, and other necessities," such as a "bolt of cloth" and jewelry; and return home by nightfall.[205] Besides the markets, in their short trips to the nearby town, the villagers could visit mosques, tombs of saints and Sufi leaders, *derviş* lodges, schools, public baths, shops, coffeehouses, bakeries, mills, slaughterhouses, warehouses, government buildings, military barracks, and public water houses, which provided the town's water supply.[206]

NOTES

1. Barbara Jelavich, *History of the Balkans: Eighteenth and Nineteenth Centuries* (Cambridge: Cambridge University Press, 1983), 62.

2. Ibid.

3. Alan Mikhail, "The Heart's Desire: Gender, Urban Space and the Ottoman Coffee House," in *Ottoman Tulips, Ottoman Coffee Leisure and Lifestyle in the Eighteenth Century*, ed. Dana Sajdi (London: Tauris Academic Studies, 2007), 143–44.

4. Cem Behar, *A Neighborhood in Ottoman Istanbul: Fruit Vendors and Civil Servants in the Kasap Ilyas Mahalle* (Albany: State University of New York, 2003), 6.

5. Mikhail, "The Heart's Desire," 144.

6. Ibid.

7. Ibid.

8. Dennis P. Hupchick, *The Bulgarians in the Seventeenth Century* (Jefferson, NC: McFarland & Company, 1993), 39.

9. Ibid., 40.

10. Ibid., 38.

11. Ibid.

12. Ibid.

13. Ibid., 39.

14. Suraiya Faroqhi, *Subjects of the Sultan: Culture and Daily Life in the Ottoman Empire* (New York: I. B. Tauris, 2007),159.

15. Mikhail, "The Heart's Desire," 146.

16. Evliya Çelebi, *Evliya Çelebi in Albania,* trans. Robert Dankoff and Robert Elsie (Leiden: Brill, 2000), 5:167.

17. Ibid.

18. Ibid.

19. Julia Pardoe, *The City of the Sultan and Domestic Manners of the Turks in 1836,* 3 vols. (London: Henry Colburn Publisher, 1838), 1:86.

20. Michael Worth Davison, ed., *Everyday Life Through the Ages* (London: Reader's Digest Association Far East Limited, 1992), 175.

21. Ibid.

22. Pardoe, *The City of the Sultan,* 1:86.

23. Ibid., 1:87.

24. Ibid.

25. Ibid.

26. Mark Mazower, *Salonica: City of Ghosts, Christians, Muslims, and Jews* (New York: Random House, 2006), 35.

27. Bernard O'Kane, *Treasures of Islam: Artistic Glories of the Muslim World* (London: Duncan Baird Publishers, 2007), 166.

28. Ibid., 169.

29. Ibid., 176.

30. Ibid.

31. Mazower, *Salonica,* 39.

32. Ibid., 33.

33. Bernard Lewis, *Istanbul and the Civilization of the Ottoman Empire* (Norman: University of Oklahoma Press, 1963), 100.

34. Ibid., 100–101.

35. Mazower, *Salonica,* 36.

36. Halil Inalcik, *The Ottoman Empire, The Classical Age 1300–1600* (New York: Praeger Publishers, 1973), 142.

37. Ibid.

38. Mazower, *Salonica,* 39.

39. Bruce Masters, "Markets," in *Encyclopedia of the Ottoman Empire,* eds. Gábor Ágoston and Bruce Masters (New York: Facts On File, 2009), 349–50.

40. Ibid., 350.

41. Huri Islamoğlu-Inan, *State & Peasant in the Ottoman Empire, Agrarian Power Relations & Regional Economic Development in Ottoman Anatolia During the Sixteenth Century* (Leiden: E. J. Brill, 1994), 240.

42. Ibid.

43. Ibid.

44. Ibn Battuta, *The Travels of Ibn Battuta,* trans. H.A.R. Gibb (Cambridge: Cambridge University Press, 1962), 450.

45. Lucy Mary Jane Garnett, *Turkey of the Ottomans* (New York: Charles Scribner's Sons, 1915), 163–64.

46. Julia Pardoe, *Beauties of the Bosphorus* (London: George Virtue, 1839), 30.

47. Justin McCarthy, *The Ottoman Turks: An Introductory History to 1923* (London, New York: Wesley Longman Limited, 1997), 254.

48. Ibid.

49. Ibid.

50. Ibid.

51. Ibid.

52. Inalcik, *The Ottoman Empire*, 151.

53. Garnett, *Turkey of the Ottomans*, 162.

54. Tom Brosnahan and Pat Yale, *Turkey* (Hawthorn, Australia: Lonely Planet Publications, 1996), 163.

55. Masters, "Markets," 351.

56. Ibid.

57. Ibid.

58. Ibid.

59. Ibid.

60. Behar, *A Neighborhood in Ottoman Istanbul*, 6.

61. Inalcik, *The Ottoman Empire*, 161–62.

62. Ibid., 162.

63. Peter F. Sugar, *Southeastern Europe under Ottoman Rule: 1354–1804* (Seattle: University of Washington Press, 1996), 84.

64. Inalcik, *The Ottoman Empire*, 162, 223.

65. Ibid., 162, 218.

66. Sugar, *Southeastern Europe under Ottoman Rule*, 85.

67. Ibid.

68. Ibid.

69. Ibid.

70. Inalcik, *The Ottoman Empire*, 162.

71. Evliya Efendi (Çelebi), *Narratives of Travels in Europe, Asia, and Africa in the Seventeenth Century*, trans. Ritter Joseph Von Hammer (London: Parbury, Allen, & Co., 1834), 1:104.

72. Ibid., 1:51.

73. Garnett, *Turkey of the Ottomans*, 159.

74. Isabel Böcking, Laura Salm-Reifferscheidt, and Moritz Stipsicz, *The Bazaars of Istanbul* (New York: Thames & Hudson, 2009), 52.

75. Ibid.

76. Suraiya N. Faroqhi, "Guildsmen and Handicraft Producers," in *The Cambridge History of Turkey, The Later Ottoman Empire, 1603–1839*, 4 vols. (Cambridge: Cambridge University Press, 2006), 3:336.

77. Halil Inalcik, "Periods in Ottoman History: State, Society, Economy," in *Ottoman Civilization*, eds. Halil Inalcik and Günsel Renda, 2 vols. (Istanbul: Republic of Turkey Ministry of Culture Publications, 2003), 1:205.

78. Faroqhi, "Guildsmen," 3:336. Inalcik, "Periods in Ottoman History," 205.

79. Inalcik, "Periods in Ottoman History," 205. Faroqhi, "Guildsmen," 3:336–37.

80. Faroqhi, "Guildsmen," 3:344.

81. Ibid.

82. Ibid., 3:345.

83. Ibid., 3:338.

84. Ibid.

85. Ibid.

86. Böcking, Salm-Reifferscheidt, and Stipsicz, *The Bazaars of Istanbul*, 52.

87. Özdemir Nutku, "Sinf," in *The Encyclopaedia of Islam*, eds. C.E.E. Bosworth, E. van Donzel, W. P. Heinrichs, and G. Lecomte (Leiden: Brill, 1997), 646.

88. Ibid.

89. Ibid.

90. Böcking, Salm-Reifferscheidt, and Stipsicz, *The Bazaars of Istanbul*, 52; Inalcik, *The Ottoman Empire*, 223, 225.

91. Ibid., 52–3.

92. Ibid., 53.

93. Inalcik, *The Ottoman Empire*, 153.

94. Ibid.

95. Ibid., 154.

96. Ibid., 153.

97. Reuben Levy, *The Social Structure of Islam* (Cambridge: Cambridge University Press, 1969), 334.

98. Ibid., 336.

99. Ibid., 334.

100. Ibid.

101. Inalcik, *The Ottoman Empire*, 154.

102. Böcking, Salm-Reifferscheidt, and Stipsicz, *The Bazaars of Istanbul*, 53.

103. Richard Davey, *The Sultan and His Subjects*, 2 vols. (London: Chapman and Hall LD., 1897), 2:304–5.

104. Bruce Masters, "Bathhouse," in *Encyclopedia of the Ottoman Empire*, 79.

105. Ibid.

106. Ibid.

107. Ibid.

108. Ibn Battuta, *Travels*, 450.

109. Davison, *Everyday Life Through The Ages*, 175.

110. Mazower, *Salonica*, 39.

111. Ibid., 39–40.

112. Çelebi, *Evliya Çelebi in Albania*, 5:153.

113. Pardoe, *Beauties of the Bosphorus*, 13–14.

114. Ibid., 15.

115. Masters, "Bathhouse," 80.

116. Pardoe, *Beauties of the Bosphorus*, 15.

117. Masters, "Bathhouse," 80.

118. Pardoe, *Beauties of the Bosphorus*, 15.

119. Ibid.

120. Ibid., 16.

121. Ibid.

122. Ibid.

123. Ibid.

124. N. Elisséeff, "Khan," in *The Encyclopaedia of Islam*, eds. C. E. Bosworth, E. Van Donzel, B. Lewis, C. H. Pellat (Leiden: E. J. Brill, 1977), 1010.

125. Ibid., 1015.

126. Bruce Masters, "Caravansary (Han, Khan)," in *Encyclopedia of the Ottoman Empire*, 120.

127. Ibid.

128. Mazower, *Salonica*, 41.

129. Pardoe, *Beauties of the Bosphorus*, 138.

130. Fernand Braudel, *The Perspective of the World: Civilization & Capitalism 15th–18th Century*, trans. Sian Reynolds, 3 vols. (New York: Harper & Row Publishers, 1979), 3:472.

131. Pardoe, *Beauties of the Bosphorus*, 138.

132. Ibid., 138.

133. Ibid., 138–39.

134. Ibid., 138.

135. Ibid., 141.

136. Ibid.

137. Islamoğlu-Inan, *State & Peasant in the Ottoman Empire*, 56.

138. Halil Inalcik, *The Middle East and the Balkans under the Ottoman Empire Essays on Economy and Society* (Bloomington: Indiana University Turkish Studies, 1993), 142.

139. Ibid.

140. Islamoğlu-Inan, *State & Peasant in the Ottoman Empire*, 56–57.

141. Ibid., 218.

142. Inalcik, *The Ottoman Empire*, 110.

143. Ibid., 109.

144. Ibid.

145. Islamoğlu-Inan, *State & Peasant in the Ottoman Empire*, 57.

146. Ibid., 57–8.

147. Inalcik, *The Ottoman Empire*, 225.

148. Islamoğlu-Inan, *State & Peasant in the Ottoman Empire*, 57.

149. Inalcik, *The Ottoman Empire*, 110.

150. Ibid., 111.

151. Ibid.

152. McCarthy, *The Ottoman Turks*, 226.

153. Ibid.

154. Ibid.

155. Ibid., 227.

156. Ibid., 229.

157. Ibid.

158. Ibid., 229.

159. Ibid.

160. Metin And, "The Social Life of the Ottomans in the Sixteenth Century," in *Ottoman Civilization*, ed. Halil Inalcik and Günsel Renda, 2 vols. (Istanbul: Republic of Turkey Ministry of Culture Publications, 2003), 1:429.

161. McCarthy, *The Ottoman Turks*, 232.

162. Halidé Adivar Edib, *Memoirs of Halidé Edib* (New York: Gorgias Press, 2004), 15.

163. McCarthy, *The Ottoman Turks*, 232.

164. And, "The Social Life of the Ottomans," 1:429.

165. Ibid.

166. Ibid.

167. Edward William Lane, *An Account of the Manners and Customs of the Modern Egyptians* (New York: Dover Publications, 1973), 21.

168. Ibid.

169. Ibid.

170. Ibid.

171. Ibid.

172. Ibid.

173. Ibid.

174. McCarthy, *The Ottoman Turks*, 235.

175. Ibid., 235–36.

176. Ibid., 226.

177. Ibid.

178. Ibid.

179. Ibid.

180. Ibid.

181. Garnett, *Turkey of the Ottomans*, 180.

182. Ibid.

183. Inalcik, "Periods in Ottoman History," 172.

184. Ibid., 173.

185. Inalcik, *The Middle East and the Balkans Under the Ottoman Empire*, 141.

186. Ahmet Yaşar ar Ocak, "Social, Cultural and Intellectual Life, 1071–1453," in *The Cambridge History of Turkey: Byzantium to Turkey 1071–1453*, 4 vols. (Cambridge: Cambridge University Press, 2009), 1:372.

187. Ibid., 370, 372.

188. McCarthy, *The Ottoman Turks*, 272.

189. Ibid.

190. Ibid., 273.

191. Ibid.

192. Inalcik, *The Middle East and the Balkans under the Ottoman Empire*, 142.

193. Ibid.

194. McCarthy, *The Ottoman Turks*, 276.

195. Ibid.

196. Ibid.

197. Ibid., 277.

198. Ibid.

199. Ibid.

200. Jelavich, *History of the Balkans*, 48.

201. Ibid.

202. Ibid.

203. McCarthy, *The Ottoman Turks*, 236.

204. Ibid.

205. Ibid.

206. Ibid.

5

RELIGIOUS COMMUNITIES

The Ottoman Empire was vast and contained numerous religious, ethnic, and linguistic communities such as Turks, Tatars, Arabs, Kurds, Circassians, Armenians, Greeks, Albanians, Serbs, Bosnians, Croatians, Bulgarians, Romanians, Hungarians, Jews, and many others. In "the Balkan Peninsula, Slavonic, Greek and Albanian speakers were undoubtedly in the majority, but besides these, there were substantial minorities of Turks and romance-speaking Vlachs."[1] In Anatolia, the majority of the population spoke Turkish, but there were also significant Greek-, Armenian-, and Kurdish-speaking communities. In "Syria, Iraq, Arabia, Egypt and north Africa, most of the population spoke dialects of Arabic."[2] In the urban centers of the empire, the population included Muslims, Christians, and Jews. As the religion of the Ottoman sultans and the ruling elite, Islam was the empire's dominant creed. The Greek and Armenian Orthodox churches, however, retained an important place within its political structure and ministered to large Christian communities, which in many areas outnumbered Muslims. There was also a substantial community of Jews scattered throughout the empire. Aside from these main religious groups, numerous other Christian and non-Christian communities resided throughout the empire.

To impose its rule over such a diverse population and maintain peace and security for its subjects, the Ottoman state downplayed ethnic and linguistic differences and instead emphasized religion as the primary form of identity. The central government organized the non-Muslim population "into three officially sanctioned millets: Greek orthodox, headed by the ecumenical patriarch, Armenians, headed by the Armenian patriarch of Istanbul, and Jews, who after 1835 were headed by the *hahambaşi* [chief rabbi] in Istanbul."[3] Each religious community, or *millet*, enjoyed cultural and legal autonomy and managed its own internal affairs under the leadership of its own religious hierarchy.[4] Unlike "the Christian churches, the Jews of the empire did not have a pre-existing clerical hierarchy."[5] Instead of patriarchs and bishops, the Jews of an Ottoman town or city governed their community autonomously. Since Islam was the official religion of the Ottoman Empire, the Muslims were not considered a separate *millet*. The Muslim community was, however, organized in the same manner as the Christian communities.[6]

As a self-governing body, which was responsible for managing its own internal affairs, each *millet* elected its own leader, who received the blessing and approval of the sultan. The state vested sufficient executive power in each *millet* leader to enable him to collect taxes from the members of his community.[7] The tolerance displayed by the Ottoman sultans did not mean that the Jews and Christians of the empire were viewed and treated as equal to Muslims. In accordance with Islamic law, or *şeriat* (Arabic: *sharia*), Jews and Christians were "People of the Book" and considered *zimmi* (Arabic: *dhimmi*), or protected religious communities that lived under the authority of a Muslim sovereign. The sultan was required to protect the lives and property of his Jewish and Christian subjects, who were obligated to pay the Ottoman government a poll tax, or *cizye*, in return for not serving in the military. In all legal matters, Islamic law had precedence and Islamic courts were open to all subjects of the sultan.[8]

CHRISTIANS

The Christian population of the Ottoman Empire was heterogeneous. The central government recognized two principal Christian *millets*, namely, the Orthodox and the Armenian Gregorian. Other Christian communities such as the Maronites, Nestorians, and Syrian Orthodox were not recognized as *millets*, although, for all practical purposes, they functioned as autonomous religious communities under their own leaders.[9] The Ottoman state did not concern itself with the daily life, customs, and rituals of its Christian subjects.[10]

Instead of dealing with individuals and their religious needs and demands, the Ottomans showed a clear preference for using religious hierarchies and local elites as intermediaries, who would control their own communities and, at times of crisis, could be blamed for problems and shortcomings.[11] Thus, indirect and decentralized rule was the hallmark of the Ottoman political culture.

ORTHODOX CHRISTIAN MILLET

Military conquests in the Balkan Peninsula in the 14th and 15th centuries resulted in Ottoman rule over vast territories inhabited by Orthodox Christians. Regardless of their ethnic, linguistic, and cultural differences, all Orthodox Christians; namely Greeks, Bulgarians, Serbs, Montenegrins, Macedonians, Romanians, and Albanian Christians, were viewed as members of the same *millet*. The religious hierarchy and the power structure within the Orthodox religious community was, however, dominated by the Ecumenical Patriarch of Istanbul, who served as the religious head of all Orthodox subjects of the sultan. After conquering Constantinople, Mehmed II appointed the influential Byzantine scholar-monk Bishop Gennadios Scholarius as the patriarch of the Orthodox Church because of his strong opposition to union with Rome and the Latin West.

The system created by the Ottomans allowed the patriarch, who enjoyed full control over all Orthodox churches in the empire and their property, to be elected by the Holy Synod (a high council of bishops, which acted as the ruling body of the church) and then confirmed by the sultan.[12] Other church administrators were appointed and dismissed by the synod and the patriarch with the approval of the sultan.[13]

With the imposition of direct Ottoman rule over the Balkans, former civil administrations disintegrated and those who resisted Muslim Turkish rule either fled or were killed or excluded from office.[14] In their place, Ottoman authorities empowered local religious leaders and clergymen who were willing to cooperate with the new Ottoman provincial administration.[15] An alliance with the Orthodox Church provided the Ottoman state with a golden opportunity to legitimize its rule. By utilizing institutions of the Orthodox Church, such as the many monasteries that played a central role in the daily lives of Orthodox Christians, the Ottoman government consolidated its legitimacy with the populations it had conquered. Faced with possible subordination to or forced union with its traditional rival and enemy, the Roman Catholic Church, the Orthodox Church chose to survive by aligning itself with the sultan. The Ottoman state allowed the Orthodox clergy to work under the jurisdiction of their own religious courts, and they were exempt from taxation.[16] Each church ensured its own financial welfare and security through assessing various fees, soliciting donations, and receiving income from property it owned.

By the beginning of the 18th century, the power and authority of the patriarch of Istanbul had become significant. He was not only the head of the Orthodox Christian *millet* but also the *ethnarch* (secular ruler) of the entire Orthodox population. The Ottoman government held him responsible "for the behavior and loyalty of his flock."[17] With the blessing and support from the sultan, the Orthodox Church taxed its constituency in accordance with its own administrative regulations and arrangements. In judicial matters, the church enjoyed full jurisdiction over a wide range of functions, such as marriage, divorce, and even commercial cases involving Christians, and, though criminal cases such as murder and theft came under the Muslim judicial system, the Orthodox courts handled them as well, as long as a Muslim was not involved.[18] Using "canon law, Byzantine statuary law, local customs, and church writings and traditions," orthodox religious courts, which were preferred by the Orthodox Christian population, "handed out penalties such as imprisonment, fines, along with denial of the sacraments and excommunication."[19] The Greek War of Independence (1821–1831) and the creation of an independent Greek state in 1832 significantly undermined the prestige and power of the "Orthodox ecumenical patriarch in Istanbul," effectively ending "the special relationship that had existed between the Greek Orthodox Church and the sultan."[20]

SERBIAN ORTHODOX CHURCH

At the time of the Ottoman conquest of Constantinople in 1453, there were two other autocephalous churches in existence: in Peć (Hungarian: *Pécs*), for the Serbs, and in Ohrid, for the Bulgarians.[21] As the power of the Orthodox Church in Istanbul—backed and supported by the Ottoman government—increased, the authority and influence of the Serbian and Bulgarian churches waned, allowing the patriarch to secure their abolition in 1463.[22] Serbian and Bulgarian bishops were replaced by Greek priests, who were dispatched by the patriarch from Istanbul. This policy ignited deep resentment among the local clerical establishment and the native population, who would later accuse the Greek clergy of trying to assimilate them by banning Serbian and Bulgarian liturgy and imposing Greek language and culture.

The Serbian people, who had inhabited vast areas in modern-day southern Hungary, Kosovo, Serbia, Montenegro, Bosnia-Herzegovina, and Croatia, were unified under a single institution, namely the Serbian Orthodox Church, and its religious hierarchy, which constituted an important segment of the Serbian elite.[23] Established in 1219 as an autocephalous member of the Orthodox communion, the Serbian Orthodox Church followed the traditions of Orthodox Christianity but was not subordinate to an external patriarch, such as the ecumenical patriarch in Istanbul. Serbian Orthodox religious texts were written in the old Serbian-Slavonic language, in which services were also conducted.

The Serbian state established by the Nemanjić dynasty in the 12th century reached the zenith of its power under Stephen Dušan (1331–1355), who elevated the Serbian Orthodox Church "to the rank of patriarchate with its seat in Peć."[24] Though the Serbian prince Lazar (1371–1389) was defeated and killed at the battle of Kosovo Polje in 1389, the Serbs resisted direct Ottoman rule for decades before they were fully conquered in 1459. The memory of the defeat and martyrdom of Serbia's last independent monarch was, however, preserved by the Serbian Orthodox Church. During long centuries of Ottoman occupation, the Patriarchate of Pec´ "felt itself the heir to the medieval Serbian kingdom and was well aware of its national mission."[25] The church referred to lands under its ecclesiastical jurisdiction as "Serbian Lands" despite the varying religious and ethnic characters the territories exhibited. In this manner, the Serbian Orthodox church became the repository of the national ideal and kept alive in the minds of the Serbian faithful their unique identity and glorious past. Through their membership and participation in their church, the Serbian people preserved their religion, as well as their language and historical identity, which distinguished them from their neighbors such as the Hungarians and Albanians.

To appease the Serbs, Süleyman the Magnificent restored the Serbian Patriarchate in 1557 and appointed a relative of his grand vizier, Sokollu Mehmed Paşa (Mehmed Paşa Sokolović), as the patriarch. This restoration played an important role in safeguarding the Serbian national and cultural identity under a unified religious authority. During the Long War of 1593–1606, the Ottoman war against the Holy League (1683–1699), and the Habsburg-Ottoman wars of 1716–1718, 1736–1739, 1788–1791, however, the Serbs "took an active part as opponents of the Ottomans" and "suffered severe consequences."[26] One result was that the Ottoman government abolished the Serbian patriarchate in 1766 and placed it under the jurisdiction of the Ecumenical Patriarch of Istanbul, igniting strong anti-Greek sentiment among the Serbs, who resented the increasing power of Greek bishops. The resistance of Serbian churches to Ottoman rule led to Serbian Orthodoxy becoming inextricably linked with Serbian national identity and the new autonomous Serbian principality that emerged after the first Serbian national uprising (1804–1813) led by George Petrović or Karageorge (Karadjordje). The Serbian Orthodox Church finally regained its status as an autocephalous church in 1879, a year after Serbia gained its full independence.

BULGARIAN ORTHODOX CHURCH

In A.D. 679, "a small tribe of Proto-Bulgars" arrived in the Balkans under the leadership of their khan, Asparukh, and settled in "an area near the mouth of the Danube."[27] These Proto-Bulgars, who were originally a Turkic/Turanian people from Central Asia and who "had once inhabited an area between the Sea of Azov and Kuban," entered "into an alliance with the Slovanic tribes" who had already settled in southeast Europe in the 6th and 7th centuries, and "a Slavo-Bulgar state was set up, in which, in spite of the numerical superiority of the Slavs, the Proto-Bulgars provided the leadership."[28] By the time the Bulgarian ruler Khan Boris Michael I (867–889) adopted Christianity, "the Proto-Bulgars had been completely absorbed by the more numerous Slavs."[29] The "reign of Boris's son, Simeon (893–927)" has been generally recognized "as the Golden Age of Bulgarian literature."[30] It also marks "the zenith of Bulgaria's territorial expansion" when the country's frontiers "stretched from the Black Sea to the Adriatic, embracing most of Serbia, Albania and Southern Macedonia."[31] The first Bulgarian empire elevated the Bulgarian church into a patriarchate in 927.[32] As in Serbia, the Bulgarian Orthodox Church played a central role in preserving the Slavonic liturgy and the Bulgarian language and history. Although their country came under Byzantine rule in 1018, the Bulgarians managed to regain their independence in 1185 and established the second Bulgarian empire (czardom), which granted the Bulgarian Church "the rank of patriarchate again" in 1235.[33] The power of the Bulgarian state, however, waned soon after, and by the end of the 14th century, the territory of the empire had fallen into the hands of rival nobles and feudal lords who were ultimately manipulated and conquered by the Ottoman Turks. On the eve of the Ottoman conquest, "the Second Bulgarian Empire had split into three more or less independent States."[34] The Ottomans captured Plovdiv (Philippopolis) in 1363 and Sofia in 1385. The conquest of Turnovo in 1393 and Vidin in 1398 by Bayezid I brought any hope of Bulgarian independence to an end. The Bulgarian territory was divided into the three *sancaks,* or administrative units, of Vidin, Nicopolois, and Silistria, each governed by a *sancak bey.*[35] Though the Ottomans did not force the Christian population to renounce and abandon their religion, a large number of Bulgarians, particularly in the Rhodopes, converted to Islam. Today, these Muslim Bulgarians or Pomaks constitute the second-largest population group in Bulgaria.

In 1454 when Mehmed II appointed the Greek bishop Gennadios Scholarios as the head of Orthodox Christian *millet,* he assumed that the office of the new patriarch represented the "interests of all Orthodox subjects in his empire."[36] But not all Orthodox Christians were Greeks. Bulgarians, like the Serbs, possessed their own native church hierarchies and organizations, which were taken over by the Greek appointees of Istanbul's patriarchate. Greek "interests and culture came to pervade the Orthodox *millet*" to the increased exclusion of the Bulgarian and Serbian churches.[37] Greek "bishops and Greek liturgical books replaced the Bulgarian bishops who were banished."[38] As a sense of Greek superiority emerged within the church hierarchy, its Slavic faithful grew increasingly resentful. Their ethnic and cultural self-awareness grew correspondingly, and a deep-seated animosity toward Greek superiority began to make itself felt within the Orthodox *millet.* It was the Bulgarian religious leaders and monks from remote monasteries and spiritual enclaves who called for throwing off the supremacy of the Greek clergy and Greek language. If the Bulgarians wished to establish Bulgarian schools and liturgy, they needed an independent ecclesiastical system. In 1557, when Süleyman the Magnificent reconstituted the Serbian Patriarchate of Peć, the Ottomans placed the Bulgarian eparchies under its authority. The Peć Patriarchate was, however, abolished by the Ottoman government in 1766. In the 19th century, as the authority of the Ottoman central government waned, the Bulgarians demanded "church services in Bulgarian, Bulgarian-speaking high clergy, the establishment of a national church, and a form of political autonomy."[39] The first "major struggles" for Bulgarian cultural independence were waged against "the domination of the Greek clergy" in the 1820s, and they were organized around the refusal of the Bulgarian people to pay taxes demanded by Greek bishops and a call to create an independent educational system with modern Bulgarian as the language of instruction.[40] By "the beginning of the 1870s, more than 1,600 Bulgarian language schools had been founded."[41] The most important aspect of this movement was the popular demand for the creation of an independent Bulgarian ecclesiastical hierarchy.[42] Finally, "in 1870, the sultan issued a decree authorizing the establishment of a Bulgarian exarchate."[43]

ARMENIAN MILLET

Armenians constituted the oldest and the largest non-Muslim community in the eastern provinces of the Ottoman Empire. There were also Armenian communities in the urban centers of the empire, particularly in Istanbul.

The Arsacid (Arshakuni) Kingdom of Armenia was the first state in history to adopt Christianity as its religion. In A.D. 301, Trdat (Tiridates) III converted to Christianity by Grigor Lusavorich (Gregory the Illuminator), and in A.D. 314, Grigor Lusavorich was ordained as the first bishop of Armenia.[44] For Armenians, their church emerged as the focal point of communal identity that preserved their unity in face of threats, domination, and conquest by larger and stronger neighbors.[45] Sometime around A.D. 400, an Armenian alphabet was invented, ushering in the golden age of Armenian culture and civilization, when numerous books and manuscripts in foreign languages, including the Bible, were translated into Armenian.[46] Starting in the last decade of the 4th century, Armenia lost its independence to the Byzantine and the Sassanid Persian empires, which partitioned the country. Despite several attempts to reestablish their independence, the Armenians lost their sovereignty as the Arab Muslims, and later the Seljuk Turks, Mongols, Ottomans, and Safavid Iranians invaded and occupied their ancient homeland.

During the long Byzantine rule, the Armenian Apostolic Church was not allowed to operate in Constantinople because the Greek Orthodox Church viewed it as heretical. Persecution by the Byzantine authorities only strengthened the separate and distinct Armenian identity. After the Ottoman conquest of Constantinople,

Mehmed II was determined to make his new capital a "universal metropolis" by "officially recognizing the spiritual leaders of the Greek Orthodox, Armenian, and Jewish communities" under his rule.[47] He aspired to establish an Armenian patriarchate of Istanbul, but he faced a problem in the case of Armenians that did not arise with either the Orthodox Christians or Jews.[48] At the time of the conquest, the majority of the Armenian population did not live under the authority of the sultan. The most important center of the Gregorian Church and the seat of the Armenian Patriarch, the *Catholicos* at Echmiadzin (Ejmiatsin) was "outside the borders of the Ottoman Empire, in adjacent hostile territory."[49] In 1461, Mehmed II appointed Bishop Hovakim of Bursa as the first Armenian patriarch of Istanbul and the religious and secular leader of all Armenians living in the Ottoman domains.

The Armenian *millet* differed from the Orthodox not only in certain beliefs, rituals, and customs, but also in that its members were all from one ethnic group and the majority lived far from the urban centers of the empire in eastern Anatolia and the south Caucasus, which were contested by the Ottoman and Safavid empires. The devastating wars between the Ottoman Empire and the Safavid dynasty in Iran partitioned Armenian-populated territory. The south Caucasus, including the seat of the Armenian Patriarch, the *Catholicos* at Echmiadzin, was incorporated into the Iranian state, and eastern Anatolia remained under Ottoman rule. During the Ottoman-Iranian wars, the Armenian population suffered. Armenian towns and villages were destroyed, harvest was burnt, and water wells were filled by the Iranians who forcibly moved entire communities and settled them in the interior of their territory so that they would not supply the Ottoman forces with food and shelter. Many Armenians were never allowed to return. Others helped the Safavid monarch Shah Abbas (1587–1629) and his successors divert the silk trade from a land route, which would have benefited the Ottomans, to a sea route, which skipped Ottoman territory to establish a direct link between Iran and the Christian powers of Europe.

Meanwhile, the Armenian population living under Ottoman rule was also depleted by military campaigns, the anarchy caused by internal revolts (i.e., *celali* revolts) in the 17th century, and emigration. The vacated lands and villages of the Armenians were mostly occupied and repopulated by various Kurdish tribes from eastern Anatolia. Since the central government in Istanbul viewed the borderland between western Iran and eastern Anatolia as strategically vital, Ottoman sultans rewarded the Kurds, who fought against the Iranians, by dividing the region into administrative units called *sancaks* and appointing loyal Kurdish tribal chiefs as hereditary governors (*sancak beys*), responsible for collecting taxes and maintaining order. Thus, while Ottoman rule restored peace and tranquility, it forced the Armenians to live under the dominance of their mortal enemies, the Kurds. As long as the central government was strong and could protect Armenian communities through its local officials, a certain balance was maintained between the Kurds and the Armenians. But in the 18th and 19th centuries, as the power of the state waned, Kurdish tribal chiefs "had matters all their own way and the Armenians suffered accordingly."[50]

The demand for an independent Armenian state began in the 19th century, when the Armenian communities in the Ottoman Empire and the Caucasus experienced a cultural revival.[51] The study of Armenian language and history became increasingly popular, the Bible was published in the vernacular, and Armenian intellectuals developed a new literary language that made their works accessible to the masses.[52] Wealthy families began to send their children to study in Europe, where a new class of young and educated Armenians became fluent in European languages and imbued with modern ideologies of nationalism, liberalism, and socialism.

Inspired by the rise and success of the 19th century nationalist movements in the Balkans, a small group of Armenian intellectuals began to question the leadership of the Armenian Church and called for the introduction of secular education.[53] Some went one step further and joined the Young Ottomans in their demand for the creation of a constitutional form of government that would grant all subjects of the sultan equal rights and protection under law. When the Congress of Berlin granted independence and/or autonomy to several Balkan states, a small group of Armenian officers who served in the Russian army began to advocate the creation of an independent Armenian state with support from the Russian tsar.[54] Two Armenian organizations—the Social Democratic Hnchakian Party, which published the newspaper *Hnchak* (Bell), founded by Armenian students in Geneva, Switzerland in 1887; and the Armenian Revolutionary Federation (ARF or Dashnak Party), created in Tbilisi, Georgia, in 1890—played a central role in advocating Armenian independence.[55]

Starting in the 1890s, the tension between the Armenian and Muslim communities in eastern Anatolia intensified, as Armenian nationalists and Ottoman forces clashed. Abdülhamid II ordered a crackdown on the wealthy Armenian families in Istanbul and organized the Hamidiye regiment that included Kurdish tribal units. From 1890 to 1893, the Hamidiye regiments were unleashed against the Armenian communities in eastern Anatolia with devastating results. Thousands of Armenians living in Sasun were murdered in the summer of 1894. The attacks and mass killings continued in "Trebizond, Urfa, and Erzurum in autumn 1895, and Diarbekir, Arabkir, Kharpert, and Kayseri in November 1895."[56] In response, the Hnchaks organized demonstrations in Istanbul and appealed to European embassies to intervene. Similar protests were organized in towns across eastern Anatolia. The situation worsened in 1895 and 1896, as clashes between the Hamidiye regiments and Armenian nationalists intensified. In August 1896, armed Armenians seized the Ottoman Bank in Istanbul, threatening to blow it up. Other terrorist attacks against government offices and officials followed. The sultan himself was attacked when bombs were set off as he walked to Aya Sofya for his Friday prayer. Some twenty Ottoman policemen were killed in the attack. Throughout the conflict with the Ottoman government, the Armenians pinned their hopes on intervention by European powers, particularly the British and the Russians. Tsar Nicholas II, however, opposed British intervention in the region, which he viewed as a sphere of Russian influence. He also feared the establishment of an Armenian state led by revolutionaries who could infect his own Armenian subjects with such radical ideas as nationalism and socialism.

As the First World War began and fighting erupted in eastern Anatolia, many Armenian officers and soldiers serving in the Ottoman army defected, joining the Russians with the hope that the defeat and collapse of the Ottoman state would lead to the establishment of an independent Armenian state.[57] The defections were followed by an uprising of the Armenians in the city of Van in April 1915. The Ottoman government responded by adopting a policy of forcibly relocating the Armenian population to the Syrian desert.[58] Starting in May 1915, virtually the entire Armenian population of central and eastern Anatolia was removed from their homes. Hundreds of thousands of Armenians perished from starvation, disease, and exposure, and many more were brutalized by Ottoman army units and the irregular Kurdish regiments who robbed, raped, and killed the defenseless refugees.

Today, after the passage of almost a century, the plight of the Armenian people continues to ignite intense emotional debate between Armenians and Turks, centering on the number of casualties, the causes for the deportations, and the intent of the perpetrators.[59] Armenians claim that nearly a million and a half people lost their lives in a genocide designed at the highest levels of the Ottoman government. Turks, by contrast, posit the "disloyalty" and "traitorous activities" of many Armenians who defected from the Ottoman state and joined the Russian army, which had invaded the Ottoman homeland. They also claim that the majority of Armenian deaths were caused by irregular armed Kurdish units, who felt threatened by the prospect of living as a minority community under a newly established Armenian state.[60] According to this argument, the Ottoman government can be held responsible for failing to prevent the inter-communal violence between the Kurds and the Armenians, but it cannot be blamed for atrocities that were committed by the local Muslim population during the fog and agony of civil war. Regardless, there is little doubt that a small inner circle within the Ottoman government, known as *Teşkilat-i Mahsusa* or Special Organization operating under the ministry of defense since January 1914, designed and implemented the plan for relocating the Armenian population in order to affect a "permanent solution" to the question of Armenian nationalism in Ottoman lands.[61]

JEWISH MILLET

Numerous Jewish communities lived scattered throughout the Ottoman Empire. Although "the Jews were recognized as a separate religious community by both Muslim legal scholars and Ottoman officials," they "did not seek formal status as a *millet* until 1835, when the Ottoman government, in its attempt to standardize the way it dealt with each of the minority religious communities, pushed the Jewish community leaders to name a chief rabbi (*hahambaşi*) for the empire."[62] The Jews of the Ottoman Empire governed their own affairs, just as the Orthodox Christians and Armenians did, under their local rabbis who were elected by their congregation and confirmed in office by the sultan.

The Jewish population of the empire did not constitute a monolith. It contained original communities in various parts of the Middle East and the Balkans, as well as the Ashkenazic and Sephardic Jews who arrived in the Ottoman Empire in the 15th and 16th centuries. The original Jewish communities were divided into Rabbanites, or those who revered the Talmud (Commentaries), and the Karaites, or those who accepted the Bible as the only source of authority, did not recognize Hanukkah as a holiday, and permitted first cousins to marry.[63]

Linguistically, the Jews of the Ottoman Empire were divided into four main groups: Romiotes, Sephardic Jews, Ashkenazic Jews, and Arabic-speaking Jews.[64] Some smaller Jewish communities in the Kurdish-populated regions spoke either Kurdish or Aramaic, while others in North Africa spoke Berber (Tamazight). Romiotes or Greek-speaking descendants of the Jews, who had settled in the former Byzantine Empire, formed the core Jewish population encountered by the Ottomans in the early centuries of building their empire. The Sephardic Jews who were refugees from Spain and Portugal "spoke a dialect of Castilian Spanish" called "Ladino or Judezmo," while the Ashkenazic Jews who were originally from central and eastern Europe "spoke either German or the Jewish dialect of medieval German known as Yiddish."[65] Arabic-speaking Jews resided in all the major cities of the Middle East and North Africa, but the largest communities were to be found in Cairo, Aleppo, Damascus, and Baghdad. Baghdad served "as a major center of learning for Arabic-speaking Jews," and rabbis trained in the city "were in demand" both in Egypt and Syria.[66] All educated Ottoman Jews knew Hebrew, which served as the language of worship and prayer, of intellectual life and, in some cases, of trade and commerce.

The arrival of the Sephardic Jews who were expelled from the Iberian Peninsula in 1492, and the influx of the Ashkenazic Jews from central Europe, only intensified the diversity and the internal divisions within the Jewish community. These divisions were the result of significant differences in language, rituals, and even prayer books. Thus, far from being a unified religious group, the Jewish community was a mosaic of subgroups each identified by its own unique linguistic and cultural characteristics. The Ottoman *millet* system recognized neither the fundamental differences between the Ashkenazic and the Sephardic communities, nor the unique characteristics of the subgroups that existed within each group. However, it would be impossible to deny that, for centuries, the Jews of the Ottoman Empire lived under far more tolerant political and cultural conditions than the Jews of Christian Europe. The protection and tolerance offered by the Ottoman state allowed both Ashkenazic and Sephardic communities to preserve their languages, rituals, customs, and traditions.[67]

The Ashkenazic Jews were descended from the medieval Jewish communities of Rhineland in Germany and had moved east, settling in Poland, Russia, Hungary, and other countries of

Eastern Europe. Seeking a refuge from anti-Jewish attacks and persecution, many migrated to the Ottoman Empire in the 15th and 16th centuries. There they sought, and received, the protection of Ottoman sultans who "encouraged the immigration of Jews from Europe, as an element bringing trade and wealth."[68] The "welcome that the Ottoman sultans gave these Jewish immigrants is evident in the permissions granted to build new synagogues in the cities in which they settled."[69] By the second half of the 16th century, there were vibrant Ashkenazic communities in Istanbul, Edirne, Sofia, Pleven, Vidin, Trikala, Arta, and Salonika, which had been established in the Ottoman domain during the reigns of the conqueror of Constantinople, Mehmed II, and his successor Bayezid II.[70] By 1477, the Jews "formed the third largest section of Istanbul's population after Muslims and Greeks."[71] Many sent letters home describing how much their lives had improved under Ottoman rule and encouraged family and friends to join them.[72] The news that Jews were welcome in the Ottoman Empire travelled quickly, and immigrants began to arrive not only from the countries of central and western Europe, but also from Hungary, Moldavia, the Crimea, and even parts of Asia.[73] Many of these new immigrants set out for Palestine despite the opposition from the Franciscans of Jerusalem who "talked the Pope into forbidding the Venetians to carry Jewish passengers to the Holy Land."[74]

In sharp contrast to the Ashkenazic Jews, the Sephardic Jews lived originally in Spain and Portugal and fled to North Africa and the Middle East during the Spanish Inquisition, seeking economic security and religious freedom under the protection of Muslim rule.[75] The new immigrants from the Iberian Peninsula included the so-called *Maraños* (Muranos), Jews who had expediently converted to Catholicism to escape persecution but upon arriving in Ottoman territory abandoned their disguise and merged back into the Sephardic congregation. Many settled in Istanbul and Edirne, as well as other cities of the empire, in the 15th and 16th centuries. There were Sephardic communities in the urban centers of the Balkans such as Sarajevo, Travnik, Mostar, Banja Luka, and Salonika, where the largest Jewish community of nearly thirty thousand resided. Salonika alone had some thirty different congregations, including Aragonese, Castilian, Portuguese, and Apulian communities.[76] Many "Jewish males were employed in Salonika's woolen industry," where they used "the techniques brought from Spain and Italy" to supply the imperial palace in Istanbul and the Ottoman army with most of the cloth they consumed.[77] The urban centers of Anatolia such as Izmir, Bursa, Amasya, and Tokat, also witnessed a significant influx of Sephardic Jews. In each urban center, the Jewish community was divided into separate congregations that formed around the unique traditions and customs the immigrants had brought with them from various regions of Spain and Portugal. As with the Ashkenazic Jews, many Sephardic immigrants also headed to the shores of Palestine and settled in Jerusalem, Gaza, and Safad in Galilee, which served as "a center for the study of the Jewish mystical tradition of the Kabbalah."[78] Smaller groups chose Syria, particularly Damascus, and Egypt, where they settled mostly in Alexandria and Cairo.

In 1517, when the Ottomans defeated the ruling Mamluk dynasty and conquered Egypt, Selim I decreed new laws for the Jews. At the time, the Egyptian Jews were led by their *nagid,* or *reis,* a rabbi and prince-judge whose authority was similar to that conferred on the *hahambaşi* in Istanbul. Selim abolished the office of *nagid* "to prevent his becoming a rival to the chief rabbi in Istanbul," and Selim's son, Süleyman the Magnificent, reasserted the authority of the *hahambaşi* as the representative of all Jews in the empire.[79] Süleyman also appointed an officer (*kahya*), a Jew himself, who enjoyed direct access to the sultan, the grand vizier, and his cabinet, and "to whose notice he could bring cases of injustice" suffered by the members of the Jewish community "at the hands of either provincial governors or of fanatical Christians."[80]

The Sephardic Jewish population played important roles in the everyday life of the Ottoman state as merchants, artisans, and physicians. Determined to preserve their traditions, they organized their social activities around synagogues and community centers, where Hebrew was taught and the Torah and Talmud studied. Ottoman tolerance allowed them to emerge as one of the most educated and literate population groups in the empire.[81] Rabbinical schools such as the one founded in Sarajevo in 1786 by Rabbi David Pardo, played an important role in preserving Jewish religious and cultural traditions and customs.[82] In these schools, the students learned classical Hebrew, though in their day-to-day life they continued to use Ladino, the Jewish-Spanish language they had brought with them from Spain.

The massive migration of Spanish Jewry to the Ottoman Empire included many Jewish merchants who were active in transatlantic trade and introduced to the empire New World plants and fruits such as chili peppers. Thus, the Turkish name for the hot peppers, *biber aci,* derives from the Caribbean *ají.*[83] The Ottoman sultans welcomed the arrival of the new immigrants, particularly the artisans, merchants, and scholars, as men of enterprise and energy who knew precisely those arts and crafts that were in highest demand in the empire, such as "medical knowledge, woolen industry, metalworking, glassmaking, the secrets of the manufacture of arms, the import and export trade, retail trade and distribution, and so on."[84] Each Jewish immigrant community was known for excellence in a unique profession, trade, or craft. The *Maraños* (Muranos) were respected as manufacturers of weapons of war, while those of the medical school of Salamanca were much in demand as doctors.[85] Many were also recruited as translators and interpreters because of their international connections and knowledge of Europe.[86]

It was in trade and commerce, however, that the Jewish community, particularly those who resided in the Balkans, excelled. Their prominent role in the economic life of the empire was observed by an 18th-century English visitor who wrote that most of the wealthy merchants in the empire were Jews and they enjoyed many privileges that ordinary Turks did not. They had "drawn the whole trade of the empire into their hands," and every Ottoman high official had his Jewish "homme d'affaires" to whom he entrusted all his business affairs and interactions.[87] By the beginning of the 18th century, the Jewish presence and participation in the commercial life of the empire was so central and critical that the English, French, and Venetian merchants negotiated with the Ottomans through their intercession.[88] The economic power of the Jewish merchants allowed the community to form a strong commonwealth, which was ruled by its own laws.[89]

Both the Ashkenazim and Sephardim produced numerous statesmen, physicians, merchants, and craftsmen. The most influential Sephardic Jew in the Ottoman Empire was Joseph Nasi (1515–1579), the product of a *Maraño* family, who had arrived in Istanbul from Portugal in 1554. Before reaching Istanbul, he had lived for a time in Antwerp, modern-day Belgium, where he joined his aunt Gracia Nasi Mendes. The Mendes family was one of the most powerful and influential banking families in Europe. When Nasi's aunt moved to Istanbul in 1553, Joseph decided to leave Antwerp and settle with her in the Ottoman capital. Both "aunt and nephew shed their identity as Marranos" and "openly embraced the practice of Judaism," emerging as "important supporters of Jewish charities and scholarship."[90] Nasi also befriended the

Ottoman sultan Selim II (1566–1574) and the sultan's powerful grand vizier Sokollu Mehmed, who appointed Nasi as the Duke of Naxos, the largest island in the Cyclades island group in the Aegean. As an advocate of war against Venice, Nasi encouraged an invasion of the island of Cyprus, which was attacked and captured by the Ottoman forces in 1570.[91] When "he died in 1579, Joseph Nasi was probably one of the wealthiest men in the Ottoman Empire."[92] Another Sephardic Jew, Solomon Abenayish (1520–1603) was appointed the Duke of the Greek island of Lesbos.

The best-known Ashkenazic Jew in the Ottoman state was the Italian-born Solomon Ashkenazi (1520–1603), who served as the physician and confidant of the grand vizier Sokollu Mehmed. Since Ashkenazi had lived both in various Italian states and Poland before his arrival in the Ottoman Empire, the grand vizier sought his advice on Polish- and Venetian-related matters. Sokollu Mehmed demonstrated his trust and confidence in the Jewish physician when he appointed him as the Ottoman ambassador to Venice.[93]

In the 17th, and increasingly, in the 18th century, during the decline of the Ottoman power and the rise of Islamic conservatism, Jews began to suffer at the hands of Muslim religious authorities. After "the great fire of 1660, in which large swathes of Istanbul were destroyed, Jews in the city were not given permission to rebuild" some of their synagogues "as Muslim judges ruled that the permission they had originally received to build them was illegal."[94] A strict interpretation of Islamic law also influenced the outcome of the case of Shabbatai Zvi when the self-proclaimed Jewish messiah was forced to convert to Islam or face death for treason. Additionally, relations between Jewish and Christian communities began to deteriorate as attacks by Christian mobs against Jewish businesses and neighborhoods increased. During the Damascus Incident of 1840, for example, authorities arrested and tortured prominent Damascus Jews after Christians accused them of murdering a Roman Catholic priest.

In the 19th century as nationalist uprisings erupted in the Balkans, links between the empire's Jewish communities and the Ottoman sultans grew stronger. Most Jews feared that any new state formed on the basis of one nation, one language, and one church would be far less tolerant than the Ottoman imperial rule. The nationalist ideologies propagated by various separatist movements in the Balkans espoused Orthodox Christianity as essential to national identity and characterized the Jews as outsiders. The worst fears of the Jews were realized when at the start of the Greek War of Independence in 1821, Greek nationalists massacred both Muslim and Jewish civilians.

NOTES

1. Colin Imber, *The Ottoman Empire, 1300–1650: The Structure of Power* (New York: Palgrave Macmillan, 2002), 2.
2. Ibid.
3. Bruce Masters, "Millet," in *Encyclopedia of the Ottoman Empire,* eds. Gábor Ágoston and Bruce Masters (New York: Facts On File, 2009), 383.
4. Imber, *The Ottoman Empire,* 216; See Benjamin Braude and Bernard Lewis, eds. *Christians and Jews in the Ottoman Empire,* 2 vols. (New York: Holmes & Meier, 1982).
5. Masters, "Millet," 384.
6. Justin McCarthy, *The Ottoman Turks: An Introductory History to 1923* (London, New York: Wesley Longman Limited, 1997), 128.
7. Gustave E. Von Grunebaum, *Medieval Islam: A Study in Cultural Orientation* (Chicago: Chicago University Press, 1962), 185.
8. Imber, *The Ottoman Empire,* 217.
9. McCarthy, *The Ottoman Turks,* 130.
10. Barbara Jelavich, *History of the Balkans: Eighteenth and Nineteenth Centuries* (Cambridge: Cambridge University Press, 1983), 48.
11. Ibid.
12. Ibid., 50.
13. Ibid.
14. Ibid., 48–49.
15. Ibid.
16. Ibid., 50.
17. Ibid.
18. Ibid.
19. Ibid.
20. Masters, "Millet," 384.
21. Jelavich, *History of the Balkans,* 49.
22. Ibid.
23. Aleksandar Fotić, "Serbia," in *Encyclopedia of the Ottoman Empire,* 517–18.
24. Ibid., 519.
25. Jelavich, *History of the Balkans,* 91.
26. Fotić, "Serbia," 518.
27. Mercia Macdermott, *A History of Bulgaria 1393–1885* (London: George Allen & Unwin Ltd, 1962), 16; Jelavich, *History of the Balkans,* 15.

28. Macdermott, *A History of Bulgaria*, 16. Jelavich, *History of the Balkans*, 15.

29. Ibid.

30. Ibid., 18.

31. Ibid.

32. Rossitsa Gradeva, "Bulgarian Orthodox Church," in *Encyclopedia of the Ottoman Empire*, 103.

33. Ibid.

34. Macdermott, *A History of Bulgaria*, 20–21.

35. Stanley G. Evans, *A Short History of Bulgaria* (London: Lawrence & Wishart Ltd. 1960), 75.

36. Dennis P. Hupchik, *The Bulgarians in the Seventeenth Century: Slavic Orthodox Society and Culture under Ottoman Rule* (Jefferson, NC: McFarland, 1993), 9.

37. Ibid.

38. Evans, *A Short History of Bulgaria*, 77.

39. Gradeva, "Bulgarian Orthodox Church," 104.

40. Macdermott, *A History of Bulgaria*, 144; Rossitsa Gradeva, "Bulgarian National Awakening (Bulgarian National revival)," in *Encyclopedia of the Ottoman Empire*, 102–3.

41. Rossitsa Gradeva, "Bulgarian National Awakening," 103.

42. Ibid.

43. Gradeva, "Bulgarian Orthodox Church," 104.

44. Rouben Paul Adalian, *Historical Dictionary of Armenia* (Lanham, MD: The Scarecrow Press, Inc., 2002), xxviii, 367–69.

45. McCarthy, *The Ottoman Turks*, 129.

46. George A. Bournoutian, *A Concise History of the Armenian People* (Costa Mesa, CA: Mazda Publishers, 2002), 54–55.

47. Halil Inalcik, *The Ottoman Empire, The Classical Age 1300–1600* (New York: Praeger Publishers, 1973), 141.

48. H.A.R. Gibb and Harold Bowen, *Islamic Society and the West: A Study of the Impact of Western Civilization on Moslem Culture in the Near East*, 2 vols. (London: Oxford University Press, 1957), 1:220.

49. Bournoutian, *A Concise History of the Armenian People*, 187.

50. Gibb and Bowen, *Islamic Society and the West*, 1:227.

51. Simon Payaslian, *The History of Armenia* (New York: Palgrave MacMillan, 2007), 117–19; Shaw, *History of the Ottoman Empire*, 2:202.

52. Payaslian, *The History of Armenia*, 117–19; Shaw, *History of the Ottoman Empire*, 2:202.

53. Payaslian, *The History of Armenia*, 117–19; Shaw, *History of the Ottoman Empire*, 2:202.

54. Shaw, *History of the Ottoman Empire*, 2:202.

55. Payaslian, *The History of Armenia*, 119–20; Adalian, *Historical Dictionary of Armenia*, 72–77, 353–55.

56. Payaslian, *The History of Armenia*, 120.

57. Zürcher, *Turkey*, 114.

58. Ibid., 114–15.

59. Ibid., 115.

60. Ibid.

61. See Taner Akçam, *From Empire to Republic: Turkish Nationalism and the Armenian Genocide* (London: Zed Books, 2004), 143–45, 158–75; Guenter Lewy, *The Armenian Massacres in Ottoman Turkey* (Salt Lake City: The University of Utah Press, 2005), 82–89.

62. Masters, "Millet," 384.

63. Bruce Masters, "Karaites," in *Encyclopedia of the Ottoman Empire*, 308.

64. Bruce Masters, "Jews," in *Encyclopedia of the Ottoman Empire*, 300.

65. Ibid.

66. Ibid.

67. Peter F. Sugar, *Southeastern Europe under Ottoman Rule: 1354–1804* (Seattle: University of Washington Press, 1996), 69.

68. Inalcik, *The Ottoman Empire*, 141.

69. Masters, "Jews," 302.

70. Sugar, *Southeastern Europe under Ottoman Rule*, 267.

71. Inalcik, *The Ottoman Empire*, 141.

72. Sugar, *Southeastern Europe under Ottoman Rule*, 267.

73. Gibb and Bowen, *Islamic Society and the West*, 1:219.

74. Ibid., 1:225.

75. Itzhak Ben-Zvi, "Eretz Yisrael under Ottoman Rule, 1517–1917," in Louis Finkelstein, ed., *The Jews Their History, Culture, and Religion* (New York: Harpers & Brothers Publishers, 1960), 602.

76. Cecil Roth, "The European Age in Jewish History," in Louis Finkelstein, *The Jews Their History*, 246–47.

77. Masters, "Jews," 302.

78. Ibid., 301.

79. Gibb and Bowen, *Islamic Society and the West*, 1:226; See also, Inalcik, *The Ottoman Empire*, 141.

80. Ibid.

81. Ivan Lovrenović, *Bosnia: A Cultural History* (New York: New York University Press, 2001), 145.

82. Ibid.

83. Michael Krondl, *The Taste of Conquest: The Rise and Fall of the Three Great Cities of Spice* (New York: Ballantine Books, 2007), 174.

84. Lovrenović, *Bosnia*, 245; See also Ben-Zvi, "Eretz Yisrael Under Ottoman Rule," 603.

85. Gibb and Bowen, *Islamic Society and the West*, 1:220.

86. Ibid.

87. Lady Mary Wortley Montagu, *The Turkish Embassy Letters* (London: Virago Press, 2007), 93.

88. Ibid.

89. Ibid.

90. Masters, "Jews," 302.

91. Sugar, *Southeastern Europe under Ottoman Rule*, 267.

92. Masters, "Jews," 302.

93. Sugar, *Southeastern Europe under Ottoman Rule*, 267. See also, Roth, "The European Age in Jewish History," 255–56.

94. Masters, "Jews," 302.

6

MUSLIMS

The defense, protection, and expansion of Islam served as the ideological foundation and unifying principle for the Ottoman ruling elite. From its inception, the Ottoman Empire acted as an Islamic state dedicated to the defense and expansion of Islam against infidels.[1] In the parlance of government officials and writers, the Ottoman sultan was "the sovereign of Islam, its armies were armies of Islam, its laws were the laws of Islam, which it was the sultan's duty to uphold and administer."[2]

Islam was the dominant religion among Turks, Arabs, Kurds, Albanians, and Bosnians. During the long period when the Ottoman Empire ruled the Balkans, the Muslims constituted the second-largest religious community in the empire, after Orthodox Christians. With the loss of European provinces in the 17th, 18th, and 19th centuries, however, Muslims emerged as the majority religious group, particularly after the Congress of Berlin in 1878 and the loss of Serbia, Romania, and Bulgaria.

FIVE PILLARS OF ISLAM

Turks converted to Islam as they entered Central Asia and swept through Iran on their way to Anatolia. For them, Islam represented a simple faith that provided daily structure and discipline through a set of beliefs, rules, and practices. The religion is based on six articles of belief, namely: belief in God, belief in all messengers of God, belief in the angels, belief in holy books sent by God, belief in the day of judgment and resurrection, and belief in destiny. In addition to adhering to these six fundamentals of belief, every Muslim is also required to perform the five pillars of Islam.

Declaration of Faith

The first pillar, declaration of faith, requires Muslims to reaffirm their belief daily by stating; "I bear witness that there is no god but God, I bear witness that Muhammad is the messenger of God." Far from a merely ritualistic and obligatory utterance, the first part of the declaration reminds the Muslim that Allah (God) is the creator of the universe and all living beings and, therefore, the only majesty to be obeyed and worshipped. The second part reaffirms the principle that Muhammad is the messenger through whom God (Allah) revealed the holy Quran. He also serves as a model and exemplar for all Muslims.

Prayer

The second pillar of Islam is prayer, or *namaz* (Arabic: *salat*), which is performed five times a day at set hours while facing in the direction of the holy city of Mecca in western Arabia (modern-day Saudi Arabia). These five prayers impose a structure and discipline on the daily life of a Muslim. They are performed in the early morning after dawn, in the afternoon after mid-day, in the late afternoon before sunset, after the sunset, and at night before sleeping. *Ezan* (Arabic: *adhan*), or the call to prayer, summons believers by means of a repeated announcement. The muezzin, who utters the call to prayer, ascends the minaret of a mosque five times a day to recite the call: "God is great" (repeated four times), "I bear witness that there is no god but God" (repeated twice), "I bear witness that Muhammad is the messenger of God" (repeated twice), "Come to worship/prayer" (repeated twice), "Come to success" (repeated twice), "Prayer is better than sleep" (repeated twice; only for the dawn prayer), "God is great" (repeated twice), and "I bear witness that there is no god but God."

Each prayer is preceded by ablution since a Muslim can not stand before God with a dirty body. In front of every mosque there are a number of taps and cisterns of water where the worshipper has to wash before he can perform his prayer. The ablution begins with the person declaring the intention that his self-cleansing is for the purpose of worship and purity. He then washes his hands up to the wrists three times, followed by rinsing the mouth three times with water, cleansing his nostrils by sniffing water into them three times, washing the whole face three times with both hands or at times with the right hand only, washing the right and then the left arm up to the far end of the elbow three times, wiping the head with a wet hand once, wiping the inner section of the ears with the forefingers and the outer section with wet thumbs, wiping the neck with wet hands, and finally washing both feet up to the ankles three times starting with the right foot. The cleanliness of the average Muslim in the Ottoman Empire was mentioned repeatedly by European travelers, who observed that Islam was a "hygienic religion" and that in the eyes of the faithful, cleanliness was part of godliness.[3]

The ablution is nullified by natural discharges such as urine, stools, gas, or vomiting, falling asleep, and becoming intoxicated. When the person is sick or does not have access to water or the water is contaminated and its usage can harm the worshipper, it is permissible to perform *tayammum*, or substitute ablution, which involves putting one's hands into earth or sand or on a stone, shaking the hands off and wiping the face with them once and touching the earth or sand again and wiping the right arm to the elbow with the left hand and the left arm with the right hand.

Prayers can be performed anywhere, for God is believed to be present everywhere. While the daily prayers can be performed alone, the Friday prayer is always a group ritual, that includes the members of the community at a local mosque. Women did not usually pray at a mosque. Instead, they performed their prayers at home, but they underwent the same preparation and the *wuzu*, or the ablution, without which it would be improper to pray.

The call to prayer is made a short time before the prayer starts, providing the faithful ample time to perform ablutions and arrive at the mosque. When all worshippers have converged and the prayer is about to begin, the *iqamah* is called to make all in attendance aware that the prayer is getting underway. The content of the *iqamah* is similar to the *ezan*, but it is often recited at a faster pace: "God is great, I bear witness that there is no god but God, I bear witness that Muhammad is the messenger of God, Come to worship/prayer, Come to success, Prayer is better than sleep." The Friday prayer is led by an *imam* (leader) who also reads the *hutbe*

(Arabic: *khutbah*), or sermon. During the Ottoman era, the name of the reigning Ottoman sultan was mentioned in the *hutbe*. During the communal prayer, the worshippers stand, kneel, and prostrate themselves in straight parallel rows behind the imam. They face the *kibla* (Arabic: *qibla*) or the direction of prayer towards Mecca. Those standing at prayer represent the equality of all Muslims before God and their solidarity as a unified community.

Zakat

The third pillar of Islam is *zakat* (giving alms to the poor or the act of sharing wealth), which requires Muslims to pay a percentage of their income as religious tax to the poor, orphans, debtors, travelers, slaves, and beggars. In the Ottoman era, the tax was payable at different rates on harvests and merchandise, but for gold and silver that was included in an individual's personal assets, the rate was two and a half percent. Islam views all wealth as emanating from God and therefore belonging to him. This does not prohibit Muslims from producing wealth and using it to obtain their own goods as long as the wealth is not gained through coercion, cheating, and theft. Islam teaches, however, that human beings descend to the level of animals if they hoard wealth and do not share it with fellow Muslims. *Zakat* is often given by the believer to the recipients of his choice.

Fasting

The fourth pillar of Islam is fasting during the month of *Ramazan* (Arabic: *Ramadan*), the ninth month in the Islamic calendar, and requires that Muslims abstain from food, drink, smoke, snuff, and sexual activities every day from sunrise to sunset. Fasting is not obligatory for children before the onset of puberty, people with an illness or medical condition, nursing and pregnant women, travelers, and those fighting on the battlefield. Despite these rules, children, pregnant women, travelers, and soldiers in the Ottoman era fasted during the entire month.

Though the duties of the holy month are arduous, members of all social classes in the Ottoman era observed them with exceeding devotion and zeal, and they condemned any open and public infraction with uncommon severity.[4] The Venetian ambassador to Istanbul, Ottaviano Bon, reported that on one occasion the grand vizier, Nasuh Paşa (1611–1614), who was riding on the street, de-

tected a drunken man who was immediately detained, and subsequently tortured and killed when the *paşa's* men poured boiling
lead down his throat.[5]

Most shops remained either shut or bereft of shopkeepers.
Merchants did not buy and students did not study as the faithful
chose to sleep during the daylight hours. The mosques were bril-
liantly illuminated, and they were crowded with worshippers.
Cords were "slung from minaret to minaret," to which lamps were
attached and "the rising or lowering of these cords," produced
magical transitions.[6] As a European visitor to the Ottoman capital observed, these unique lamps rendered "the illuminations of
Istanbul unlike those of any European capital."[7] *Ramazan* is a month
of self-cleansing and meditation, and the faithful are expected to
refrain from waging warfare, becoming angry, lusting for money
and sex, and making offensive or sarcastic gestures and utter-
ances. Purifying one's thoughts and actions means treating fellow
Muslims with added kindness, compassion, and generosity.

As the hour of sunset approaches, people prepare themselves
for the sound of the cannon and the cry of the muezzin, calling
the faithful to prayer. The second cannon discharge signals *iftar,*
or breaking of the fast, with an evening meal that includes family
and friends. The poor often ate a large meal at once, while the rich
broke the fast with a light meal—a morsel of bread with yogurt,
dates, fresh or dried fruit, especially watermelon, sweetmeats,
and *muhallabi*, "a thin jelly of milk, starch, and rice flour," washed
down with water or lemonade.[8] The evening prayer is performed
after breaking the fast. At times, the faithful smoked a pipe,
drank a cup of coffee or a glass of sherbet before performing the
evening prayer. Then he sat down with family and friends to the
main meal.

After the meal, streets became crowded with throngs of people. Some spent their time in a coffeehouse smoking water-pipes
filled with tobacco and listening to storytellers and singers, while
others walked through gardens, sitting in the moonlight and
enjoying cakes, toasted grains, coffee, and sugared drinks as they
watched the performance of the Karagöz shadow puppet theater.[9]
Many walked to a mosque and listened to prayers and recitations from the local imam, while others spent part of the evening
with local *dervişes* at a Sufi lodge (*tekke*) although during the holy
month, *zikrs* (literally remembrance of God), or ecstatic worship
through devotional singing, were rarely performed.[10] The rich
spent the entire night in festivities, while the poor tried to get as

much food, drink, and rest as possible because they were obliged to work at daybreak.

Shortly before midnight came the call to prayer, at which time the late wanderers returned home to prepare for a morning meal.[11] In the large urban centers such as Istanbul and Cairo, shortly after the arrival of midnight, the cannon sounded a warning to the faithful that it was time to eat their morning meal.[12] In small towns and villages, drummers walked through narrow streets and alleys warning the faithful to eat their early morning meal before the sunrise. The morning meal was usually eaten an hour before the morning prayer. In homes of the rich and powerful, the servants brought water for ablution, spread the leather cloth (*sofra,* Arabic: *sufrah*)—well tanned and generally of a yellow color bordered with black—and placed a meal on it which at times included remnants of the evening's meal.[13] Then sounded the *salam,* or blessing on the prophet, an introduction to the call of morning prayer.[14] Many took the last puff on their pipes. A second gun was fired as a sign of *imsak,* or the order to abstain from eating and drinking.[15] Then the faithful waited for the call to prayer, which was followed by a ceremony called "purpose" or "intention" (*niyet/niyat*).[16] For instance, the worshipper could say to himself, silently or audibly, that he intended to pray two bows of prayer to God. He then proceeded with his prayers and went to sleep immediately. Different schools of Islamic jurisprudence required different forms of *niyet.*

When the month of fasting fell in winter, the wealthy families of the Ottoman capital, particularly the women, spent much of their time in chatting and embroidery work until "about six o'clock in the evening when the cry of the muezzin from the minarets proclaimed that one of the out watchers had caught a glimpse of the moon."[17] Instantly, the entire household went into motion; the "preliminary arrangements" had been so "carefully made" that not a second was lost and as a servant "announced dinner," the entire harem followed the matriarch of the family "to a smaller apartment," which served as the dining room.[18] In the center of the square-shaped and unfurnished dining room was "a carpet, on which stood a wooden frame, about two feet in height, supporting an immense round plated tray, with the edge slightly raised."[19] In the center of the tray "was placed a capacious white basin, filled with a kind of cold bread soup and around it were ranged a circle of small porcelain saucers, filled with sliced cheese, anchovies, caviars, and sweetmeats of every description; among these were scattered spoons of box-wood, and goblets of pink and white sherbet, whose rose-scented contents perfumed the apartment."[20] The outer section of the tray "was covered with fragments of unleavened bread, torn asunder, and portions of the Ramazan cake," a dry paste "glazed with the whites of eggs, and stewed over with aniseeds."[21]

After spreading richly fringed napkins on their laps and munching on this starter tray, the household sat quietly as servants served them with "fish embedded in rice," dishes of meat and poultry, which were eaten with fingers with each individual "fishing up, or breaking away" a piece of the meat and handing one to the guest as a courtesy.[22] One European observer, who was invited to one of these sumptuous meals, counted "nineteen dishes of fish, flesh, fowl, pastry, and creams, succeeding each other in the most heterogeneous manner," all culminating with "a pyramid of pilaf."[23] Once the meal had been finished, water, sherbet, and coffee were served. As the family and guests rose from the table, "a slave presented herself, holding a basin and strainer of wrought metal, while a second poured tepid water" over everyone's hands "from an elegantly-formed vase of the same materials"; and a third handed "embroidered napkins of great beauty."[24] Returning from the dining room to "the principal apartment," the family gathered to listen to a storyteller who was invited to relieve the tedium of the long evening with her narrations.[25]

Some among high government officials celebrated the arrival of the holy month by opening the doors of their homes and showering their dependents and servants with kindness and generosity. In his *Book of Travels*, Evliya Çelebi wrote that at the beginning of *Ramazan*, his patron, Melek Ahmed Paşa, distributed various precious goods from his treasury such as expensive garments, vessels, weapons, armor, jeweled muskets, swords, sable furs, and coral prayer beads to his servants and *ağas*, in return for a complete Quran recital and their prayers and invocations.[26] Every Monday and Friday evening during the month, the doors of his home were opened to the public, who were served fruit syrups and musky sweetmeats of pistachios and almonds, while they listened to recitations of prayers from the Quran.[27]

The sultan and his officials used *Ramazan* as an occasion to sacrifice a variety of animals either at a mosque or at a public place such as an open street or the main gates of the city. The meat was distributed among ordinary people, particularly the poor and the needy. Numerous religious ceremonies and observances also took place throughout the holy month. On the fifteenth of *Ramazan*, the sultan and high government officials went to pay homage to the relics of the prophet Muhammad, which they held in great veneration. These included the prophet's mantle, "a black woolen jacket, measuring 124 centimeters, with wide sleeves and cream-colored wool lining," his flag and battle standard, the hair from his beard, a piece of his tooth, and his footprint set in a piece of stone.[28] The ceremonial uncovering, display, and veneration of these relics followed the noon prayer. Though conducted privately, the ceremony was nonetheless an occasion of great religious significance.

Ramazan Bayrami

The end of *Ramazan* was marked with a three-day Islamic holiday called *Ramazan Bayrami* (Ramazan Festival) or *Şeker Bayrami* (Sugar Festival) also known in Arabic as *Eid ul-Fitr* or *Eid us-Sagheer*, Minor Festival. The month of fasting ended and the festivities began with the first appearance of the new moon heralding the month of *Shawwal*.[29] At times, the *bayram* was delayed if the weather was cloudy and the new moon did not appear in the sky. If the sky remained cloudy and the moon was obscured, it was simply presumed that the new moon was present and the month of fasting had ended. In Istanbul, the end of *Ramazan* was officially proclaimed with discharging of cannons at the imperial palace. The lights and lamps on the minarets were extinguished, and drums and trumpets were played in public places and the homes of high government officials and court dignitaries.[30]

Even before the arrival of the *bayram*, the sultan—as well as the rich and powerful who surrounded him—demonstrated their devotion, charity, and piety by distributing alms to the poor. Some families prepared a variety of dishes and sent them to their neighbors, as well as to the poor and the needy. In the courtyards of the main mosques, markets were set up to sell meat, fruits, vegetables, sweets, clothing, fabrics, candles, toys, and a host of other popular goods. On the first day of *Shawwal*, the tenth month in the Islamic calendar, came the *Ramazan* celebration.

At the palace, the entrance leading to the apartments of the chief eunuch, who commanded the royal pages, was adorned with rich carpets, cushions, and furniture. A few hours before daybreak, the grand vizier and other high officials and court dignitaries assembled at the palace, where shortly after sunrise the sultan mounted his horse and rode passed his officials to attend prayers at Aya Sofya. After performing his prayers, the sultan returned to the palace and entered the royal chamber, where he sat on the throne with the grand vizier standing on his right and the chief eunuch standing on his left. The sons of the Han of Crimea, who lived as hostages at the Ottoman court, were the first to wish the sultan a happy *bayram* as they kissed the hem of his sleeve. To show his respect for them, the sultan walked three paces to meet them. Once the Tatar princes had retired, the grand vizier followed by kneeling in front of the sultan, kissing the hem of the sleeve of his royal master, and wishing him, on behalf of the entire government, happy and healthy festivities. After the grand vizier, the *şeyhülislam* led a delegation of religious dignitaries such as the *kadiaskers* (the highest religious judges under *şeyhülislam*), and the prominent Muslim scholars and preachers. The *şeyhülislam* approached the sultan, bowed his head to the ground, and, holding his hand on his girdle, kissed the sultan on the left shoulder. To express his respect for the religious establishment, the sultan walked one step forward to meet the *şeyhülislam*.

Once these high dignitaries had expressed their wishes for a happy *bayram*, the sultan returned to his throne. Other high officials and dignitaries then followed as the grand vizier called out their names. The last to appear was always the commander of the janissary corps. With the end of this ceremony, the sultan retired to his harem, where the four principal pages responsible for the royal chambers (privy, treasury, larder, and campaign), followed by the chief eunuch and other pages, wished their royal master a happy *bayram*. Meanwhile, a sumptuous dinner was served in the divan for the grand vizier, his ministers, and other state dignitaries. The ceremony concluded after dinner, when the sultan presented a sable vest as a gift to each high government official.[31] When the dignitaries had retired, the royal harem, including the mother and wives of the sultan, visited him to offer their homage and best wishes.

Outside the palace, before the arrival of the new month, the faithful who had fasted for 30 days made their customary fast offering. Such an offering required them to distribute among the poor and the needy a certain amount of wheat, barley, dates, and fruit. This purified their fast for it was believed that until a

Muslim had distributed these gifts, or their equivalent in money, god kept his fasting suspended between heaven and earth. Among the wealthy and powerful families, every member of the household, including servants and slaves, received a valuable present according to their status, "the length and difficulty of their services," or "the degree of favor in which" they "were held."[32]

In the Arab provinces of the empire, where this practice was called *sadaqat ul-Fitr* or *zakat ul-Fitr*, the alms were distributed one or even two nights before the end of *Ramazan*. The head of household was responsible to pay the alms on behalf of every member of his family. Approximately two kilograms of grains was distributed on behalf of each family member. Some among the rich and powerful chose to distribute money instead of grains or dates.

On the first day of the new month, men bathed, perfumed, and dressed in their finest clothing to attend congregational prayer. Having distributed their required alms, worshippers assembled outside their town or village in a large space especially set aside for the large congregation who attended the *bayram* prayer. There, led by an imam, they performed prayers. After the end of the prayer, the imam ascended the pulpit and delivered a sermon.[33] The prayer marking the new month had no call to prayer and no *iqama*, which was called to make all in attendance aware that the prayer was getting underway. Once prayers had ended, all worshippers embraced and wished one another a happy and healthy *bayram*. They then returned to their homes, taking a different road from the one they had taken coming to the prayer.

On the occasion of the arrival of the *bayram*, parents bought new clothes for their children, who proudly displayed them as they walked through the streets. Women wore their best jewelry and most splendid dress. The rich and powerful distributed presents among their servants, dependents, and the poor. During congratulatory visits, the young kissed the right hands of the older members of the family, who gave them sweets.

An important part of the *bayram* was the restoration of friendship between those who had quarreled or hurt each other's feelings. After the mid-day service at the mosque and exchange of visits, some people set off for cemeteries, where temporary markets were set up to sell flowers, prayer books, and water for watering the plants around the grave. The rest of the day was spent in relaxation and amusement, such as listening to performances by the janissary marching band (*mehtaran*) or watching the popular *Karagöz* and *Hacivat* shadow theater.

Hajj

The fifth pillar of Islam is *hac* (Arabic: *hajj*), or pilgrimage to the holy city of Mecca in western Arabia. The journey is required of every Muslim who is physically and financially able. Islam allows those who can not tolerate the hardship of the journey to Mecca to perform it by proxy, requesting another Muslim, typically a friend or a relative, to act as a substitute. *Hac* serves as a unifying force by bringing Muslims of diverse racial, ethnic, and linguistic backgrounds together in a common set of religious rites. Once a believer has performed the pilgrimage, he adds the title of *haci* (*hajji*) to his name. The pilgrimage rite follows the pattern established by the prophet Muhammad during his life.

In the Ottoman era, before the pilgrim entered Mecca, he wore the *ihram* garments, consisting of two white seamless sheets without any ornamentation with one piece wrapped round the loins and the other covering the left shoulder and passed under the right armpit. He also took vows to avoid "quarrels, immorality, bad language, and light conversation," while demonstrating his respect for the holy sanctuary "by sparing the trees" and not plucking "a single blade of grass."[34] The pilgrim was also obligated to abstain from using "all oils, perfumes, and unguents; from washing the head with mallow or with lote leaves;" and from "dyeing, shaving, cutting" his hair.[35] For "each infraction of these ordinances," he had to sacrifice a sheep.[36] After a complete ablution and assuming the *ihram*, the pilgrims performed prayers, and recited the meritorious sentences beginning with the words, "Here I am, O God, here I am . . ."[37]

Once he had arrived in Mecca, the pilgrim walked around the *Ka'ba* seven times, kissed the Black Stone (*Hajar al-Aswad*), prayed twice, and walked seven times between Mount Safa and Mount Marwa. On the seventh of *Zilhice*, the last month in the Islamic calendar, the pilgrim was reminded of his duties. During the second stage of the *hac*, which took place between the eighth and the twelfth days of the month, the pilgrim visited the holy places outside Mecca and sacrificed an animal in commemoration of Abraham's sacrifice. Men shaved their heads, and after throwing seven stones at each of the three pillars at *Mina* that represented the devil, the pilgrims returned to Mecca to perform the farewell *tawaf*, or circling of the *Ka'ba*, before leaving the city.

The number of those who performed the *hac* every year is unknown, but at least one European writer who lived in Istanbul in the 1660s estimated the total number of the pilgrims to be "about fifty thousand souls."[38] The sultan did not perform the pilgrimage in person, but he appointed a commander of the pilgrims, who carried a letter of compliments and greetings from the sultan to the Sharif of Mecca, who acted as the governor of the city. The commander of the pilgrims was accompanied by a large military escort, which was responsible for transporting the royal gifts that were sent to Mecca and Medina for the relief of the poor and for the bribe paid to the Bedouin tribesmen who raided and looted pilgrim caravans. The royal caravan and its military escort also carried a new *kiswah*, or the cloth covering for the *Ka'ba*.[39] As the old hanging was pulled down, the pilgrims tore it into pieces and carried it home as a relic and token of their pilgrimage. Two royal camels, decorated with flowers and other ornaments, were the most attractive features of the procession. The first camel carried "a high pinnacled litter" called the *mahmil*, which represented the sultan's authority.[40] The second camel's green velvet and silver saddle was intended to resemble the prophet Muhammad's own saddle. On the appearance of the two camels, a great stir moved through the crowd who shouted: "Allah Allah" in welcome. The camels were followed by an army of grooms and attendants carrying supplies, including the tents that provided protection and covering for the sultan's *mahmil*.[41] After the end of the procession, the camels, which had performed the journey, were declared exempt from all labor and service.

KURBAN BAYRAMI

Muslims across the empire celebrated the *Kurban Bayrami* (the Feast of Sacrifice) or *Büyük Bayrami* (Greater Festival) (Arabic: *Eid ul-Adha*) on the tenth of *Zilhice* (Arabic: *Dhu-l Hijjah*), the last month in the Islamic calendar. The four-day festivities commemorated Abraham's unflinching devotion to God by his willingness to sacrifice his son Ishmael (substituted for Isaac in the Muslim version of the story). In Istanbul, for several days prior to the feast, shepherds from all over Anatolia brought thousands of sheep into the open space in front of the Bayezid Mosque, where heads of households gathered. A sheep, with its fleece colored with henna or cochineal and its horns covered with gold leaf, was taken home with help from the children of the family, who were responsible for its food and water.[42]

In the morning of the festival, Muslims gathered in a place outside the city, town, or village, to perform their prayers. Once everyone had assembled, the imam took his place in front of the congregation and led them in prayer. After the prayer had ended, the imam ascended the pulpit and delivered a sermon on the meaning and significance of the festival. When he had finished his sermon, the attendants returned home, where the head of the family took the sheep and, at times, the goat, camel, or cow, he had bought and turned its head toward Mecca, said a prayer, uttered the *takbir* ("Allahu Akbar" or "God is great") three times and requested "the gracious acceptance of the sacrifice," by uttering *bismillah* (in the name of Allah/God).[43] He then slaughtered the animal. Every head of a family sacrificed "an animal with his own hands and every male member of his household" was "at liberty to indulge his piety in a similar manner," but the head of the family was "bound to observe" the ceremony.[44]

No animal was lawful food unless it was slaughtered according to the Islamic law. The Muslim had to draw the knife across the throat and cut the windpipe, the carotid arteries, and the gullet repeating at the same time *bismillah,* and *Allahu akbar.*[45] The meat was divided into three portions, of which one was shared with the poor, another was given to relatives, and the third was kept for home consumption.[46] The animal had to be "of a fixed age and be free" from "certain blemishes" (lack of an eye, lameness, etc.).[47]

The sultan celebrated the opening of the Feast of Sacrifice surrounded by government officials and court dignitaries, who attended the ceremonies with him at an imperial mosque, while the crowds cheered. Upon returning to his palace, the sultan put on "a sacrificial dress," and slaughtered an animal with his own hands.[48] The first sheep he slaughtered was for himself, but he afterwards offered one for each member of the royal family.[49] At the conclusion of this ceremony, the sultan hosted a grand reception for state officials and grandees, as well as foreign ambassadors and dignitaries, who offered him their congratulations.

All Muslims, rich and poor, young and old, were expected to celebrate the holiday by wearing their best clothes and participating in congregational prayer at a mosque. The rich bestowed gifts and alms, while children were offered sweets, fruits, and toys, which were sold by Christian and Jewish vendors. A European visitor, who was in Istanbul in 1836, described the splendor and rejoicing with which the festival of sacrifice was celebrated by "all the population of the capital." She wrote that the harbor of Istanbul was beautifully "decked out with flags," all business was suspended, men grasped each other by the hand in the streets and uttered "a fraternal greeting," and the poor were seen

"hastening from house to house to secure the flesh of the sacrifices."[50] Another Western resident of Istanbul who watched the
festivities at the dawn of the First World War observed that as
"evening faded into night," the whole of Istanbul began "to glit-
ter with the lights of myriads of tiny oil lamps hung around the
windows of houses, festooned from minaret to minaret, or encircl-
ing, in double or triple coronals, their surrounding balconies and
pinnacles."[51]

The people of Istanbul celebrated both *Ramazan Bayrami* and
Kurban Bayrami with "extraordinary public entertainments," "eating
in the streets," and "prayers and illuminations in the mosques."[52]
One of the most popular amusements throughout the city, day and
night, was playing on swings, although "there were occasional
directives prohibiting" them "on the grounds of public morality."[53] According to an Italian traveler who visited the capital in
1614–1615, the swings were suspended from "very high beams, put
up under canvas for this purpose, and all decorated with leaves,
flowers, tinsel, festoons, and other colored adornments."[54] Young
and old; men and women; Muslim, Christian, and Jew sat on the
swing and were pushed by the ropes high into the air as they listened to music playing nearby.[55] Young men used the opportunity to take off their "outside garment" and, at times, long shirts,
to show off their skills, agility, and physique—especially if a lady
were present and watching.[56] At times the swings were set in pairs
at a short distance from each other, one individual took one and
another the other; and if they were men, they tried "to kick each
other" as they passed, while if they were women, they tried "to
embrace each other in mid-air and hook the other by legs, or capture in their hands some of the fruit attached on high."[57] Another
form of popular entertainment was spinning on large wooden
wheels that revolved, "some crosswise like millstones, and others
from on high down like the wheel of fortune," with people enjoying the sensation of "being swept up high and down again" very
fast, and then "going up again." When a person shouted, panicked,
or felt dizzy from the movement and the speed of the wheel, he
was immediately sprinkled with jugs of rose water.[58]

HOLY NIGHTS

The Ottoman Empire used the Islamic calendar, a lunar calendar
based on 12 months in a year of 354 or 355 days. With the *Hijra,*
or the flight of the prophet Muhammad from Mecca to Medina

in A.D. 622, designated as its first year, the calendar was used by Muslims to determine the proper day on which to celebrate important religious holidays and festivals. The months began when the first crescent of a new moon was sighted. Since the lunar calendar year was 11 to 12 days shorter, the months migrated and moved throughout seasons.

Besides the two great *bayrams*, several important holy nights and religious holidays were celebrated with an impressive display of prayer and meditation by all Muslims. Unlike the two main *bayrams* that were celebrated with public festivities, however, during the holy nights of the year, the faithful focused on solemn prayers, meditation, participation in chanting ceremonies, and feasting and celebrations in the privacy of their homes. The first of these holy nights was the feast of the birth of Muhammad, the prophet of Islam, and it was celebrated by Sunni Muslims on the 12th of *Rabi ul-Awwal* and by the Shia Muslims on the 17th of *Rabi ul-Awwal*, the third month in the Islamic calendar. The second great holy night celebrated the night of Muhammad's conception on the fourth of *Receb* (Arabic: *Rajab*), the fifth month in the Islamic calendar. On each of these holy nights, mosques were illuminated and special foods prepared.

The third holy night in the Islamic calendar was the Night of Ascension that commemorated the prophet Muhammad's ascent to heaven. Sometimes known as Muhammad's Night Journey, the story on which the holiday was based illustrates the scriptural and narrative connections between Islam, Christianity, and Judaism. The Night of Ascension was traditionally celebrated on the 27th of *Receb*. On this night, mosques and minarets were lighted, and families visited a main mosque where children sat and listened attentively to the story of the Prophet's journey. After listening to the story of Muhammad's night journey, children joined their parents in a communal prayer, followed by food and special treats. One of these treats, *kandil simit*, or ring-shaped sweet bread covered by sesame seeds, was served at each of the commemorations of major events in the life of the prophet Muhammad, such as his birth, the first revelation he received, and his ascension to heaven.

The fourth important holy night was the Night of Record and Day of Forgiveness, celebrated on the 14th of *Sha'ban*, the eighth month in the Islamic calendar. As with other holy nights of the year, the faithful gathered in mosques to pray. The worshippers believed that on this night, God registered all the actions of mankind to be performed during the coming year. They also acknowledged a tree in heaven that shed several leaves on this night, each one containing the name of someone destined to die within the year. The mercy of God also descended on this night, and sinners who repented were likely to obtain forgiveness. Muslims remained awake and prayed for much of the night. A day-long fast followed.

The most important of all holy nights was the Night of Power, which was observed on the 27th of *Ramazan*, the ninth month in the Islamic calendar. It celebrated the angels' descent to earth with the Holy Quran and the Angel Gabriel's revelation of it to the prophet Muhammad. The night was also significant because it was believed that special blessings were sent down to the truly devout from heaven. Upon the arrival of the Night of Power, a solemn and meditative spirit overcame every Muslim household. From the large urban centers to the humblest village, young and old, men and women, state officials, merchants, artisans and peasant farmers, participated in night prayers, for they believed that on this night the fate of every devout Muslim was shaped for the following year.[59] Muslim men generally avoided sexual intercourse during all holy nights, but on the Night of Power, the sultan slept with a slave girl at the royal harem, and if a baby was conceived, it was regarded as a symbol of the power and the glory of the Ottoman ruling house.[60]

The Muslim communities of Anatolia and the Balkans also celebrated non-Islamic festivals with great joy and enthusiasm. *Nevruz*, also known as *Sultan Nevruz*, marked the beginning of spring and was celebrated on the day of the astronomical vernal equinox. The celebration was particularly popular among the Kurdish and Alevi communities of Anatolia, Iraq, and Syria, who greeted the arrival of the New Year by exchanging the greeting "May your *Nevruz* be victorious." While the devout shunned dancing, Muslims living in the rural and mountain communities of Bosnia, Albania, and the Kurdish-populated regions of southeast Anatolia, northern Iraq, and northern Syria, danced frequently during weddings, various festivities, and even religious ceremonies connected with pilgrimages to the tombs of holy men and saints. Among many Kurdish communities, men and women danced *chubi*, which brought together a group of dancers joining hands and balancing "their bodies backwards and forwards, marking time, first with one foot and then with the other, accompanying their movements at intervals with wild cries."[61] Men danced first, followed by women who removed their veils and wore long dresses "resplendent in gold spangles and parti-colored silks."[62]

At weddings, *surnay* or *zurna*, double-reed outdoor wind instruments, accompanied by a bass drum and reed flutes, were played in unison as men and women danced for hours.

NOTES

1. Bernard Lewis, *Istanbul and the Civilization of the Ottoman Empire* (Norman: University of Oklahoma Press, 1963), 145.

2. Ibid.

3. Sir Edwin Pears, *Turkey and Its People* (London: Methuen Co. Ltd., 1912), 47.

4. Richard F. Burton, *Personal Narrative of a Pilgrimage to Al-Madinah and Meccah*, 2 vols. (New York: Dover Publications, 1964), 1:74.

5. Ottaviano Bon, *The Sultan's Seraglio: An Intimate Portrait of Life at the Ottoman Court* (London: Saqi Books, 1996), 136.

6. Julia Pardoe, *The City of the Sultan and Domestic Manners of the Turks in 1836*, 3 vols. (London: Henry Colburn Publisher, 1838), 1:9.

7. Ibid.

8. Burton, *Personal Narrative of a Pilgrimage*, 79. Burton's description focuses on Cairo; however, the activities he mentions among the populace were also popular among the residents of Istanbul and other urban centers of the Ottoman Empire.

9. Ibid., 81.

10. Ibid., 85–86.

11. Ibid., 88.

12. Ibid.

13. Ibid., 76.

14. Ibid.

15. Ibid.

16. Ibid., 76–77.

17. Pardoe, *The City of the Sultan*, 1:20.

18. Ibid.

19. Ibid.

20. Ibid., 1:20–21.

21. Ibid., 1:21.

22. Ibid., 1:22.

23. Ibid.

24. Ibid., 1:24.

25. Ibid.

26. Çelebi, *The Intimate Life of an Ottoman Statesman*, trans., Robert Dankoff (Albany: State University of New York Press, 1991), 280.

27. Ibid.

28. Süleyman Beyolu, "The Ottomans and the Islamic Sacred Relics," in *The Great Ottoman-Turkish Civilization*, ed. Kemal Çiçek, 4 vols. (Ankara: 2000), 4:37–38.

29. Paul Rycaut, *The Present State of the Ottoman Empire* (New York: Arno Press, 1971), 162.

30. Ibid.

31. Ibid., 163.

32. Pardoe, *The City of the Sultan,* 1:111.

33. Thomas Patrick Hughes, *Dictionary of Islam* (New Delhi: Munshiram Manoharlal Publishers, 1999), 194–95.

34. Burton, *Personal Narrative of a Pilgrimage,* 2:140.

35. Ibid.

36. Ibid.

37. Ibid., 139.

38. Rycaut, *The Present State of the Ottoman Empire,* 161.

39. Ibid.

40. Raphaela Lewis, *Everyday Life in Ottoman Turkey* (London: B. T. Batsford Ltd., 1971), 122.

41. Ibid.

42. Lucy Mary Jane Garnett, *Turkey of the Ottomans* (New York: Charles Scribner's Sons, 1915), 262.

43. E. Mittwoch, "ID Al-ADHA," in *Encyclopaedia of Islam,* eds. B. Lewis, V. L. Me'nage, C. H. Pellat, and J. Schacht, (Leiden: E. J. Brill, 1969), 3:1007.

44. Pardoe, *The City of the Sultan,* 1:168.

45. Hughes, *Dictionary of Islam,* 130.

46. Mittwoch, "ID Al-ADHA," 3:1007.

47. Ibid.

48. Pardoe, *The City of the Sultan,* 1:168.

49. Ibid.

50. Ibid., 1:168–69.

51. Garnett, *Turkey of the Ottomans,* 263.

52. Pietro Della Valle, *The Pilgrim: The Journeys of Pietro Della Valle,* trans. George Bull (London: The Folio Society, 1989), 23.

53. Suraiya Faroqhi, *Subjects of the Sultan: Culture and Daily Life in the Ottoman Empire* (New York: I. B. Tauris, 2007), 184.

54. Della Valle, *The Pilgrim,* 23.

55. Ibid.

56. Ibid.

57. Ibid.

58. Ibid., 24.

59. Lewis, *Everyday Life in Ottoman Turkey,* 122.

60. Ibid.

61. Garnett, *Turkey of the Ottomans,* 270.

62. Ibid.

7

ISLAMIC LAW
AND EDUCATION

The Ottomans did not rule as a colonial empire but as an Islamic state where the sacred law of Islam, or *şeriat* (Arabic: *sharia*), ruled supreme. The *şeriat* provided the legal framework for public as well as private aspects of daily life, including all personal, political, social, and economic activities. It also regulated the personal and ethical conduct of the individual and applied to both civil and criminal cases. The Quran and the *sunnah* (the way and the manners of the prophet Muhammad, including his statements, actions, and practices) constituted the primary sources of Islamic law. In performing his responsibilities as a Muslim sovereign, the sultan "was assisted by a hierarchy of scholars and divines, the custodians of the Islamic holy law."[1] Thus, parallel with the palace and the administrative and military structure was the Islamic religious establishment and the legal and educational system of the empire, which was exclusively run by freeborn Muslims.

ULEMA

The interpretation and application of the *şeriat* belonged to the ulema, who were recognized as the learned men of religion, "the doctors of the Muslim canon," and "the jurist-divines of Islam."[2]

"Law, education, and the supervision of the Muslim community's moral and religious life were in their care," and since "the basis of the state was religion, their duties gave them prestige and power."[3] They "were to apply the sheriat and to further the principles of Islam through their educational and religious institutions."[4] The "dogmas of faith, the rules of ritual and worship, the civil and criminal law—all emanated from the same authority and were buttressed by the same ultimate sanctions."[5] Those who were experts in them "followed different specializations in the same basic discipline of knowledge."[6] That knowledge, "in Arabic *Ilm,*" was the domain of the ulema—"those who know" and are therefore learned.[7] Under the Ottoman system, their hierarchy was called *Ilmiye.*[8] The everyday work of the ulema "was concerned with two main subjects, theology and law and their talents were exercised in two great professions, education and justice."[9] They were led by the *şeyhülislam,* or the head of the ulema, who was appointed by the sultan, "but who held in fact an independent position."[10] He "could issue a *fetva,* which was an opinion or interpretation dealing with the question whether acts performed by the government conformed to Muslim principles."[11] The *şeyhülislam* "could not enforce his decisions, but his judgment had an important hold on public opinion."[12] He "could and sometimes did determine the fate of a sultan."[13]

From among the ranks of the ulema came the muftis, who interpreted the Islamic law, and the *kadis* who executed it.[14] Acting as the interpreters of the Islamic law "and the sultan's decrees," the muftis "were consulted when the meaning of a law was in dispute," while *kadis* "were dispatched throughout the provincial administration to enforce" both the *şeriat* and the sultan's laws.[15] The *kadis* enjoyed "jurisdiction over all Muslims and over Christians except in those sectors reserved for the Christian church authorities."[16]

In the eyes of the ulema, the state existed to serve as the tool for the application of Islamic law and was, therefore, subordinate to religion.[17] *Fiqh,* or Islamic jurisprudence, which was an extension of Islamic law and based directly on the Quran and the *sunnah,* dealt with supervising and legislating the everyday observance of public morals, rituals, and practices.

The brand of Islam that the Ottomans espoused was Sunni, as distinct from the Shia Islam that the rival Safavid Empire imposed as the official religion of neighboring Iran in 1501.[18] Sunni Islam recognized four schools of Islamic jurisprudence: the Hanafi, Shafi'i, Maliki, and Hanbali schools of legal interpretation. The principal differences between the four schools centered on religious rituals,

such as ablution before the five daily prayers and personal and con-
tractual issues, such as marriage, divorce, and inheritance.[19] The
Ottoman ruling class, as well as the majority of the Muslim population in the Balkans and the Sunni Turkish-speaking communities
of Anatolia, observed the Hanafi school of law, while the majority
of the North African subjects of the sultan, as well as those in Upper Egypt, followed the Maliki school. The Shafi'i school was dominant in western Arabia (Hejaz), Yemen, Lower Egypt, and the
Kurdish-populated regions of the empire. The Hanbalis were confined to the Wahhabi-held territory in Arabia.[20] Though the Ottomans did not try to impose the Hanafi school of jurisprudence on
non-Hanafi Muslim communities, the *kadis* or religious judges they
appointed followed the Hanafi legal interpretation.[21]

RELIGIOUS EDUCATION

The education of a young Muslim began at primary schools, or
sibyan mektepleri, which were usually "established by the sultans,
or by prominent statesmen or philanthropists" and "were generally located within a *külliye* (mosque complex), or in freestanding
buildings in many villages and city quarters."[22] The freestanding
schools were often "established and operated through charitable
foundation or endowment system and might be co-educational or
segregated by sex, according to the stipulation in the deed establishing the school."[23] Children "aged five or older" attended these
schools and enrolled in classes often taught by "religious function-
aries, such as the imam (prayer leader), the muezzin (person who
calls the faithful to prayer), or the caretaker of the mosque."[24] Educated women "who had memorized the Quran were also eligible
to teach in the schools for girls."[25] The principal objective of the
mektep education was "to teach children how to read, write, and
perform the four basic arithmetic operations, and to have them
memorize passages from the Quran and the precepts of Islam."[26]
In their last year at the *mektep,* the students studied "dictionaries in
Arabic and Persian."[27]

From the *mektep,* the pupils moved on to a *medrese* (Arabic:
madrassa), or a higher institute of Islamic education, where students
memorized the Quran and studied Quranic interpretation, Islamic
law, the sayings of the prophet Muhammad, logic, and the principles of Islamic jurisprudence. The *medreses* were usually established in the large urban centers of the empire, where they were
supported by *vakifs,* or religious endowments, which were grants

of "land or other source of revenue given in mortmain for pious or charitable purposes."[28]

The founder of a *medrese* was usually a sultan, a prince or princess of the royal family, a member of the ruling elite such as a grand vizier, a high government official, a provincial governor, or a member of the ulema. The *medreses* were divided into lower or exterior (*hariç*) *medreses,* which served as preparatory schools, and the interior (*dahil*) schools that provided instruction in advanced religious sciences. Each of these two institutions was further subdivided in accordance with the particular topics, texts, and areas of study that they offered. Thus, at the lower preparatory schools the students learned "the rudiments of Arabic grammar and syntax, logic, scholastic theology, astronomy, geometry and rhetoric."[29] Later, they could move to a higher rank institution and study rhetoric and literary sciences, and eventually attend an even more advanced school and enroll in classes on scholastic theology and jurisprudence.[30] At the *medreses* where higher knowledge and advanced Islamic sciences were taught, students began by studying Quranic exegesis and ultimately moved to the highest-level *semaniye medreses,* where they enrolled in "a group of three subjects—Islamic jurisprudence, Koranic exegesis or scholastic theology, rhetoric, and related studies—and received specialized training."[31]

Many of the prestigious schools and centers of Islamic learning were attached to the grand mosques. These could include elementary schools for boys, schools for reading the Quran, or ones for studying the traditions and statements attributed to the prophet Muhammad. Charitable and public services, along with institutions such as hospitals, insane asylums, soup kitchens for the poor that provided a loaf of bread and a dish of food every day, and bathhouses, could also be attached to large mosques built by a sultan, members of the ruling dynasty, or high officials of the central government.[32]

As with some *mekteps,* many *medreses* were located within the *külliye* or mosque complexes. The *külliye* "included a hospital, lodgings, and a soup kitchen that served the needy."[33] The "Süleymaniye building complex" in Istanbul named for Süleyman the Magnificent (1520–1566), "who ordered its construction," marked "the zenith of Ottoman culture and education."[34] Its architectural design included *mekteps, medreses,* "a hospital, a public kitchen, a convalescence hospital, and a pharmacy, all built around the central mosque."[35] Instruction was conducted "at different levels in the complex and included two specialized medreses," *dar ul-hadis* or "the school where the traditions of the Prophet were taught and Tarüttib (the school of medicine)."[36] The *dar ul-hadis* "was considered the highest-ranking" *medrese* "in the empire and its teachers were the most honored, as is evident from the high wages they received."[37]

The ulema were recruited from the higher and advanced *medreses*. The muftis, who were the official interpreters of Islamic law and issued legal opinions, came from the ranks of the ulema and were assigned by the *şeyhülislam* to the provinces of the empire. The *kadis*, or judges, who enforced the Islamic law and the *kanun* (the laws issued by the sultan), and administered the courts throughout the empire, were also appointed by the *şeyhülislam* from among the ulema.[38]

Starting in the second half of the 18th century and continuing until the First World War, "the Ottoman Empire went through a period of continuous change" that often included governmental reforms.[39] One of the most important aspects of these reforms was the introduction of modern educational institutions borrowed from European countries. The educational reform "began in the army, born out of the need to prevent further defeats on the battlefields and to regain Ottoman military superiority."[40] New "methods and technology, as well as experts to teach them, were brought from Europe to modernize the Ottoman army."[41] This "modernization project focused initially on three areas: shipbuilding techniques, engineering, and modern medical education," culminating in the establishment of the Darülfünun Şahane (Imperial University) in 1900 and a full-fledged university in 1909.[42]

EDUCATION OF GIRLS AND WOMEN

Women who lived in the palace or were born and raised in ulema families constituted the main segments of the female population that received education. Women educated at the palace learned how to read and write Ottoman Turkish. They also studied the fundamental tenets of Islam, including the basic elements of Islamic law, as well as the arts of sewing, embroidering, singing, and playing various musical instruments. At times, the ladies of the harem, particularly the mothers, wives, and daughters of sultans, memorized the Quran by heart and studied Arabic and Persian literature. They also wrote poetry. The daughters of the ulema were typically taught at home by their fathers and grandfathers. Many memorized the Quran and some became accomplished poets.

Outside of the palace and the home of the ulema, small schools attached to mosques offered classes that taught young girls the Arabic alphabet, the art of reading and reciting the Quran, and the proper performance of the daily prayers. Students also learned how to write and the basics of arithmetic. These schools were funded and supported by the religious endowments or pious foundations. Starting in the second half of the 19th century, the state allowed the establishment of modern schools for girls and many elite families welcomed the opportunity. Before sending their daughters to school, these households celebrated a young girl's "entrance into learning (*başlanmak*)" with a ceremony.[43] Families who could afford an expensive *başlmanlak* "spent large sums in the effort to have a grander ceremony than their neighbors."[44] They arranged for poor children in the neighborhood to participate in the ceremony and would thereafter pay for their schooling, "as well as that of their own child."[45] On the first day of school, the young girl "was dressed in silk covered with jewels, and a gold-embroidered bag, with an alphabet inside, was hung round her neck with a gold tasseled cord."[46] She was seated in an "open carriage, with a damask silk cushion at her feet."[47]

All the young students of the school "walked in procession after the carriage, forming two long tails on either side."[48] The older students sang a popular hymn, "The rivers of paradise, as they flow, murmur, 'Allah Allah.' The angels in paradise, as they walk, sing, 'Allah, Allah.'" At the end of each song hundreds of children shouted, "*Amin, amin.*"[49] The children marched through several streets in this way, drawing into the procession children from other neighborhoods until they reached the school. When they arrived in school, the new student "knelt on her damask cushion before a square table, facing the teacher."[50] She then kissed the hand of her teacher and repeated the alphabet after her. Sweetmeats were then served to the children, and each student "received a bright new coin given by the parents" of the new pupil.[51] With this ceremony, which "was as important as a wedding," the young girls were initiated into the school.[52] From that day on, the girl went to school every day "fetched by the *kalfa*, an attendant who went from one house to another collecting the children from the different houses."[53]

In some cases, the wealthy and powerful father of a girl from an elite family could decide that her daughter should receive private lessons at home before enrolling at school. On these occasions, he arranged for a tutor to come to the house and give his child lessons that focused on reading Arabic and the holy Quran.[54] Before the first private lesson began, a sumptuous dinner was prepared and served to a group of male acquaintances, co-workers, and neighbors who were invited to the house by the father of the girl. The ceremony began after the men had performed their evening prayer.[55] The girl was dressed in a silk frock and a soft silk veil of the same color. She then walked to the hall where everyone had assembled for the ceremony.[56] A young boy "chanted" the Quran.[57] The girl had to kneel and repeat the first letters of the alphabet.[58] She then kissed the hand of her teacher.[59] The lessons she received took place in the *selamlik,* before the same table and in the same kneeling attitude as was first assumed at the *başlanmak.*[60]

TRADITIONAL BELIEFS AND SUPERSTITIONS

Although Islam denounced irrational customs and traditions, superstitious beliefs and practices remained popular among all social classes from all religious backgrounds. Muslims, Christians, and Jews, of both sexes and every age, believed in the power of amulets, talismans, or charms of some kind. Indeed, charms and magical formulas covered the smallest contingencies of daily life. The most common charms were "of stone or metal, strips of paper, parchment, leather, and gems, which were specially valuable as talismans."[61] Writings of any kind, particularly those containing verses of the Quran, were popularly regarded as a charm of greatest magic and power. The "best talisman of all" was a copy of the holy Quran; "sometimes a small one was worn in an embroidered leather or velvet case carried on a silk cord which passed over the left shoulder and across the body; very powerful too were the ninety-nine names of God."[62] Other "written charms included the names of saints and angels, or magic squares, or diagrams and combinations of numerals, and sometimes the words of an incantation were interpolated" between verses from the opening sura of the Quran.[63] These written charms "were worn by adults and children, hung on cradles and round the necks or on the foreheads of animals, and suspended in houses and shops; in fact they were used everywhere as protection from evil."[64] Written charms and incantations were used to exorcise evil spirits, procure aid from unknown powers, separate a boy and a girl who had fallen in love, prevent a man from leaving his wife for another woman, and cure a serious ailment.

In Albania, where "a childless marriage" was "considered a great misfortune and a woman living on her own, without a husband and children" was "quite inconceivable," it was "believed that sterility in women could be overcome by the wearing of amulets."[65] Various herbs "were also used and numerous holy places were visited," including the beaches of Kavajë and Durrës in western Albania, where women bathed "to ensure pregnancy."[66] And there were additional stratagems in popular use when it was desired to grant blessings, to lay a curse, to ward off diseases of cattle, to bring success in a difficult enterprise, to come out on top in a business bargain, or to compel someone to do something.

Aside from belief in written charms, the Muslims of the empire attributed miraculous power to the dust from the tomb of the prophet Muhammad in Medina. A "cake composed of dust from the Prophet's tomb" was "sowed up" in a leather case and "worn as an amulet."[67] Muslims also believed in the magical power of the water from the sacred well of Zamzam in the holy city of Mecca. A toothbrush dipped in the water of Zamzam was thought to clean a person's teeth and protect them from pain and decay.[68] The holy water was also sprinkled on the shroud of the dead. Pieces of the curtain covering the sacred *Ka'ba* were also greatly valued. Every year, "on the first day of the Great Festival, which immediately" followed "the pilgrimage, a new covering" was hung on the holy shrine, while the old one was cut up and sold to the pilgrims.[69] The proper use of charms was usually "in the hands of the wise men and women, of which every community possessed at least one, a feared but essential element in society, who would be consulted on the choice of propitious times and suitable matches and who made up spells and antidotes."[70]

From the elite to the ordinary people, everyone believed in the devastating impact of an evil eye. If anything in the world could overcome fate, it was an evil eye. If an individual praised the beauty of a Turkish child without prefacing his admiration with *mashallah* (in the name of God), which was "considered sufficient to counteract the power of all malignant spirits," and if the child became ill or met with an accident, it was at once decided that the person who had uttered the compliment had smitten the child with the evil eye.[71] When "by accident the Greeks" alluded "to their own good health or good fortune," they immediately spat on "their breast to avert the malign influence" of evil eye.[72] The Turks decorated the roof of their homes, the prow of their boats, the caps of their children, and the necks of their horses with charms against the evil eye.[73] One of "the most powerful antidotes" was garlic, which was sent "to the mother of a new born infant as a safeguard both to herself and her little one."[74] To protect Sultan Mahmud II (1808–1839) from the power of the evil eye during his processions on the streets of Istanbul, a "head-dress was invented for the imperial boy-pages, whose ornamented plumes were of such large dimensions" as "to form a screen" around the monarch.[75]

NOTES

1. Bernard Lewis, *Istanbul and the Civilization of the Ottoman Empire* (Norman: University of Oklahoma Press, 1963), 145.

2. Halil Inalcik, *The Ottoman Empire, The Classical Age 1300–1600* (New York: Praeger Publishers, 1973), 226; Lewis, *Istanbul*, 146.

3. Barbara Jelavich, *History of the Balkans: Eighteenth and Nineteenth Centuries* (Cambridge: Cambridge University Press, 1983), 43.

4. Ibid.

5. Lewis, *Istanbul*, 146.

6. Ibid.

7. Ibid.

8. Ibid.

9. Ibid.

10. Jelavich, *History of the Balkans*, 43.

11. Ibid.

12. Ibid.

13. Ibid.

14. Halil Inalcik, *The Ottoman Empire, The Classical Age 1300–1600* (New York: Praeger Publishers, 1973), 171.

15. Jelavich, *History of the Balkans*, 43.

16. Ibid.

17. Inalcik, *The Ottoman Empire*, 171.

18. Jane Hathaway, *Beshir Agha: Chief Eunuch of the Ottoman Imperial Harem* (Oxford: Oneworld Publications, 2005), xiii.

19. Ibid.

20. Gustave E. Von Grunebaum, *Medieval Islam: A Study in Cultural Orientation* (Chicago: Chicago University Press, 1962), 153.

21. Hathaway, *Beshir Agha*, xiii.

22. Ekmeleddin Ihsanoglu, "Education," in *Encyclopedia of the Ottoman Empire*, eds. Gábor Ágoston and Bruce Masters (New York: Facts On File, 2009), 199.

23. Ibid.

24. Ibid.

25. Ibid.

26. Ibid.

27. Ibid.

28. Inalcik, *The Ottoman Empire*, 226.

29. Ibid., 168.

30. Ibid.

31. Ibid., 169.

32. Evliya Efendi (Çelebi), *Narratives of Travels in Europe, Asia, and Africa in the Seventeenth Century,* trans. Ritter Joseph Von Hammer (London: Parbury, Allen, & Co., 1834), 1:171–75.

33. Ihsanoglu, "Education," 199.

34. Ibid., 200.

35. Ibid.

36. Ibid.

37. Ibid.

38. H.A.R. Gibb and Harold Bowen, *Islamic Society and the West: A Study of the Impact of Western Civilization on Moslem Culture in the Near East,* 2 vols. (London: Oxford University Press, 1957), 1:121–22; Inalcik, *The Ottoman Empire,* 169–72.

39. Ihsanoglu, "Education," 200.

40. Ibid.

41. Ibid.

42. Ibid., 200, 204.

43. Halidé Adivar Edib, *Memoirs of Halidé Edib* (New York: Gorgias Press, 2004), 86.

44. Ibid., 87.

45. Ibid.

46. Ibid., 86.

47. Ibid.

48. Ibid.

49. Ibid.

50. Ibid.

51. Ibid.

52. Ibid., 87.

53. Ibid., 86.

54. Ibid., 87.

55. Ibid.

56. Ibid., 88.

57. Ibid.

58. Ibid.

59. Ibid.

60. Ibid.

61. Sir Edwin Pears, *Turkey and Its People* (London: Methuen Co. Ltd., 1912), 80.

62. Raphaela Lewis, *Everyday Life in Ottoman Turkey* (London: B. T. Batsford Ltd., 1971), 52.

63. Ibid.

64. Ibid.

65. Robert Elsie, *A Dictionary of Albanian Religion, Mythology, and Folk Culture* (New York: New York University Press, 2001), 36.

66. Ibid., 36–37.

67. Edward William Lane, *An Account of the Manners and Customs of the Modern Egyptians* (New York: Dover Publications, 1973), 255.

68. Ibid.

69. Ibid.

70. Lewis, *Everyday Life in Ottoman Turkey*, 52–53.

71. Julia Pardoe, *The City of the Sultan and Domestic Manners of the Turks in 1836*, 3 vols. (London: Henry Colburn Publisher, 1838), 1:273.

72. Ibid.

73. Ibid.

74. Ibid., 1:274.

75. Ibid., 1:275.

8

SUFI ORDERS AND POPULAR CULTURE

Despite the enormous power and influence of official Islam, Ottoman culture and civilization was not a linear projection of Quranic
scripture. Throughout the long reign of the Ottoman dynasty, religious orthodoxy had to wage a constant battle for primacy against
the heterodox interpretations of faith as articulated and preached
by numerous Sufi mystical orders and brotherhoods, which enjoyed
enormous popularity among the ruling elite and the masses. Each
brotherhood was dedicated to its own unique mystical path, called
tarikat, and "had its own form of ecstatic worship, called *zikr.*"[1] The
heterodox beliefs and practices of the Sufis left a profound impact
on the popular culture and the everyday life of the masses. The
"Sufi brotherhoods and lodges" played "a central role in Ottoman
social life" and "provided an important space for socialization outside the home."[2] The "space was exclusively Muslim" and contained
within it sections for men and women, active members, and curi-
ous visitors.[3]

The privileged position of the ulema, their close alliance with the
Ottoman ruling family, the rigidity of their Islam, and "the cold le-
galism of their doctrine, failed to satisfy" the "spiritual and social
needs of many Muslims, who turned for sustenance and guidance"
to mysticism and Sufi brotherhoods.[4] The diverse and heterodox
beliefs and practices of various Sufi orders provided men and

women with unique spiritual experiences, which transcended the unbending and impersonal rules and practices that a Muslim was obligated to follow at home and at a mosque.

Greatly influenced by Zoroastrian, Manichean, Buddhist, Gnostic, and Neoplatonist ideas, Sufism, or Islamic mysticism, emerged in the first century of Muslim rule as a protest against the rigid, intolerant, and politicized interpretations of Islam. The ulema, who acted as the representatives of official Islam, defended the Islamic law as the essence of Islamic thought and emphasized *tawhid* (monotheism), or the oneness of God. In sharp contrast, the Sufis preached an ascetic lifestyle that rejected the distinction between the Creator (God) and the created by teaching that the creation was a manifestation of the Creator.[5] For Sufi masters, removing the distinction between the Creator and the created allowed man to attain perfection and unity with God and the divine truth.[6] By God, the Sufis did not mean an anthropomorphic entity that possessed human qualities and was man-made. For them, God was the absolute being, and the whole universe was a manifestation of that Being. As everything was a manifestation of God, to love God was to love God's creatures and His entire creation.

In their journey to reach union with God, Sufis sought out knowledge and interpretation related to the inner and esoteric (*batini*) aspects of Islam. This was in sharp contrast with the ulema and the *medreses,* or religious schools, where the outer and exoteric (*zahiri*) knowledge of Islam was emphasized. The Sufis did not, however, view mysticism as an intellectual activity confined to elaborating esoteric concepts such as detachment from the world. For them, such concepts could be understood only when one embarked on the spiritual journey towards union with God. In this context, Sufism was essentially a human enterprise, one that combated and neutralized the dry, and, at times, harsh aspects of official Islam by allowing the seeker to design and initiate his own unique journey to spiritual peace and salvation.

In contrast to the ulema, who asserted the absolute and unassailable superiority of Islam over other religions and religious traditions, many Sufis viewed all religions and religious leaders as fellow travelers on the same mystic path, seeking Gnostic wisdom (*maarifet*) by submitting themselves to the way of Truth (*tarik-i hak*). Thus, in the poetry of many Sufi masters, Moses and Jesus were praised as great men of knowledge, humanity, spirituality, and integrity, whose lives and actions provided exemplary models for Muslims and all of humanity. The teachings and practices of some

Sufi orders, therefore, contained a strong element of respect, appreciation, and tolerance toward non-Muslims and stood in sharp contrast to the rigid interpretations of Islam by the ulema, who viewed Christians and Jews as dirty, inferior, and unequal to Muslims.

Even in their public appearance, the ulema and Sufi masters stood at diametrically opposite poles. The ulema appeared in public with pomp and ceremony, dressed in beautiful and expensive clothing, and surrounded by followers, servants, and attendants, ranging from menial domestics and bodyguards to companions and agents. In sharp contrast, the Sufi leaders adhered to the principles of simplicity and humility. They generally wore a simple white tunic made of wool or, less commonly, linen, and refused to adorn themselves with precious stones. Some "wandering mendicant" *dervişes* "deliberately flouted Muslim opinion by shaving their beards, hair, and eyebrows and by throwing off the restraints of the Holy Law and most others."[7] Turning their backs to the vanities of this world, they renounced all human obsessions and small satisfactions of riches and empty honors. Instead, they chose a solitary life of contemplation, meditation, humility, and silence. In choosing solitude and silence, they emphasized the limitations of language to express inner experience and attributed a peripheral significance to religious piety. They ridiculed the pretentious religiosity of the ulema and their pompous public postures and sermons, which for the Sufis were another sad manifestation of man's ego. Sufi masters considered the ulema's religious dogmatism, narrow-mindedness, and intolerance, the cause of most calamities, including that of fanaticism and oppression.

The Sufis demonstrated their tolerant attitude by absorbing Islamic heresies, as well as Shia and Christian beliefs and practices.[8] It is not surprising, therefore, that the Sunni ulema viewed the activities of Sufi teachers with apprehension and trepidation, and frequently denounced them as hypocrites, innovators, and heretics. In particular, the Sunni religious establishment detested the pantheistic beliefs and doctrines of various Sufi orders, "which seemed to impugn the transcendental unity of God," as well as "their idolatrous worship of saints and holy places; their thaumaturgic practices and suspect methods of inducing ecstasy," and "their laxness in observing the divine law."[9]

Throughout the long history of the Ottoman Empire, the philosophical and doctrinal conflict between the ulema and the Sufi orders ignited rivalries and jealousies between prominent religious leaders and influential Sufi masters. The antagonism between the two camps was also reflected in unrelenting battles over consumption of coffee and tobacco, which the religious establishment condemned and the Sufi orders defended.[10]

Each Sufi brotherhood was founded around loyalty, devotion, and belief in the teachings of a particular Sufi master (*şeyh*/*sheikh*), who was at times revered as a saint. During their life on earth, each *şeyh* had, through his teachings and practices, established a distinct pathway to attainment of spiritual truth and union with God. His followers, who had adopted him as their guide (*murşid*), gathered in a Sufi lodge (*tekke*) for communal prayer and ecstatic worship (*zikr*), as well as a set of distinct practices prescribed by their spiritual leader. These lodges served as spiritual retreats and hospices for travelers. Financed by contributions from their members, they usually had a mausoleum (*türbe*), where the veneration of the saints and founders of the order took place, a "hall for prayers and rituals (*tevhidhane, semahane,* or *meydan*)" and a "kitchen (*matbah, aş evi, mutfak*)."[11] Because serving food to travelers and the poor constituted one of the principal functions of the Sufi orders, the kitchen occupied a central role in *derviş* lodges. Among some orders, such as those of the Mevlevis and Bektaşis, the kitchen was used as a space "for training and initiation" of new recruits.[12]

In the 17th century when coffee drinking spread among the masses, many Sufi establishments, "particularly in the Balkans, incorporated a special room for the preparation of coffee, known as the *kahve ocağu*."[13] Many large *tekkes* also had baths, libraries, "reception and meeting halls (*mosafer odasi, meydan odasi*), cells or chambers for the *şeyh* and dervishes (*hücerat*), and often one or several small spaces, generally without windows, for spiritual seclusion (*halvet odasi, halvethane, çilehane*)."[14] Large Sufi lodges and hospices contained homes and apartments for the family of the *şeyh*, and some were attached to a mosque and a garden that they kept immaculate. Thus, *derviş* lodges "were not only places of worship, but also housing complexes where people lived and carried out the routines of everyday life."[15] As late as 1885, 1,091 men and 1,184 women lived in 260 *tekkes* in Istanbul.[16]

In earlier Ottoman times, lodges and hospices established and run by *ahis*, or semireligious/semimystical fraternities in Anatolia, provided food, shelter, and hospitality to all travelers regardless of social background. As the North African traveler Ibn Battuta described, the *ahis* built hospices and guesthouses and furnished them with rugs, lamps, and other equipments they required.[17] The members of the brotherhood worked "during the day to gain their livelihood, and after the afternoon prayer," gathered "their collective earnings"; with this they bought "fruit, food, and the other things needed for consumption in the hospice."[18] Whenever a traveler arrived at the hospice, they served him food and lodging, while Quran readers recited the holy book, and if no newcomer arrived, the members of the brotherhood assembled, ate, and, after eating, sang and danced.[19] In the later Ottoman period, many Sufi convents followed the same traditions and practices, providing food, lodging, and hospitality to travelers from far and near. Devout *dervişes*—barefoot and bareheaded, and dressed in rough, patched woolen cloaks—pursued a life of poverty, withdrawal, isolation, and quiet meditation. As they "were expected to provide a bowl of soup" for the visiting guests, "the cauldron, on the boil day and night, became a symbol of hospitality."[20]

Some of the early Ottoman sultans were followers of Sufi masters who participated in various Ottoman military campaigns and provided the ruler and his troops with spiritual support and guidance. It was their alliance with the Ottoman state that allowed Sufi brotherhoods to establish themselves in the Balkans. Given their close interaction and association with various Sufi orders, it is not surprising that the Islam of the early Ottomans, and the *gazis* who supported them, lacked the theological sophistication of the Muslim ulema who dominated the mosques and seminaries of Anatolia's urban centers. The religious beliefs of these Ottoman rulers were simple, personal, unorthodox, eclectic, and mystical.[21] One of the earliest accounts of the rise of Osman, the founder of the Ottoman state, describes how he received a blessing from Şeyh Edebali, a prominent Sufi leader, who handed him the sword of a *gazi* and prophesied that his descendants would rule the world.[22] When Osman died, the ceremony that decided the succession of his son, Orhan, to the throne took place at a *zaviye*, a hospice run and managed by *dervişes* for travelers.[23]

With the rise of the empire and the establishment of Ottoman power in the urban centers of Anatolia where Sunni Islam dominated the social and cultural life of the Muslim community, the state became increasingly identified with the official Islam of the ulema. Sufi traditions and practices were never abandoned, however, and mystical orders continued to enjoy great popularity and respect, allowing them to play a prominent role in the daily life of many Muslims in the empire.

This popularity and mass appeal may explain why Sufi mystics and *derviş* leaders led several major uprisings against the Ottoman state. For example, the revolt of Şeyh Bedreddin in 1416 against the authority of the Ottoman sultan, Mehmed I (1413–1421), brought the empire to the verge of extinction. Influenced by the mystical writings of such prominent philosophers and Sufi writers as Ibn Arabi (1165–1240), Bedreddin believed that the world was ancient, without a beginning, without an end, and not created in time.[24] If the physical world disappeared, the spiritual world would disappear as well; "creation and destruction" was "an eternal process," and "this world and the next, in their entirety" were "imaginary fantasies."[25] The revolutionary Sufi *şeyh* rejected heaven and hell, as well as the Day of Judgment, and the resurrection of the body.[26] He also dismissed any difference between Muslims and non-Muslims, allowed his followers to drink wine, and advocated distribution of land among his followers, who included landless peasants. The ulema accused him of ignoring the Islamic law and denounced him as a heretic. Şeyh Bedreddin's revolt was crushed by Ottoman troops, and he was executed by order of Mehmed I in 1416.

Bedreddin's followers, however, continued to preach, and one of his disciples, Börklüce Mustafa, organized a revolt against the Ottoman government by instigating an uprising among Turcoman tribal groups in a region near Izmir in western Anatolia. Börklüce "preached that all things, except for women, were common property."[27] As with Bedreddin, he also rejected the inequality between Muslims and Christians and declared that any Muslim who called a Christian an infidel was himself an infidel.[28] Once again, the Ottoman government sent its forces against the rebellious Sufi *şeyh*, who was captured and executed together with hundreds of his followers.

BEKTAŞIS

The first major Sufi brotherhood in the Ottoman state, that of the Bektaşi Sufi order, emerged as a powerful social and political force in Anatolia during the 14th century. The order continued to play a prominent role in the daily life of the empire until the establishment of the Turkish Republic in 1923. The leaders (*babas/dedes*) of the order acted as the chaplains to the janissary corps, and the brotherhood recruited heavily from manufacturing guilds in Istanbul and other large urban centers of the Ottoman Empire. The alliance between the Bektaşi order and the janissaries was symbolized in various public events and parades as the chaplains of the brotherhood marched near the commander of the infantry corps reciting prayers and incantations with their daggers drawn from their sheaths.[29] It is not surprising, therefore, that the power of the Bektaşi order diminished after Sultan Mahmud II disbanded the janissary corps in 1826 and closed down many of the brotherhood's centers.

The Bektaşis traced the origins of their order to the Persian Sufi master Haci Bektaş Veli (Haji Baktash Vali), who is believed to have lived in the 13th century. His teachings, which were given a definite form by Balim Sultan, the leader of the order in the 16th century, were greatly influenced by the beliefs, customs, and practices prevalent in Shia Islam, as well as in certain Sufi doctrines of the Hurufi movement that had spread from northeastern Iran to Azerbaijan and Anatolia in the 14th and 15th centuries.

The Bektaşis acknowledged the 12 Shia imams and venerated the first Shia imam, Ali, the cousin and son-in-law of the prophet Muhammad, whom they believed to be one with God (Allah) and Muhammad in a single united entity. Though denied by the Bektaşis, many observers referred to this unity as a form of belief in trinity.[30] As with the Twelver Shia (*Ithna Asharis*) in Iran and elsewhere, the Bektaşis also mourned the death of Husayn, the third Shia Imam and the son of Ali and Fatima (the daughter of the prophet Muhammad), whose martyrdom was commemorated every year on the tenth of *Muharram*, the first month in the Islamic calendar. To share in the suffering of Husayn and his family, mourners beat their chests with fists and chains, and cut and repeatedly struck their foreheads with swords and knives. From the first to the tenth of *Muharram*, the Bektaşis also celebrated the nights of mourning for the Shia martyrs and especially those Shia figures who had perished in infancy.[31] In their daily rituals, the Bektaşis showed a general disregard for Muslim rituals such as the daily prayers. They believed that the holy Quran contained two levels of knowledge and meaning: the first was the outer and exoteric (*zahir*), and the second was the inner and esoteric (*batin*), which constituted the eternal meaning of the holy book.[32] This inner meaning was only available to a very few and was the meaning and instruction sought by Sufis. The Bektaşis were led by their leader (*çelebi*) who lived in the monastery (*tekke*) of Pir Evi (The Tomb of the Founder) at Haci Bektaş in central Anatolia. The head of each Bektaşi *tekke* was called *baba* (father).

The Bektaşis absorbed certain pre-Islamic and Christian practices and rituals, which explains their acceptance, popularity, and success among many urban and rural communities of the Balkans, particularly in Albania. Using Holy Communion as a model, they served wine, bread, and cheese when new members joined the order. The members of the order also confessed to their sins and sought absolution from their *murşid* (spiritual guide). In sharp contrast to Muslims who prescribed strict separation between the two sexes, Bektaşi women participated in the order's rituals without covering their faces. A small group within the order swore to celibacy and wore earrings as a distinctive mark. Under Ottoman rule, Bektaşi leaders introduced the teachings of their order to various regions of the Balkans, Anatolia, and the Arab Middle East, including Egypt. As the convents of the order spread throughout the Balkan region, many Christians in Albania, Kosovo, and Macedonia converted to Islam through Bektaşi teachings and activities. Evliya Çelebi wrote that the Muslims of Gjirokaster in southern Albania were so devoted to the first Shia imam, Ali, that, when sitting down or standing up, they uttered *"Ya Ali"* ("Oh Ali"). According to Evliya Çelebi, these Albanians studied and read Persian and, in sharp contrast to Muslims who shunned alcohol consumption and public demonstrations of physical intimacy with the opposite sex, they "were very fond of pleasure and carousing" as well as "shamelessly" drinking wine and other intoxicating beverages.[33] The Bektaşis also celebrated weddings and the two Muslim feasts of *bayrams*, as well as Persian Zoroastrian and various Christian festivals, such as *Nevruz* (Persian New Year) and the days of St. George, St. Nicholas, and St. Demetrius, by dancing and drinking, a behavior that was denounced by the devout traveler and writer as "shameless" and "characteristic of the infidels."[34]

In his *Book of Travels*, Çelebi left his readers with a vivid description of a "love intoxicated" Bektaşi *derviş*:

Meanwhile I took a close look at this dervish. He was barefooted and bareheaded and raggedy. But his face and his eyes gleamed with light, and his speech sparkled with pearls of wit. He was extremely eloquent and quick witted. On his head perched a "water pot" headgear, with the turban awry and adorned with twelve ruby-colored brands, like appliqué roses, standing for the twelve leaders of the *Bektaşi* order, and signifying his love for the dynasty (of Ali) and his devotion to the twelve *imams*. . . . On his shirtless and guileless pure and saintly chest were marks of flagellation he had received in Tabriz [a city in northwestern Iran] during the Aşura ceremonies marking the martyrdom of el-Huseyn. . . . He removed the "water pot" from his head revealing, just above his forehead, a "brand of submission" the size of a piaster [a coin]. His purpose in displaying it to us was to demonstrate that he was an adept in the holy law (*şeriat*), in the mystic path (*tarikat*), in the mystic truth (*hakikat*), and in Gnostic wisdom (*marifet*), and that he had submitted to the way of Truth (*tarik-i hak*). On both arms were wounds and gashes of the four companions of the Prophet, and on his left arm were brands and lashes of the plain of Kerbela. He was mad, pure, wild, and radiant, but not exactly naked. He was shaven in the saintly "four strokes" manner to indicate that he was free of all forbidden things—thus there was no trace of hair, whether on his head, mustache, beard, brow, or eyelashes. But his face was shining. In short, the apron round his waist, the staff in his hand, the words "Oh Beloved of hearts" on his tongue, the sling of David in his waistband, the *palheng*-stone ("a carved stone the size of a hand with twelve flutings worn at the waist") of Moses, pomp of Ali, the decorative plumes, bells, and other ornaments [all these indicated that he was] a companion of the foot-travelers, they were the outfittings and instruments of poverty of the noble dervishes, and he himself was the perfect mystic.[35]

MEVLEVIS

The greatest rival of the Bektaşis was the Mevlevi order, which enjoyed immense popularity among the members of the Ottoman ruling elite. The founder of the order, and one of the most beloved Persian poets, was Mevlana Celaledin Rumi (Persian: Mowlana Jalaludin Mohammad Balkhi, also known as Mowlavi), born in 1207 in Balkh in today's northern Afghanistan. His father, Bahauddin Walad, a renowned scholar, theologian, and mystic, fled his home before the arrival of the Mongols in 1215 and took his family to Konya, the capital of the Rum Seljuk state in central Anatolia. Rumi lived, wrote, and taught in Konya until his death in 1273. His body was buried beside his father under a green tomb, which was constructed soon after his death. The mausoleum has served as a shrine for pilgrims from the four corners of the Islamic world, as well as those of other faiths who revere his teachings and mystical poetry.

Rumi would have been an ordinary mystic and poet had it not been for an accidental encounter in 1244 with the wandering Persian Sufi master Shams-i Tabrizi, who hailed from Tabriz, a city in northwestern Iran. Shams inspired Rumi to compose one of the masterpieces of Persian poetry, *Divan-i Shams-i Tabrizi* (The Divan of Shams of Tabriz), in which Rumi expresses his deep love, admiration, and devotion for Shams, who had transformed his life. This was followed by the *Masnavi* (Turkish: *Mesnevi*), a multivolume book of poetical genius and fantastic tales, fables, and personal reflections that Rumi completed after the disappearance of Shams. Rumi's poetry transcends national, ethnic, and even religious boundaries, and focuses primarily on the spiritual journey to seek union with God. Love for fellow human beings is presented in his poems as the essence of the mystical journey.

The mystical order that was established during Rumi's lifetime (which came to be known as Mevleviyya) was distinguished from other Sufi orders by the significance it gave to *sema*, a music and whirling/dancing ritual performed in a circular hall called *sema hane*. Imitating their master's love for the musical ceremony that inspired singing and dancing, Mevlana's followers employed spinning and whirling to reach a trance-like state. While the majority of Muslims shunned singing and dancing, the Mevlevi *dervişes* made music and dancing the hallmark and central tenet of their order.

Because of its popularity, power, and influence, the Mevlevi order was subjected to frequent attacks and persecution from the ulema, who denounced their use of music and dancing as un-Islamic. Thus,

Derwych houkechan, Derviches Tournans.

Dancing dervishes. Anonymous, c. 1810. (Bildarchiv Preussischer Kulturbesitz / Art Resource, NY)

in 1516, when Selim I was moving against the Safavid dynasty in Iran, the *şeyhülislam* persuaded the sultan to order the destruction of Rumi's mausoleum in Konya, which served as the physical heart of the order. Fortunately for the Mevlevis, the order was repealed and the mausoleum and center were spared.[36]

Despite numerous campaigns of harassment by the members of the religious establishment, Ottoman sultans and government officials continued to show their respect and reverence for the Mevlavi order by showering its leaders with gifts and favors. For example, in 1634, Murad IV assigned the poll tax paid by non-Muslims of Konya to the head of the Mevlevi order.[37] In 1648, the chief of the Mevlevi order "officiated, for the first time, at the ceremony of the girding on of the sword of Osman, which marked the accession of a new sultan," a privilege that remained with the order until the end of the Ottoman dynasty.[38] The close relationship between Ottoman sultans and the leaders of the Mevlevi order continued into the 19th century. The reform-minded Selim III (1789–1807) visited the Mevlevi *tekkes* so frequently that the musical ceremony, which had been performed only on Tuesdays and Fridays, was performed daily in a different *tekke* on each day of the week. Outside Istanbul, however, the ceremony continued to be performed only on Fridays.[39] This visible support allowed the order not only to survive against attacks from the ulema but also grow and expand into the four corners of the Ottoman Empire.

NAKŞBANDIS

A latecomer among the Sufi orders in Istanbul was the *Nakşbandiyya (Naqshbandiyya)* Sufi order, which arrived in the Ottoman Empire from Central Asia in the late 15th century. The order traced its origins to the Persian mystic and teacher Khawjah Bahauddin Naqshband (d.1389), who lived and taught in Central Asia in the 14th century. The order immediately attracted a large following because, more than any other mystical brotherhood, its teachings and practices corresponded with the established rules and practices of Sunni Islam. Greatly influenced by the writings of the Persian theologian, mystic, philosopher, and jurist Ghazali (1058–1111), the Nakşbandis believed that mysticism could not negate anything that was taught by the Quran and the examples, deeds, sayings, and customary practices (*sunnah*) of the prophet Muhammad.[40] The members of the order closely observed the daily prayers, fasts, and other observances prescribed by the Islamic law.[41]

In sharp contrast to other Sufi orders, the Nakşbandis did not "engage in any outward performance" of their *zikr*, "the act by which" Sufis meditated and sought "a union with God."[42] Instead, they engaged in what they called, the silent *zikr*, as they believed that "the sort of physical exercise characteristic of other order's practice" of *zikr* was "theatrical diversion from the true purpose of the act."[43] Also unlike other Sufi orders, the Nakşbandis did not "have a long process of spiritual internship that required those seeking to join the order to pursue a series of stages under the guidance of a master before being judged worthy of admittance."[44] They believed that a person only approached the order for admittance if he had already reached a sufficient level of religious enlightenment internally and thus knew that he was ready.[45]

At times, the enormous power and popularity of the Nakşbandiyya order ignited the jealousy and insecurity of Ottoman sultans. For example, in 1639, Murad IV "executed a şeyh of the *Nakşbandi* order of dervishes, called Mahmud, who had grown too influential."[46] Despite the sporadic persecution of the order, the Nakşbandis continued with their missionary activities and spread the teachings of the order to the four corners of the Ottoman Empire. The order "received a major boost from the teachings of Sheikh Ziya al-Din Khalid (d. 1827)," who "was a Kurd from the Shahrizor district in present-day Iraq."[47] He "rejected the anti-Sufi stance" of radical Muslim reformers such as Muhammad ibn Abd al-Wahhab (1703–1791), the founder of the Wahhabi movement in Arabia, who "condemned all Sufis as heretics," but the sheikh also criticized "what he believed to be the divergence from 'true' Islam that most Sufi orders of his day represented."[48] Sheikh Khaled "saw his mission as nothing short of the revival of Sunni Islam in the Ottoman Empire through strict adherence to Islamic law, grounded in a certainty of purpose that could only come to the believer through the mystical experience."[49] His movement gained popular support among the masses. In particular, the order played an important role in shaping the culture of the Kurdish-populated region in southeastern Anatolia, northern Iraq, and northern Syria.

Many among the elite and the subject classes viewed the Sufi masters as holy men who possessed miraculous powers.[50] When a Sufi master of great standing appeared in a town, townspeople rushed to touch or kiss the hem of his mantle or skirt, or even his feet.[51] The tombs of Sufi masters were places of pilgrimage. When a Sufi şeyh passed away, the tomb would be enclosed and a dome was built over it, attracting pilgrims from near and far away lands. Cults and myths often arose around the tomb of a Sufi master who was venerated for his spiritual purity and power. In order to attract the attention and blessings of a saint or Sufi master buried in a tomb, pious visitors, the sick, the ailing, impotent men, women unable to bear children, pregnant women fearful of complications in childbirth, and mothers pleading for a cure for their children's infirmity offered prayers and supplications by tying scraps of material, "shreds of cotton, woolen, and silk morsels of ribbon and tape" to the railings of the mausoleum or the nearby bushes and trees.[52] Many lit candles as they pleaded for a cure, while others donated metal candelabra or carpets for the floor of the mausoleum as a sign of their humility and devotion. Some who could not find a remedy to their illness slept near or on a tomb for a few hours or up to forty days if their ailment was serious.[53] At times, even trees, rocks, or fountains in the garden of the shrine became holy objects with magical power.

The inside of mausoleum was covered with embroidered shawls and handkerchiefs, and the turban worn by the Sufi teacher in life "was affixed to the head of the coffin."[54] The relics of the deceased *şeyhs* were "suspended against the walls—their walking sticks, their rosaries and beads, and portions of their garments," and pilgrims kissed and touched these with devotion and reverence.[55] Many Sufi shrines were built on sites that already served as places of pilgrimage and worship before the arrival of the Turks and Islam. While some of the sites were important during the Christian era, the sacredness of others dated back further to pre-Christian times, when pagan cults, centered on the worship of a sun god or another natural deity, prevailed.

STORYTELLING

The overwhelming majority of the population in the Ottoman Empire could not read or write. Formal knowledge was the monopoly of a few who had received their education and training either at the palace or at the *mekteps* and *medreses,* which prepared their students for a career in the religious establishment. The same situation prevailed among the Christian and Jewish communities of the empire. Until the arrival of modern education and schooling in the 19th century, the majority of Christians and Jews who could read and write received their education at religious schools, at times attached to a church or a synagogue.

In this environment, storytelling was not merely a form of popular entertainment but also one of the most popular forms of transmitting historical knowledge and popular culture among the masses.

Ordinary people from diverse social backgrounds gathered in coffeehouses to listen to storytellers read fables, recite poetry, and use a variety of provocative methods to create and sustain suspense. In these public performances, skilled storytellers inserted pauses, switched from normal speech to chanting, moved arms and head in sweeping gestures, whispered, shouted, clapped hands, and pounded feet, as they impersonated a variety of characters and, in this way, "imparted to the audience the whole gamut of feelings and passions experienced by them."[56] Instead of relying exclusively on describing characters, the storyteller "would give an impersonation, sometimes changing headdress to suit, and using two props—a cudgel and a kerchief wrapped around his neck—to produce appropriate audible and visible effects."[57] Sometimes *dervişes* acted as "oral narrators (*meddah*) and drew on their knowledge of written culture in their stories."[58] Because of this highly specialized knowledge and their unique ability to perform in a dramatic fashion, these *derviş* storytellers were greatly esteemed among the members of the ruling elite.[59] Storytellers were divided into several categories according to their style and repertoire. Some specialized in popular romances, others in national legends, pseudo-historical romances, epic tales, individual exploits, or religious narrations.[60]

The numerous anecdotes, jokes, and stories attributed to Nassredin Hoca (Wise or Learned Nassredin), and told daily by storytellers in coffeehouses, or in gatherings with family and friends, reflected the witty and subversive nature of a culture that viewed the claims and actions of those in power with humor and skepticism. In tale after tale, Nassredin appears as a man of small means, living with his wife, or as a travelling wise man, without a regular job, wandering from one town or village to the next. He has a biting tongue and a fearless character, and cannot be easily impressed or intimidated by men of power, wealth, and influence. On one occasion he arrives in a town without a penny in his pocket and desperate to make a quick gain before he can continue his journey. Using his turban and robe to impress the people with his knowledge and education, he agrees to deliver a lecture in return for a handsome honorarium, although he does not know what he will be talking about. When he appears in front of a large crowd that is waiting enthusiastically for his presentation, he asks the audience if they know what he will be talking about. The answer from the crowd is a resounding "No," to which Nassredin responds, "Since you are so ignorant that you do not know anything about what I will talk about, I refuse to speak to you," and he walks out. He cannot, however, receive his pay unless he returns and delivers a lecture. Thus, he appears for a second time and since he still does not have anything to say, he merely repeats the same question he had asked the audience the day before: "Do you know what I will be talking to you about today?" To ensure that he does not use their negative response as an excuse to walk out again, the audience answer with a resounding, "Yes, we do," to which Nassredin responds, "Since you all know what I will be talking about there will be no need for me to waste your time," and he walks out again. Frustrated and suspicious, the townspeople decide to preempt Nassredin's she- nanigans by discussing a possible strategy that would prevent him from leaving without delivering a lecture. The decision is made that if he asks the same question, "Do you know what I will be talking to you about today?" half of the people present will say, "Yes" and the other half will say, "No." Thus, when Nassredin appears for the third time and asks the question, the crowd is ready with one group shouting, "Yes," and the second crying out, "No," to which the Hoca responds, "There is no need for me to waste your time with a lecture since those of you who know what I will talk about can tell those of you who don't."

On another occasion, Nassredin is awakened in the middle of a cold and snowy night by the sound of commotion and loud argu- ment outside his house. He tries to ignore the fight outside his window and goes back to sleep, but his wife, who has also been awakened by the noise, insists that he should get up and investi- gate the cause of the fight. Despite his best efforts to convince his wife that he should not become involved in the fight, Nassredin is finally forced to wrap himself in his quilt and go out of the house. Shivering from the freezing cold, he steps out of his house and asks the two groups arguing and fighting in front of his house what is causing the big commotion. His question ends the argument among the men who were fighting until then. They look at Nassredin for a moment, then suddenly jump on him and tear the quilt he is using to cover his body. After ripping the quilt into two halves, they run away and disappear into the darkness of the night. Having lost his quilt, Nassredin returns to his bedroom. His wife looks at the baf- fled, perplexed, and shivering Nassredin and asks him the reason for the loud argument on the street. Nassredin responds: "the fight was over my quilt."

The popular Ottoman shadow theater Karagöz and Hacivat was another means through which the society "created its world of laughter," allowing the ordinary subjects of the sultan to criticize the government and the clerical establishment "before rapturous audiences" who crowded the cafés.[61] There are many different legends and claims about the origins of shadow theater in the Ottoman Empire. Regardless of how it arrived in Istanbul, Karagöz quickly emerged as the epitome of Ottoman wit and humor and a central cultural personage in the daily life of ordinary Ottomans.[62] He was a "roughly colored diminutive figure cut out of camel's hide," who played "its merry part behind a sheet" so that "its comic outline and gorgeous coloring" would stand out against the white background.[63] Members of all social classes in the Ottoman Empire watched Karagöz, some of which "originated in the palace" and found its "way to the street," while others "conceived in local coffeehouses, were performed in the sultan's harem, transmitting the norms and wishes of the populace and poking fun at the state and its servants."[64] Removed from reality, "once through the stage, then through the puppets, and finally through their projection on a flat screen," the shadow play served "as a safety valve for venting popular dissatisfaction," ridiculing the hypocrisies of power and morality and voicing "a truth about society that hides within fiction."[65] The plays portrayed a reality that "stood in marked opposition" to the rites and rituals of the palace and the Islamic religious hierarchy, and they represented a world opposed to the one suggested by the ruling class.[66]

Not surprisingly, the sultans and their officials did not view shadow-theater as "harmless entertainment."[67] The uneasiness of the ruling elite was intensified by the fact that the majority of shadow plays were performed in coffeehouses, which served as the meeting place for the members of the lower classes.[68] It is true that shadow plays were also performed "at family celebrations like circumcisions, births and marriages," but their "greatest success came during Ramadan, when on the evening before breaking their fast, people would crowd into the coffeehouses to watch a show and shorten the time before the next meal."[69] When the performance was held after breaking the fast, "tiny cups of aromatic coffee were constantly handed round" by young men "wearing the good old costume: baggy trousers and little coils of colored linen" with "turbans heaped up on their shaven heads."[70] Once the play had ended, the spectators applauded and "bestowed doles of small coin on the two lads who came round with a platter to collect their offerings."[71] Then, "the light behind the screen disappeared as suddenly as it had shone out," and the musicians played a final crescendo as the crowd had a parting coffee before it poured out into the street.[72]

Aside from the sultan and his officials, the members of the religious class viewed the shadow play with suspicion and disgust because they dealt openly with "immoral subjects" and portrayed "female characters whose behavior left a great deal to be desired."[73] To make matters worse, Islamic law forbade the depiction of all living beings.[74] However, "with just one or two holes in the brightly painted leather puppets, it was possible to kill two birds with one stone: the actors could fit the sticks into them in order to move them, but because of the hole (which was generally in the region of the heart), the characters could not be deemed capable of life, and so they could not be considered to depict living beings."[75]

In the shadow play, the principal characters were Karagöz (literally the Black Eye), the kind, honest, straightforward, illiterate man on the street who cannot find permanent employment, and his friend and opposite, Hacivat, an intelligent, refined, and cultured man, who displayed his knowledge and education by speaking Ottoman Turkish and using traditional poetry. Karagöz was usually "eight inches high" and was "always shown in profile" with "a parrot-like nose, and a beady, glittering eye, screened by a thick projecting eyebrow."[76] He wore a huge turban, "which on the slightest provocation" was "removed by a wire, to display his cocoa-nut of a head, an exhibition always greeted with shouts of laughter."[77] Dressed in "a colored waistcoat, a short jacket, and a pair of baggy trousers, with striped stockings," his "legs and arms" were "flexible" and "moved by skillfully concealed wires," while his gestures were "clumsy but vigorous."[78] In sharp contrast, his friend and confidant, Hacivat, was "more alert in his movements."[79]

Karagöz and Hacivat were joined by a large cast of characters who caricatured "a variety of races, professions and religions."[80] Besides moving the puppets from the back by rods that he held between his fingers, the puppeteer "spoke all their parts in various voices, sang songs, made a variety of sound-effects, and into the old, familiar and well-loved plots he introduced a number of improvised comic scenes, sometimes of current or legal interest, which included a great deal of ribaldry and a number of coarse jokes."[81] Usually as the play unfolded, keen to make mischief, Karagöz grew "bolder with impunity and approbation," becoming increasingly more daring, outspoken, and intrepid "in his impropriety."[82] Special and "sedater performances" were often organized for women and children "in rich private homes."[83] Occasionally Karagöz paid a visit to the imperial palace, where he was extremely careful "not to say or do anything" that would offend the Shadow of God.[84] But Karagöz was not the only theatrical performance popular among the urban population. There was another form of theater called *orta oyunu*, "which involved improvising without a stage or set text" and "depended almost entirely on the skill of the main comic."[85]

NOTES

1. Bernard Lewis, *Istanbul and the Civilization of the Ottoman Empire* (Norman: University of Oklahoma Press, 1963), 152–53.

2. Donald Quataert, *The Ottoman Empire, 1700–1922* (Cambridge: Cambridge University Press, 2005), 162.

3. Ibid.

4. Lewis, *Istanbul*, 152.

5. Ahmet Yaşar Ocak, "Sufism, Sufis and Tariqahs, Private Dervish Lodges" in *Ottoman Civilization*, eds. Halil Inalcik and Günsel Renda, 2 vols. (Istanbul: Republic of Turkey Ministry of Culture Publications, 2003), 1:267.

6. Ibid.

7. Lewis, *Istanbul*, 154–55.

8. Ibid., 153.

9. Ibid., 153–54.

10. Ibid., 160.

11. Nathalie Clayer, "Life in an Istanbul Tekke In the Eighteenth and Nineteenth Centuries According To a 'Menakibname' of the Cerrahi Dervishes," in *The Illuminated Table, the Prosperous House: Food and Shelter in Ottoman Material Culture*, eds. Suraiya Faroqhi and Christoph K. Neumann (Würzburg: Ergon in Kommission, 2003), 221.

12. Ibid., 222.

13. Ibid.

14. Ibid.

15. Ibid., 219.

16. Ibid.

17. Ibn Battuta, *The Travels of Ibn Battuta*, trans. H.A.R. Gibb (Cambridge: Cambridge University Press, 1962), 419.

18. Ibid.

19. Ibid., 420, 450.

20. Suraiya Faroqhi, *Subjects of the Sultan: Culture and Daily Life in the Ottoman Empire* (New York: I. B. Tauris, 2007), 156.

21. Halil Inalcik, *The Ottoman Empire, The Classical Age 1300–1600* (New York: Praeger Publishers, 1973), 186.

22. Ibid., 55; Peter F. Sugar, *Southeastern Europe under Ottoman Rule: 1354–1804* (Seattle: University of Washington Press, 1996), 8.

23. Ibid., 55, 226.

24. Ibid., 189.

25. Ibid.

26. Ibid.

27. Ibid., 190.

28. Ibid.

29. Paul Rycaut, *The Present State of the Ottoman Empire* (New York: Arno Press, 1971), 149.

30. R. Tschudi, "Bektashiyya," in *The Encyclopaedia of Islam* (Leiden: E. J. Brill, 1960), 1:1162.

31. Ibid.

32. Ibid.

33. Evliya Çelebi, *Evliya Çelebi in Albania,* trans. Robert Dankoff and Robert Elsie (Leiden: Brill, 2000), 85.

34. Ibid.

35. Çelebi, *The Intimate Life of an Ottoman Statesman,* trans., Robert Dankoff (Albany: State University of New York Press, 1991), 117.

36. T. Yazici, "Muwlawiyya," in *The Encyclopaedia of Islam* (Leiden: E. J. Brill, 1991), 6:887.

37. Ibid.

38. Lewis, *Istanbul,* 157.

39. Yazici, "Muwlawiyya," 885.

40. Bruce Masters, "Naqshbandiyya Order," in *Encyclopedia of the Ottoman Empire,* eds. Gábor Ágoston and Bruce Masters (New York: Facts On File, 2009), 419.

41. Lewis, *Istanbul,* 158.

42. Masters, "Naqshbandiyya Order," 419.

43. Ibid.

44. Ibid.

45. Ibid.

46. Inalcik, *The Ottoman Empire,* 99.

47. Masters, "Naqshbandiyya Order," 419–20.

48. Ibid., 420.

49. Ibid.

50. Richard Davey, *The Sultan and His Subjects,* 2 vols. (London: Chapman and Hall LD., 1897), 1:87.

51. Ibid.

52. Julia Pardoe, *The City of the Sultan and Domestic Manners of the Turks in 1836,* 3 vols. (London: Henry Colburn Publisher, 1838), 1:267; Faroqhi, *Subjects of the Sultan,* 162.

53. Quataert, *The Ottoman Empire,* 163–64.

54. Davey, *The Sultan and His Subjects,* 1:88.

55. Ibid.

56. Metin And, "Traditional Performances in Ottoman Civilization," in *Ottoman Civilization,* ed. Halil Inalcik and Günsel Renda, 2 vols. (Istanbul: Republic of Turkey Ministry of Culture Publications, 2003), 2:990.

57. Ibid.

58. Faroqhi, *Subjects of the Sultan*, 273.

59. Ibid.

60. And, "Traditional Performances," 2:990.

61. Dror Zéevi, *Producing Desire: Changing Sexual Discourse in the Ottoman Middle East, 1500–1900* (Berkeley: University of California Press, 2006), 125; Richard Davey, *The Sultan and His Subjects*, 1:343.

62. Davey, *The Sultan and His Subjects*, 1:344.

63. Ibid.

64. Zéevi, *Producing Desire*, 125.

65. Ibid., 125–26.

66. Ibid., 126.

67. Isabel Böcking, Laura Salm-Reifferscheidt, and Moritz Stipsicz, *The Bazaars of Istanbul* (New York: Thames & Hudson, 2009), 154.

68. Ibid.

69. Ibid.

70. Davey, *The Sultan and His Subjects*, 1:345.

71. Ibid., 351.

72. Ibid., 351–52.

73. Böcking, Salm-Reifferscheidt, and Stipsicz, *The Bazaars of Istanbul*, 154.

74. Ibid.

75. Ibid.

76. Davey, *The Sultan and His Subjects*, 1:348.

77. Ibid.

78. Ibid.

79. Ibid., 349.

80. Raphaela Lewis, *Everyday Life in Ottoman Turkey* (London: B. T. Batsford Ltd., 1971), 125.

81. Ibid.

82. Davey, *The Sultan and His Subjects*, 1:345.

83. Lewis, *Everyday Life in Ottoman Turkey*, 124–25.

84. Davey, *The Sultan and His Subjects*, 1:352.

85. Faroqhi, *Subjects of the Sultan*, 260.

9

COURTSHIP
AND MARRIAGE

One of the basic teachings of Islam was the promotion of marriage and condemnation of celibacy. Only those who suffered from severe economic hardship could legitimately remain unmarried. Every Muslim was expected to marry, and celibacy was regarded as unnatural, unhealthy, and therefore, unacceptable.[1] To abstain from marriage when one had attained a sufficient age and had no physical and emotional impediments was viewed as improper and even disreputable. Girls married at an early age, and at times, soon after they had reached puberty.

The general belief among the urban and rural population was that if the young remained unmarried, their sexual instincts and desires would find an outlet outside marriage and this could cause social chaos and moral evils.[2] According to the Muslim tradition, "when an unmarried man and woman" were together, Satan was "also present."[3] There could, therefore, be "no allowance for innocence in the unsanctioned mixing of the sexes."[4] Families were often apprehensive about the sexual desires of their daughters and always concerned about their sexual purity.[5] Islamic law and tradition viewed women's sexuality as a potent force, which had to be controlled first by the father and then by a husband.[6]

The great Muslim theologian, jurist, and philosopher Ghazali (1058–1111), whose works were studied at religious schools and seminaries throughout the Ottoman Empire, had warned against "the calamity of social disorder" that followed "from the failure to control women."[7] If left uncontrolled, women's "irresistible and assertive sexual nature" could destroy "social—particularly male—equanimity" resulting in chaos and anarchy.[8] Girls were the guardians of their family's honor. They were to remain virgins until they married and their "clothing and physical mobility" had to be regulated.[9] The Ottoman religious establishment took Ghazali's position "on women's physicality" one step further and argued that "women's entire body" was "effectively pudendal," and must therefore be completely covered, including the face and hands.[10] Exception could only be made within the circle of permitted relatives or out of absolute necessity, such as for medical reasons. Violation of this honor code could result in the woman's expulsion from the household and even worse, death at the hands of her own father or brothers.

PREARRANGED MARRIAGE

Family life in the Ottoman Empire began with marriage, and all marriages were prearranged. In exceptional cases, young men escaped the marriage arranged by their parents. Young girls did not, however, have any other option but to obey the decision made by their family.[11] Marriage was a contract negotiated and executed by the families involved, and legalized by a religious judge or another available member of the religious class.

Islamic law had not fixed an age for marriage, and in the Ottoman Empire, as in other Islamic states, many families gave their young children to marriage, although girls were not allowed to move into their husband's home until they had reached puberty. The Hanafi school of Islamic law, to which the Ottomans adhered, made it very clear that a marriage could not be consummated until the bride was fit for marital sexual intercourse. Only after the establishment of the Turkish Republic were specific ages defined. The new Turkish constitution fixed 18 as the youngest marriageable age for men and 17 for women, although, even then, the courts could be asked to sanction marriage at 15 for either sex, but no earlier.

The planning for a marriage traditionally began when the father of a young man decided that the time had arrived for his son to marry. In some instances, the son initiated the process by informing his mother of his desire to marry. Regardless, the father had to agree that the time had arrived for his son to be married. Without his consent and support, the process of selecting a bride and arranging a marriage could not begin. A good marriage was a union that enhanced the economic and social status of the family. Every effort was made, therefore, to find a spouse whose family held equal, or higher, social and economic status. The family of the bride considered a husband who was a hard-working breadwinner a good catch, while the parents of the bridegroom regarded a young beautiful girl, who was well trained by her mother in housekeeping and child care, as the perfect match.

Marriage customs and traditions varied from one community and region of the empire to another, but the majority of Muslims shared many common or at least very similar traditions and rites. Marriage to cousins, particularly between children of brothers, was prevalent in many Muslim communities, particularly in Anatolia, the Arab provinces of the Middle East, and Egypt. In Egypt, when a man married his first cousin, the husband and wife continued to call each other "cousin" because it was believed that blood ties were indissoluble, but those of matrimony very fragile and precarious.[12] In most rural communities, the prospective bride was selected from within the village and in many instances, from within the immediate or extended family. Non-Muslims living in the empire followed many of these same patterns. Most marriages were arranged among co-religionists and co-ethnics who resided in the same village or neighborhood.

Many marriage arrangements followed a predictable timetable. Inquiries were made among relatives, friends, and neighbors about attractive, available, and well-bred girls. Negotiations began with a go-between or a matchmaker, who provided the family of the prospective groom with a list of young and available girls. Sometimes the matchmaker was a relative or a friend of the family of the future groom and offered her services as a favor. Once the matchmaker and the mother of the prospective groom had agreed on a short list, they visited the homes of intended brides.

In small villages and towns, parents may have thought for years about a suitable partner and spouse for their child. At times, they had already selected the ideal bride years before their son and the intended bride reached puberty and were old enough to marry.[13] Consequently, a boy's mother, who had already reached a decision, might arrive at the home of the prospective bride unannounced and request a meeting with the girl and her mother. More often, however, the mother was accompanied by relatives, friends, and a go-between, who requested a meeting with the mother of the prospective bride. If the girl's mother had any reason for opposing the proposed marriage, she gave an evasive reply, which conveyed her refusal to consider the match; otherwise she consented to a meeting and received her visitors with a show of respect and honor.

The two mothers exchanged the customary compliments before the girl entered the room dressed in her best. She kissed the hands of the visitors and with downcast eyes, served them coffee and sweetmeats. The visitors observed her physical appearance and, at times, asked frank questions. This may explain why the guests took their time finishing the coffee.[14] As long as they were drinking their coffee, the guests could continue with the inspection. Once they had finished drinking, the girl withdrew and the inspection came to an end. It was always a bad sign if the visitors finished their coffee too quickly.[15] When the girl left the room, the mothers began to negotiate, but they did not make a final decision. The mother of the girl asked the visitors about their opinion regarding her daughter, and they responded by making flattering comments about the beauty and manners of the girl, though they may have been completely untruthful.[16]

Sometimes the meeting between the mothers took place at a public bathhouse. To arrange a meeting with the bride and her mother, the groom's mother would have let it be known in advance that she would be at the bath with her relatives and friends on a certain day and time.[17] One of the main advantages of meetings at a bathhouse was that the prospective bride was obliged to appear only partially dressed, and the visiting party could then inspect her physical beauty and qualities in a more open and immediate fashion. If the boy's mother was not satisfied with the girl, or if she found serious faults and defects, she would continue with her search until the right match was found. If she returned from her inspection pleased and convinced of her choice, however, she would share the news of her visit with her husband and son.[18]

As for the girl, it was the duty of her parents to ensure that her suitor was of equal birth with them and that the match was suitable in other ways as well. If the father of the prospective bride was deceased, her oldest and closest male relative, usually an uncle or an older brother, acted as her representative. To secure the consent of the bride's father, and to reassure him of the seriousness of their commitment, the groom and his family sometimes dispatched a relative, friend, or even the matchmaker to the house of the intended bride with gifts and expressions of genuine interest.

In submitting these gifts, the intermediary or the matchmaker tried to reassure the family of the girl about their future son-in-law, often exaggerating his personal characteristics and qualifications. She told them how gracious, handsome, hardworking, and faithful the young man was, and that they had nothing to fear for the future of their daughter.

The decision to accept the gifts and the marriage proposal rested exclusively with the parents of the girl. In some instances, the father of the girl rejected a suitor if he did not come from a suitable social and professional background, or if the older daughter of the family was still waiting for a husband. In most communities, tradition called for the girls to marry according to their age and did not allow younger females to marry before their older sisters.

MEHR

Once the bride's father had expressed his satisfaction with the prospective groom, representatives from both families began to negotiate on the final details of the marriage, including the nature and the amount of the dowry, the date for the wedding, and whether the newlyweds would live at the groom's house or the bride's. The transfer of a dowry or *mehr* (Arabic: *mahr*) to the new bride sealed the marriage contract. Marriages could not be consummated without the payment of *mehr*, which was a precondition for the legality of the contract. According to Islamic law and the existing customs and traditions, the bridegroom had to promise the bride the payment of a certain sum of money in case he divorced her against her consent, or in case he died. The *mehr* was frequently paid in two portions. The first portion, generally stipulated to be two-thirds, was paid before the marriage contract was signed. The second portion was paid only if the husband divorced his wife, or if he died while they were still married. In some instances, a part of *mehr* was kept in trust for the bride to support her if the groom died or divorced her. Some parents simply took the first portion of the *mehr* as their own, treating it as a payment for the loss of their daughter's labor.[19] Regardless, once the first portion of the *mehr* had been paid, the couple was considered to be engaged.

Court registers from the 16th century indicate that at times local customs conflicted with the laws of Islam regarding marriage. On "the basis of several entries in the Ankara court registers for that period, it would seem that a certain type of betrothal, called *namzedlik* (literally, 'candidacy') was quite common."[20] In "this type of arrangement, the father would promise his daughter in marriage to someone while she was still very young and would accept money or goods in return."[21] This "sum would be used by the father; when his daughter came of age, he would hand her over to the man to whom she was betrothed."[22]

In Egypt, the *mahr* for a virgin-bride was much larger than the amount paid to a bride who was a widow or a divorced woman. The exact amount, and the terms of payment, varied from one case to another and formed a part of the premarital negotiations between families. The financial capabilities of the groom and his family, the physical beauty of the bride, and the blood relationship between the bridegroom and his intended bride were important factors in settling the amount.[23]

The bride did not usually take part in the discussions surrounding the *mehr* and the details of the upcoming wedding. Instead, she was represented by her family. As for the bridegroom, in many instances, his uncle or other close and trusted male relatives negotiated with the family of the bride over the exact amount of *mehr* and the final details, such as the expectations for both spouses and what the bride would bring into her new house in the way of linens, pots, and other household amenities.[24] These rituals and negotiations left no doubt that the consenting units were families rather than individuals. The marriage was not just between a man and a woman, and the happiness of two individuals was not viewed as the supreme concern. Out of the marriage, two families emerged as a unified team, which would support each other and look out for each other's interests.[25]

Once negotiations between the two families had reached a full agreement, the groom's mother, acting on behalf of her son, asked for the hand of the girl from her mother. Heading a group of female relatives and friends, she went to the bride's home with several yards of red silk and a basket of candies. The red silk, which would eventually be made into an undergarment for the bride, was spread on the floor so that the bride could stand on it. On this occasion, the bride had to demonstrate her respect and obedience to her future mother-in-law, into whose house she would move, by serving her coffee or tea as a sign of respect.[26] The bride would then take a bite from a candy and express sincere gratitude to her future mother-in-law by kissing her hand. The portion of the candy she had not eaten was returned to the mother of the groom, so that she could give it to her son as a symbol of the bride's commitment to share her life with him.[27] The bride also sent a package of presents to her future husband and his family. The gifts were presented to the groom and his family by an elderly female, who was usually a relative or trusted confidant of the girl's family. The presents she carried might include shawls, shirts embroidered with pearls, handkerchiefs, braces, and "candy-filled box of mother-of-pearl in tortoise-shell."[28] At times, the bride also sent a variety of special foods and dishes.

Among the affluent, the groom responded to these gifts by sending his bride and her family several trays of presents. The first contained house slippers, a silver hand mirror, perfumes, and a wedding ring that was placed inside a small silver box. The second tray carried flowers, and the third held baskets of fruit. The fourth carried baskets of sweets, spices, coffee, colored wax candles, and bags of henna from the holy city of Mecca. The fifth tray held the material for the wedding dress and other clothing material, as well as a pair of clogs, a silver basin, and a number of combs, which could be used by the bride when she went on her weekly visit to the bathhouse. Each tray was tied in muslin and decorated with ribbons.[29]

ENGAGEMENT AND WEDDING

All ethnic and religious communities in the Ottoman Empire attached considerable importance to the formalities of engagement and wedding ceremonies. Among wealthy Muslim families, weddings consisted of a week of activities, rituals, and festivities. Before the festivities began, however, the men from both families gathered and agreed to a marriage contract in the presence of an imam who had received the marriage permit from the local religious judge. The responsibility of the imam was to read the marriage contract and secure the signatures of the bride and the groom or their male representatives.

On the day of signing, the fathers of the bride and the groom or, in their absence, the male representatives of both parties, gathered at the home of the bride. In the presence of male witnesses, the imam read the conditions and clauses of the marriage contract loudly enough for the bride and her relatives and friends in the adjoining room to hear him clearly. When he had finished reading the contract, the imam asked the bride if she consented to the conditions outlined in the document. To this she simply answered, yes. Having received the consent of the bride, the imam signed the contract, congratulated both parties, and prayed for a long lasting union. He then proceeded to register the contract with the *kadi*. All marriages were recorded in the court register. Otherwise, "the man and woman concerned would be summoned to court for 'cohabiting out of wedlock' and their illegitimate relationship would be recorded in the same registry."[30] Meanwhile, the families on both sides attended a banquet celebrating the signing of the marriage contract. The festivities that followed, and included nearly a week of activities, could immediately follow the signing of the marriage contract or could be postponed to a date in the near or distant future. The following account of wedding festivities, which has been adopted from Fanny Davis's *The Ottoman Lady, A Social History from 1718 to 1918,* describes only one possible sequence of Ottoman wedding ceremonies. This description should not, however, be construed as the only possible traditional wedding organized by families in the Ottoman Empire.

On the first day of festivities, following the signing of the marriage contract, the bride's trousseau was carried in a procession from her home to the house of the groom.[31] Among royalty, as well as among the rich and powerful, this procession served as an opportunity to display the wealth and power of the bride's family. A large band of musicians played a variety of instruments, such as flutes, fifes, drums, and bagpipes. Servants and attendants carried gilded cases, like bird cages, containing all kinds of expensive gifts, carpets from every part of Anatolia and Iran, embroideries, ornaments of gold and silver, parrots, rare songbirds, jewels, fans, and sweetmeats. Each case was covered with a pink veil sufficiently transparent for the eager crowd to identify the contents.

After the gilded cases came an artificial tree (*nahil*) about sixty feet in height, the branches and leaves of which were thickly gilt and hung with presents, such as toys and ornaments suspended by colored ribbons. On one occasion at least, during the wedding procession of the daughter of Ahmed III (1703–1730), the *nahil* was so large that "it demolished the balconies of the houses on the narrow streets through which it passed."[32] These initial processions were followed by more musicians and foot soldiers. Finally came black slaves with long whips in their hands running in front of a large tent made of cloth of gold, beneath which female attendants carried the bride in a litter atop their shoulders. If the bride was a member of the royal family, the sultan graced the procession with his presence. To mark the occasion, he wore a special turban, which was decorated by a heron's plume clasped with a crescent brooch of huge diamonds. As the sultan passed, his subjects "touched the ground with their heads before him so as to avoid being dazzled by the glory of the Shadow of God."[33]

The next pre-wedding ceremony required the bride and her female companions to meet at a public bathhouse. All the female friends and relatives from both families assembled at the bathhouse, where the older and married women sat on the marble sofas, while the young and unmarried girls removed their clothing and, without any ornaments or covering other than their own long hair, braided with pearl or ribbon, prepared to receive the bride.[34] When the bride arrived with her mother and an older female relative, two of the girls led her to the gathering inside the bathhouse. Ornately dressed and shimmering with jewels, the bride was immediately undressed as two other girls "filled silver gilt pots with perfume."[35] Once finished, they began a procession with the rest of the girls following in pairs.[36] The leading girls sang "an epithalamium answered by others in chorus," while the last two ladies led the bride forward, "her eyes fixed on the ground with a charming affection of modesty."[37] In this fashion, the women marched through the large rooms of the bathhouse. After they had completed their procession, the bride was "soaped, pummeled, shampooed, scalded, and perfumed."[38] Her body hair was removed with depilatory paste, "her hair was braided in eight or ten tresses and entwined with strings of pearls and gold beads or coins," and her eyebrows were blackened.[39]

Once she had been bathed, cleaned, and prepared, the bride again was led to every matron, who saluted her with a compliment and a gift.[40] Some offered pieces of jewelry, others embroidered handkerchiefs, which the bride "thanked them for by kissing their hands."[41] The bride was then dressed in fine clothes and seated on a gilt-edged throne built of gauze and ribbon. From this seat she viewed a variety of performances by a group of gypsies, whom she paid at the end with gold coins and candies. After food and refreshments had been served, the bride and her companions departed. They had to prepare themselves for the following day, when the female relatives of the groom would come to pay a visit.

The female members of the bride's family received the female relatives of the groom at the door of the bride's home and led them to the women's quarter, where the hosts and guests were served coffee. After they had finished their coffee and exchanged compliments and niceties, the bride entered the room to greet the visitors and kiss the hand of her future mother-in-law. After she had left the room, the visitors were entertained by musicians, singers, and dancers. Neither the visitors nor the guests participated in the dancing and singing. When the guests stood up to leave, the bride appeared again to bid them farewell and was showered with coins by the visitors.

Later that evening, the women of both families assembled again to celebrate the "henna night," when the bride said farewell to her girlhood by dyeing her hands with henna paste.[42] Prior to the actual ceremony, the girl was escorted through the garden of the house with her unmarried friends, while musicians and professional dancers played and danced. The henna was applied to the bride's hands by her new mother-in-law, who rubbed a small quantity of the paste first on the bride's right hand and then her left as the guests pressed gold coins into the orange material. The hands of the bride were then wrapped in a small bag or a piece of fabric, allowing the dye to leave its orange stain.

The next day, the bride was prepared for the final procession, which would celebrate her departure from her parents' home for the house of her new husband. Her hair was braided, her face "was whitened and rouged and gold dust, spangles, even diamonds were affixed to her forehead, cheeks, and chin."[43] She also wore her wedding dress, which consisted of a fine white shirt, baggy pants, a richly embroidered long red or purple dress that she wore on top of her shirt and pants, and a pair of calfskin boots. Along with her wedding dress, she wore a pearl necklace, a pair of earrings, and bracelets and rings of precious stones that glowed on her hands and fingers. To cover her face and body, she donned a crimson- or red-colored veil, which skimmed over the top of her dress. On her head over the veil, her mother placed a bridal aigrette, tiara, or crown made of cut glass that could come in a variety of colors. Before leaving her house, the bride appeared in front of her father for the last time as a virgin. She kneeled in front of her father and kissed his hands and feet. He raised her and "clasped about her waist the bridal girdle, which might be a jeweled belt, a fine shawl, or, in late Ottoman times, simply a ribbon symbolic of the girdle."[44] During this short and highly emotional ceremony the girl cried and, at times, the father shed tears as he bid his daughter a final farewell. Meanwhile, an attendant announced that the groom and his party had arrived.

Earlier in the day, the groom had arrived at his own home, accompanied by relatives and friends, astride horses adorned with gold and silver mountings on their saddles and bridles. One European observer, who witnessed an Ottoman wedding procession, reported that entertainers, such as musicians and fire-eaters, accompanied by men carrying silver dinner services wrapped in silk cloth, followed the bridegroom and his retinue.[45] He also observed numerous pieces of sugar-candy products, bowls, pitchers, candelabras, and even animals such as horses, elephants, lions, sea creatures, and a variety of birds, participating in the march toward the wedding ceremony.[46] At the tail end of the procession, donkeys ferried household goods such as carpets and beds, intended for the newlyweds' use. While the guests were being entertained, the bridegroom's family dispatched a string of donkeys to the home of the bride to transport her clothes, personal belongings, and furniture to the new home where she would be living with her husband. The animals wore decorative harnesses and bells hung from their necks. Although "ten donkeys would have been sufficient to transport her dowry," reported one observer, "twice that number would be sent to make the procession more impressive."[47]

The bridegroom and his friends, beautifully clothed, next mounted their horses and led a procession to the house of the bride. There they met her family and requested and received the permission of her parents to bring her to the house of the groom. When the groom and company first arrived at the bride's house, however, they found the gates besieged by a crowd, who caused the young man to have to enter the house amid a storm of cheers, compliments, and benedictions. If he were particularly well to do, he responded by scattering a handful of coins to the crowd. At the entrance to the house or at the foot of the main staircase, the groom was met by his father-in-law, who embraced him, kissed him on both cheeks, and led him to the *selamlik* (the male section of the house), where he found male relatives and friends assembled. Coffee, sherbet, and other refreshments were served.

Meanwhile, in the women's harem, the bride, covered by her wedding veil, sat on a throne at the end of the room, silent as a statue. She was surrounded by the women of her family as well as friends and acquaintances, all dressed beautifully and covered with all the jewelry they could find. They ate, drank, joked, laughed, complimented the bride on her beautiful dress, and examined the bridal gifts, which were "protected by a wire grating, to prevent pilfering" because "at a Turkish wedding, according to ancient custom, the poorest woman in the street" was "allowed to come up and see the bride and her presents."[48] Amid the noise and chatter, refreshments, sweetmeats, and sugar confectionery were served, and dancers and musicians performed.

After the conclusion of festivities at the harem and the *selamlik,* the bride was escorted to her horse or carriage. Dressed in her bridal veil and curtained with a red canopy, or baldachin, over her head, she rode with pomp and ceremony to the home of the bridegroom.[49] She was accompanied by an older female relative and several male representatives who led the procession. Clowns, jesters, musicians, and dancers joined the procession and entertained the spectators, who emerged from their homes to cheer the groom and the bride. At the groom's house, women often gathered in the harem and celebrated the arrival of the bride by showering her with coins, flowers, candies, and kisses.

Across various provinces of the empire, local elites mimicked the elaborate ceremonies and rituals of the ruling classes in Istanbul. Among the rich and the powerful in Albania, for example, armed horsemen and foot soldiers were sent to fetch the bride from her home in a village or town. Great banquets welcomed the men upon their arrival at the home of the bride, and volleys of cannons and muskets were fired into the air in celebration. When the men set off again to bring the bride to the home of the bridegroom, festivities continued along the road. Muslim youth lined the road to welcome the procession with dancing, and shouted the name of God—"Allah Allah!"—as the procession passed.[50]

Among the Ottomans, particularly the wealthy classes, a sumptuous meal was served after the bridegroom and his friends had brought the bride to her new home. The menu usually included dishes of saffron rice, mutton pilafs, roasted pigeons, sweetmeats, fresh fruit, and different kinds of sherbets. After the meal, female guests accompanied the bride to the harem and the male guests joined the groom in the *selamlik,* or the male section of the house. In each place, musicians and dancers entertained. The guests did not, however, participate in dancing and singing. Dancing was frowned upon by religious authorities, and dancing by men and women together was specifically forbidden. Once the feast had ended and the guests had departed, the groom stood up and returned to his bedchamber, which had been specially decorated with carpets and cushions. This served "as the signal for the women to gather round the bride and amid laughter and joke, push her into her husband's presence."[51] Once inside the chamber, the bridegroom lifted the bride's veil and handed her a special present, which among the rich was usually a diamond that was pinned on the hair. They then exchanged candies and drank coffee. At times, an elderly woman, who had accompanied the bride to the house of the groom, remained in the room until the couple had finished drinking their coffee. To put the bride and the groom at ease, she served the couple a small meal. This was the first meal the newlyweds shared together. After the meal, the woman helped the bride to undress.

The actual wedding ceremony was usually held on a Thursday, and it was generally believed that the best time for the marriage to be consummated was Thursday evening, as Friday was the holy day in the Islamic week. On Friday morning, the newlyweds appeared before the family, "who scrutinized them to learn whether or not their stars had met."[52] The families then feasted on *paça*, or "sheep's trotters cooked in a stew"; rice; cream; and, among the rich, "the delicacies of *borek*, sweets, *dolmas*, and *hoşaf* were also served."[53]

WEDDINGS AMONG THE POOR

Ceremonies held in various rural communities and small towns of Anatolia, the Balkans, and the Arab provinces of the Middle East were far less elaborate. At times, the entire village joined the festivities as men, women, and children cooked, danced, and listened to music. In Ottoman Iraq, the bridegroom, accompanied by an imam of the neighborhood in which he lived and a number of his friends, arrived at the house of the prospective bride and asked the girl's father formally for his daughter's hand in marriage. In the course of the visit, the amount of the *mahr* paid by the groom to the bride was discussed and settled. Once the negotiations had achieved the desired result, the accompanying imam prayed, gifts were exchanged, and the trousseau was displayed, before the marriage was formalized in a ceremony presided over by a *kadi*. While women did not give any dowries to their husbands, they brought "from their homes an abundance of household goods, which may be regarded suitable, depending on the bride's status; not just the trousseau . . ., but also clothes, gold, and silver ornaments, jewels, beasts of burden, and even male and female slaves."[54]

As with Muslims, among the Armenian Christians, boys and girls were "always promised very young," but they could not see one another until three days after their marriage.[55] The bride was carried to church wearing a crown on her head, over which fell a red silky veil that covered her all over to her feet. The priest asked the bridegroom whether he was prepared to marry the young bride, "be she deaf, be she blind."[56] When the groom responded with a "yes," the bride was led to the house of her new husband "accompanied with all the friends and relatives on both sides, singing and dancing."[57] Once she had arrived at her new home, the bride was "placed on a cushion in the corner of the sofa, but her veil was not lifted up, not even by her husband," until she had been married for three days.[58]

Among the Muslim subjects of the sultan, once the bride had arrived in her new home, she was kissed and welcomed by her husband's family. She had left her home to join them, and from that moment on, she would become part of their family, although she was expected to maintain a close relationship with her own family, particularly with her parents, brothers, and sisters. Besides their husbands, fathers and brothers were the only other males with whom a woman could converse and maintain a relationship, without violating social taboos and conventions.[59] On rare occasions, when the groom was very poor and the bride's family did not have any sons, the husband would move in with his wife's family.

The prearranged marriages characteristic of the Ottoman Empire have been criticized for a lack of respect and sensitivity toward the opinions and feelings of the young men and women who were getting married. Equally troubling to modern-day critics is the absence of love as the principal reason and cause for marital union. It is important to recognize that under the Ottoman system many marriages were, in fact, based on romantic love. In rural and nomadic communities, men and women lived and worked in close proximity, and boys who caught a glimpse of a beautiful girl could request the intercession of their mothers in arranging a marriage. On these occasions, the mother of the boy initiated the process by convincing her husband that the marriage between the lovebirds would be a wise move. Once she had secured his approval, negotiations could begin in earnest with the family of the prospective bride.

At times, the mother's intercession failed, or even if the family of the boy approved, the girl might come from a family that demanded a large sum toward the payment of the bride settlement. On these occasions, when faced with parental disapproval or lack of sufficient funds to pay the *mehr*, bride stealing (*kiz kaçirma*) provided an alternative of sorts.[60] The general custom among Muslim communities in Anatolia was that a man who had seduced and stolen a virgin was obligated to marry her, because a man and a woman who had spent a night together had inevitably engaged in sexual intercourse. The standard procedure was to abduct the girl and leave her with a relative overnight. Though no sexual intercourse had taken place, the act was sufficient to force parents on both sides to agree to marriage. The danger in stealing the girl lay in the retaliation that could potentially come from her father and brother, who, in protecting their honor, might resort to violence. This possibility forced the lovers to flee the village or town and seek a hiding place where they could elope. Once children were born to such marriages, many grandparents came round and forgave their children for their youthful indiscretions.[61]

WOMEN'S LEGAL RIGHTS AFTER MARRIAGE

Ottoman jurists "viewed married couples as enjoying reciprocal, as opposed to symmetrical rights."[62] From this perspective, a husband was obliged to support his wife. He assumed full responsibility for all the expenses associated with the family home, as well as his wife's personal expenses. Accordingly then, a wife owed her husband obedience. A "husband could restrict" his wife's "freedom of movement by forbidding her to leave the house (except to visit her family) or he might insist that she accompany him on a journey."[63]

Ottoman women were viewed as full-fledged subjects of the state "as soon as they reached puberty," and they retained control over their property even after they were married.[64] Ordinary "women as well as women of the elites not only possessed moveable and immoveable property in appreciable amounts, but actively tended to their property rights."[65] They "made and dissolved contracts, sold, bequeathed, rented, leased and invested property, and they did so in substantial numbers."[66] Women could also file a complaint in front of a *kadi* at a court of law, and many appeared in person in court without an accompanying male relative. At times, rich women who had inherited land and money from their family and husbands invested in commercial ventures and became successful capitalists.[67] Indeed, court records from both early and late periods of the empire indicate that women owned flourishing businesses of considerable entrepreneurial worth. They were, however, disadvantaged by traditional beliefs and customs, which did not allow them to operate their businesses in person. Thus, female investors could not accompany the caravans in which they had invested, although they could run their business through male agents and employees. In the villages and among tribal groups of the empire, particularly in Anatolia and the Arab provinces, women played an important role in the economic life of their communities. Many, especially in villages and nomadic tribes, raised money by spinning wool or cotton and producing handicrafts.

With the introduction of capitalism in the 19th century, textile production expanded and the work of rural women assumed greater importance for businesses in search of cheap labor to produce yarn, rugs, and carpets. New textile factories in the urban centers of the empire hired Muslim and Christian women from lower classes. In the second half of the 19th and the first decade of the 20th century, the growing "participation of girls and women" was "most visible in the export industries that grew dramatically—raw silk, carpets and lace—" where they "formed a very strong majority of the knotters and probably all of the reelers and lace-makers."[68] Women also dominated "the various spinning industries, of cotton, linen and wool," with some engaged "in household spinning, weaving, knotting, embroidering and lacemaking," while others worked outside the home.[69] Aside from dominating all of the mechanized cotton-spinning and silk-reeling mills and some wool yarn plants and cloth factories, women also played an important role in other industries such as shoemaking and tobacco processing, where they received a fraction of wages obtained by men. The economic integration of women broke the old and traditional stereotypes, but the low wages and poor conditions were condemned as exploitative and inhuman.[70]

POLYGAMY

According to Islamic law, a man was entitled to four wives, while for a woman polyandry was impossible and monogamy remained the rule. In the Quran, men were told that, "you may marry other women who seem good to you: two, three, or four of them. But if you cannot maintain equality among them, marry one only or any slave-girls you may own. This will make it easier for you to avoid injustice."[71] To many Western writers, this practice, more than any other, highlighted the fundamental difference between Christian Europe and the Islamic world, and symbolized the inequality between the sexes in the Ottoman Empire and other Muslim states. Available evidence, however, indicates that, among men, monogamy was the dominant norm and that those with more than one wife constituted a minute group in the Ottoman society.[72] Saomon Schweigger, a German Protestant minister who travelled to the Ottoman Empire at the end of the 16th century, wrote: "Turks rule countries and their wives rule them. Turkish women go around and enjoy themselves much more than any others. Polygamy is absent. They must have tried it but then given it up because it leads to much trouble and expense."[73]

In the 18th century, rich and powerful families in Istanbul frowned upon men of status who married more than one wife. In some cases, the wife vehemently opposed the presence of a second woman in her husband's life and refused to allow him back into her room if he proceeded with marriage to a new wife. The news of such marital discord could spill into the public sphere and become part of everyday gossip. Many men would, therefore, avoid serious conflict within the household as well as public embarrassment and scandal by eschewing a second marriage. Protocol at court required dignitaries and high government officials to separate from former wives and concubines if they wished to marry a princess of the royal household. Lady Mary Wortley Montagu, who visited the Ottoman Empire from 1717 to 1718, wrote that although the Islamic law permitted Muslim men to marry four wives, she could find no instance "of a man of quality" who made "use of this liberty, or of a woman of rank that would suffer it."[74] Among all "the great men" at the Ottoman court, the English author could only name the imperial treasurer who kept "a number of she-slaves for his own use," and he was spoken of "as a libertine." Montagu recalled that the treasurer's wife refused to see him, though she continued "to live in his house."[75] Even when a husband established an intimate relationship with another woman, he kept his mistress in "a house apart" and visited "her as privately" as he could.[76]

By the last two decades of the 19th century, polygamy was confined to palace officials and the upper echelons of the religious establishment, but it hardly existed among the merchants and craftsmen of Ottoman society.[77] Among these latter classes, horror stories and anecdotes circulated regarding the misfortunes visited upon a family when a married man decided to take a second wife. In her memoirs, the Turkish writer Halidé Edib, who had grown up in Istanbul during the reign of Abdülhamid II (1876–1909), recounted the story of a rich and successful Ottoman merchant who "married for the second time the widowed wife of his brother," claiming that his act was out of sympathy and kindness.[78] Edib wrote that since polygamy was "rare in the families who had no slaves," this development "brought bad luck to the household."[79] Their "house was burnt down soon after in one of the big fires in Istanbul," and the wealthy merchant lost his money as well.[80] Blaming himself for his family's trials and tribulations, the man divorced his second wife and begged for forgiveness from his first wife, confessing "that all his domestic calamity was due to having made her suffer."[81]

Muslim men could marry Jewish or Christian women, provided that the man allowed his non-Muslim wife to retain her religion and attend religious services required by her faith.[82] The children of a mixed marriage were considered Muslims. A non-Muslim wife could not inherit from her Muslim husband, nor could the husband inherit from his wife.[83] Muslim women could not marry non-Muslim men. Even after the Republic of Turkey removed the prohibition of marriage between a Muslim woman and a non-Muslim man, customs strongly urged the bridegroom's conversion to Islam. Christian and Jewish men married within their respective communities. In sharp contrast to Muslim men, they could not maintain concubines, whether the woman was a Muslim, a Christian, or a Jew. If a non-Muslim man was found with a concubine, the religious judge forced him to marry her. In the Ottoman Empire, Christian women from one denomination could marry men from another Christian community. They could even marry Christian men from a European country with the consent of their parents.

NOTES

1. Justin McCarthy, *The Ottoman Turks: An Introductory History to 1923* (London, New York: Wesley Longman Limited, 1997), 262.

2. Ibid.

3. Madeline C. Zilfi, "Muslim Women in the Early Modern Era," in *The Cambridge History of Turkey: Byzantium to Turkey 1071–1453*, 4 vols. (Cambridge: Cambridge University Press, 2009), 3:232.

4. Ibid.

5. McCarthy, *The Ottoman Turks*, 262.

6. Ibid.

7. Zilfi, "Muslim Women in the Early Modern Era," 232.

8. Ibid.

9. Ibid.

10. Ibid.

11. Suraiya Faroqhi, *Subjects of the Sultan: Culture and Daily Life in the Ottoman Empire* (New York: I. B. Tauris, 2007),102.

12. Edward William Lane, *An Account of the Manners and Customs of the Modern Egyptians* (New York: Dover Publications, 1973), 156.

13. McCarthy, *The Ottoman Turks*, 263.

14. Fanny Davis, *The Ottoman Lady, A Social History from 1718 to 1918* (New York: Greenwood Press, 1986), 62.

15. Ibid.

16. Ibid.

17. Raphaela Lewis, *Everyday Life in Ottoman Turkey* (London: B. T. Batsford Ltd., 1971), 100.

18. Davis, *The Ottoman Lady*, 64.

19. Lewis, *Everyday Life in Ottoman Turkey*, 100.

20. Ilber Ortayli, "Family," in *Encyclopedia of the Ottoman Empire*, eds. Gábor Ágoston and Bruce Masters (New York: Facts On File, 2009), 213. *Namzad* is a Persian word, which has been used as an equivalent for the word fiancé in English.

21. Ibid.

22. Ibid.

23. Lewis, *Everyday Life in Ottoman Turkey*, 100.

24. McCarthy, *The Ottoman Turks*, 263.

25. Ibid., 264.

26. Ibid.

27. Davis, *The Ottoman Lady*, 66.

28. Ibid.

29. Ibid.

30. Ortayli, "Family," 213.

31. Davis, *The Ottoman Lady*, 67–68.

32. Ibid.

33. Richard Davey, *The Sultan and His Subjects*, 2 vols. (London: Chapman and Hall LD., 1897), 2:307.

34. Lady Mary Wortley Montagu, *The Turkish Embassy Letters* (London: Virago Press, 2007), 134–35.

35. Ibid., 135.

36. Ibid.

37. Ibid.

38. Davis, *The Ottoman Lady*, 70.

39. Ibid.

40. Montagu, *The Turkish Embassy Letters*, 135.

41. Ibid.

42. Davis, *The Ottoman Lady*, 71.

43. Ibid., 74.

44. Ibid.

45. Ibid.; Davis, *The Social Life of the Ottomans*, 422.

46. Ibid.

47. Ibid.

48. Davey, *The Sultan and His Subjects*, 1:231.

49. Faroqhi, *Subjects of the Sultan*, 182.

50. Evliya Çelebi, *Evliya Çelebi in Albania*, trans. Robert Dankoff and Robert Elsie (Leiden: Brill, 2000), 89.

51. Metin And, "The Social Life of the Ottomans in the Sixteenth Century," in *Ottoman Civilization*, eds. Halil Inalcik and Günsel Renda, 2 vols.

(Istanbul: Republic of Turkey Ministry of Culture Publications, 2003), 1:424.

52. Davis, *The Ottoman Lady*, 76.

53. Ibid.

54. Pietro Della Valle, *The Pilgrim: The Journeys of Pietro Della Valle*, trans. George Bull (London: The Folio Society, 1989), 111–12.

55. Montagu, *The Turkish Embassy Letters*, 139.

56. Ibid.

57. Ibid.

58. Ibid.

59. McCarthy, *The Ottoman Turks*, 264.

60. Ibid.

61. Ibid.

62. Judith E. Tucker, "Law and Gender," in *Encyclopedia of the Ottoman Empire*, 325.

63. Ibid.

64. Faroqhi, *Subjects of the Sultan*, 101.

65. Zilfi, "Muslim Women in the Early Modern Era," 238.

66. Ibid.

67. McCarthy, *The Ottoman Turks*, 275.

68. Donald Quataert, *Ottoman Manufacturing in the Age of the Industrial Revolution* (Cambridge: Cambridge University Press, 2002), 174.

69. Ibid.

70. McCarthy, *The Ottoman Turks*, 275.

71. Quran, Women, 4:1.

72. Faroqhi, *Subjects of the Sultan*, 102.

73. Ortayli, "Family," 212.

74. Montagu, *The Turkish Embassy Letters*, 72.

75. Ibid.

76. Ibid.

77. Faroqhi, *Subjects of the Sultan*, 103.

78. Halidé Adivar Edib, *Memoirs of Halidé Edib* (New York: Gorgias Press, 2004), 41.

79. Ibid.

80. Ibid.

81. Ibid., 42.

82. And, "The Social Life of the Ottomans," 422.

83. Faroqhi, *Subjects of the Sultan*, 102, 302.

10

SEX AND FAMILY

Islamic law "assigned men and women distinct social roles, and made many rights and obligations contingent upon gender identity."[1] Along "with distinctions between free and slave, and between Muslim and non-Muslim, gender difference was one of the most significant distinctions of the Islamic legal system in the Ottoman Empire."[2]

The "proper sphere" of Muslim women as articulated by classical authorities such as Ghazali was "in domestic and sexual terms."[3] According to Ghazali, the principal function of women was to obey male authority and take care of the household and satisfy their husbands' sexual desires. In the 16th century, Ottoman ulema who used Ghazali as their source and model declared that "women's obligations" were "to bake bread, clean up the dishes, do the laundry, prepare meals and the like."[4] These responsibilities to one's home were "a matter of heaven and hell for a woman" for if she failed to perform these tasks, she would be "a sinner."[5] Screened from the gaze of the outsider, decent, obedient, and pious Muslim women had to attend to the everyday needs of their husbands and children without any reservation.[6]

In Islam, marital sex was viewed as part and parcel of a believer's obligation toward God and in no way connoted sin for the Muslim believer. While heterosexuality and marriage were praised as natural, normal, and indeed necessary, the official Islam of the ulema was "violently opposed to all other ways of realizing sexual desires," which were denounced as abnormal, unnatural, and running "counter to the antithetical harmony of the sexes."[7] The curse of God rested on "the boyish woman and effeminate man, male and female homophilia, auto-eroticism, zoophilia etc."[8] By rejecting the principle of the natural male-female relationship, all these "deviations" constituted a revolt against God and the divine scriptures. Among all these ungodly deviations, the Quran regarded "male homosexuality the worst," because it was "the essence of all perversions."[9] The story of "Lot (Lut) and his city, Sodom, destroyed by God for the sexual sins of its people," was interpreted as the ultimate warning against a deviation that could lead to the end and destruction of the human family.[10] And yet, in Ottoman society male erotic attraction to males was assumed to be natural and, if not universal, sufficiently widespread to be tolerated.

The Ottoman concept of sexuality was based on the traditional medical notion that human body comprised four basic elements, namely, air, fire, earth, and water.[11] In this conception, "man and woman were virtually the same being, differing in the balance between the elements and in the degree of development."[12] Rather than "a separate sex," women were viewed "as an imperfect version of men, a form that did not reach its full development."[13] The "vagina, clitoris, and uterus were assumed to be an underdeveloped version of the male penis and scrotum, and women were believed to be able to produce semen in their ovaries and thus contribute to the creation of the fetus."[14] Because this view "of the body implied that men and women were not inherently different sexually, present-day concepts of same-sex intercourse as radically different from heterosexual intercourse were not part of the Ottoman culture."[15] Thus, "while homosexual acts were forbidden by law, as were other forms of sexual activity such as incest and fornication, same-sex intercourse was not perceived as fundamentally unnatural and abnormal."[16] Indeed, "in most circles, same-sex love and intercourse (mainly, but not exclusively, between older and younger men) were perceived as more proper."[17] Female "same-sex intercourse was known and sometimes mentioned, but largely ignored by the men responsible for almost all writing in the empire until well into the 19th century."[18] The "general preference for homoerotic ties was present most prominently in mystical Sufi circles" as "love between an initiate and a young disciple, often referred to as 'gazing upon an unbearded youth.'"[19] By "gazing upon

the beauty" of an unbearded boy (*amrad*), "the Sufi would fill his
heart with the attributes of God's splendor and learn the virtues of
unconditional love."[20]

PROSTITUTION

In addition to young beardless boys, female prostitutes provided
another important outlet for male sexual energy. As in other societies, "traffic in sexual pleasure" was widespread in the Ottoman
Empire "since its early days, and edicts and *fetvas* were published
frequently to try to contain what authorities viewed as a problem
for moral order and public health."[21] During the 16th century, the
central government tried several times to clamp down on prostitution by expelling prostitutes from Istanbul, Damascus, and
other major urban centers of the empire, "and in a famous edict
they were forbidden to follow the army as it marched to and from
the front."[22] Even in state regulations, "procurers were warned
against the use of slave girls as prostitutes in hostels around the
empire."[23]

The practice of punishing prostitutes by banishing them from
towns, and at times, even hanging them at the entrance to city markets, continued into the 17th century. While such harsh punishments
were hailed by the members of the elite who could support several
wives and female slaves, they were opposed by the poor who could
only afford cheap and publically available sex. In his *Book of Travels*,
the Ottoman writer Evliya Çelebi proudly reported that in 1652,
his patron, Melek Ahmed Paşa, who at the time served as the governor of Rumelia, banished all of the prostitutes from Sofia, Bulgaria.[24] In accordance with Islamic law and "for the reform of the
world," a few of these prostitutes "were strung up like chandeliers
to adorn the town at the street corners in the silk market."[25] To
demonstrate the popularity of his patron's act, Çelebi added that
"the notables of the province were grateful that their town was now
tranquil and free of prostitutes," but he had to admit that "for
the sake of their carnal pleasures," the local "rogues and brigands
bruited it about that the town's resources had grown scarce, and
there would now be famine and dearth, even plague."[26] And indeed,
the plague they had predicted did begin, devastating the town and
killing thousands.

Common though it may have been, prostitution in the Ottoman
Empire "was not usually practiced in formal establishments intended for the purpose."[27] The "older" and more traditional form of

prostitution portrayed in the Karagöz shadow theater was Zenne, "the lone damsel" living "in a rented house in the neighborhood and socializing with men" and symbolizing the "blurred boundaries between companionship and sexual favors."[28] It was only in the second half of the 19th century that the brothel "as a commercial enterprise" and a new space for male-female encounters emerged.[29] Indeed, throughout the 19th century, as the European urban centers of the empire grew in size and population and a "culture of public parks, cafés, beer gardens, and dance halls" spread, prostitution "assumed new proportions" and emerged as a "major industry."[30]

In 1879 in Salonika, local journalists "denounced the 'depraved women' who haunted the city's beer-halls, and demanded they be driven away," and a year later, "Christian, Jewish and Muslim community leaders protested to the municipality at their presence in the heart of the city," but by 1910, "girls of all races and religions were working its more than one hundred brothels in a separate quarter near the railway" and "neither the rabbis nor the other notables of the city seemed very concerned about the problem."[31] According to one source, there were three types of prostitutes: "the woman who had her own room, the woman who went to the room of her client, and those who consorted in the open because woman and client were both too poor to rent rooms."[32] This last category "included youths from villages who had saved up in order to walk many kilometers to the town for no other reason than sex."[33]

In addition to the brothel, the second half of the 19th century witnessed the emergence of a new phenomenon in Ottoman society, namely, the practice of keeping a mistress or the woman who lived in a clandestine apartment and served the unique sentimental and sexual needs of her lover.[34] Traditional Ottoman society had developed its own unique outlets for males who wished to have extramarital sex. In accordance with the Islamic law, "men could marry several women; richer men could own slaves and exploit them sexually; many public baths also functioned as meeting places for same-sex encounters," but as "slavery declined in the 19th century and polygamy was frowned on in certain urban circles," the new institution of mistress "often called *metres* (from French *maitresse*)" appeared and took over from Zenne, the neighborhood's "lone damsel."[35] The brothels of "the fashionable streets of Pera, Istanbul's urban center, were now in need of new venues for extramarital and premarital encounters of the modern kind."[36] According to the Islamic law, the punishment for an adulteress was death by stoning. Various schools of Islamic jurisprudence, however, introduced provisos, which made inflicting such harsh punishment in effect impossible. That "adultery had in fact been committed had to be proved through the testimony of at least four male witnesses, and a woman accused by her husband of adultery could evade punishment by denying the allegation and basing her denial on a solemn oath."[37] This "particular ruling was commonly adhered to in Ottoman jurisdiction where *kadis* generally refrained from deciding that adultery had been formally proven."[38] When residents of a neighborhood surprised a couple engaged in intercourse, "the verdict would usually be one of 'alleged adultery' and a prison term and/or condemnation to the galleys would be imposed."[39] Women "who bore illegitimate children or cohabited out of wedlock," however, "were never regarded with tolerance, and urban security officers were empowered to keep an eye on them," or place them in the custody of the local police.[40] To reduce the potential for extramarital relationships, every effort was made to "keep unmarried men out of residential districts."[41]

GIVING BIRTH

Among the Ottoman elite, astrologers and diviners were asked to take the woman's horoscope and determine whether she should get pregnant and if so, when. At times, they warned the wife against pregnancy by predicting that she would suffer and that in the end she would die in the childbirth. Sometimes, such warnings alarmed and frightened the wife to the point that she would not allow her husband to approach her. Regardless, the news of a woman's pregnancy was welcomed with joy and a great deal of trepidation. In rich and powerful households, the servants celebrated the news of a pregnancy because whenever the lady of the house gave birth, she distributed money and gifts to the members of her household.

Highly skilled midwives were indispensable to childbirth. Women who had acquired considerable experience and skill in delivering children were greatly respected at all levels of Ottoman society. Many families had their own favorite midwife, in whom they had developed enormous confidence. When the woman's labor had reached the final stage, the midwife sat her on a chair with side arms, a high back, and "a seat scooped out to facilitate the delivery of the child."[42] Just prior to the appearance of the child's head, the midwife uttered the *tekbir*, or "God is great."[43] With the arrival of the child, the midwife and all the women present proclaimed the *şehadet*: "I bear witness that there is no god but God, I bear witness that Muhammad is the messenger of God."[44] Then the midwife washed the newborn in warm water and cut the umbilical cord.

To protect the mother from evil eye, a copy of the Quran, which had been installed in an embroidered bag, was placed at the head of the couch. At its foot hung "an onion impaled on a skewer, wrapped in red muslin and ornamented with garlic and blue beads."[45] When the mother had been dressed up, her husband came to visit his wife and the new baby. He held the child toward Mecca and uttered the Muslim's declaration of faith in his right ear: "I bear witness that there is no god but God. I bear witness that Muhammad is the messenger of God."[46] He then chanted the *bismillah* ("In the name of God") in the baby's left ear and three times announced the child's name. Shortly after a successful delivery, and sometimes the day after the baby was born, a messenger bearing the good news visited the homes of relatives and friends. At each home, he was rewarded with a tip.

Childbirth in the Ottoman Empire could be extremely dangerous—even when the woman giving birth was a member of the Ottoman ruling family. In his writings, the Ottoman traveler Evliya Çelebi described the pregnancy of Kaya Sultan, the daughter of Sultan Murad IV, who was married to Evliya's patron, Melek Ahmed Paşa. As the time for delivery arrived, close female relatives and friends, and all the experienced women and skilled midwives, arrived. Forty Quran recitals and 4,000 invocations of the prophet Muhammad were recited, and after she had given birth to a daughter, her husband gave away 10 purses of his own and 40 purses of Kaya Sultan's money to the poor and the needy, as alms and a sincere expression of gratitude. Melek Ahmed Paşa also "clothed 500 men in all sorts of garments and they responded by showering him with benedictions."[47] But as Çelebi had to admit, God did not answer these prayers and "the placenta," which was "supposed to come down the uterus and exit the mother's womb as the afterbirth," remained "stuck in the womb."[48] The women and the midwives placed the Kaya Sultan "in blankets and shook her mercilessly."[49] Twice "they suspended her upside down," and they "filled a honey barrel with orange-flower water and put her inside."[50] To make a long and sad story short, the women "tortured" Kaya Sultan "for three days and nights" without finding a remedy.[51] Finally, "the bloody midwives came with their arms smeared in almond oil and stuck their oily arms up into the sultana's uterus all the way to their elbows" and "brought out a piece of skin."[52] But they were not willing to release their patient. One midwife insisted that there was still some skin left inside and "stuck her hand up the vagina and brought out several items that looked like pieces of wet skin."[53] At last, four days after giving birth to a girl, the princess died.

If the delivery moved along without any complications and if the mother was well enough to receive guests, a reception was organized following the birth. Female relatives and friends were invited to visit the mother and the baby. Every guest arrived knowing that, according to the prevailing custom, she could not admire the baby or praise his/her beauty and vigor, as this could invoke the evil eye and undermine the fragile health of the newborn. In fact, the guests tried to ignore the baby, who lay on a cushion of embroidered satin, or called him/her "an ugly thing," although they often brought charms, cookies, and candies, as well as gold and silver pieces for the infant.

During the reception, the attention of the guests was focused primarily on the mother. Coffee, sherbets, and sweetmeats were served, while women played a variety of musical instruments and sang happy songs. When the reception ended and the guests departed, the midwife "fumigated the room against an evil eye they might have brought in by throwing into the brazier a clove for each guest," and if "one of the cloves exploded, that meant the evil eye was indeed present."[54] At times, to exorcise the house, the midwife threw into the brazier "a strand of the mother's hair and a piece of the child's (if it had any) and, if it could be secured, a scrap of the clothing of the person suspected."[55] While these were burning, she prayed and recited incantations.

The mother rested for nearly a week. During this period, she could not drink water but only sherbets. At the end of the seventh day, the family read to the child the *Mevlüd,* or the poem celebrating the birth of the prophet Muhammad. The mother's bed was removed, and the baby's maternal grandmother delivered a wooden cradle. A urinal was also provided, "which consisted of a tube that led from between the baby's legs to a receptacle."[56] Now, the life of a normal infant began with the mother gently singing lullabies. Attendants and servants (if the woman was from a wealthy family) burned incense day and night to ward off the evil eye.

As late as the second half of the 19th century, Turks believed that a woman who had given birth to a child was "dangerously exposed" to evil spirits for 40 days, and it was, therefore, "not safe for her to be left alone for a moment."[57] If the woman "was poor and had no servants a neighbor would come in to stay in her room and would leave a broom behind the door if called out in an emergency;" the broom kept the evil spirits away.[58] To ensure the health of the mother and protect her from dangerous spirits, a copy of the Quran was placed on her pillow. Additionally, she wore a red ribbon on her hair, and every evening, incense was "burned beside her to keep the evil ones at a distance."[59] After 40 days, during which she had been watched over by a midwife, female relatives, and friends, as well as servants and attendants, the woman left her home for a public bathhouse. On her walk to the bathhouse, the new mother was accompanied by her own mother, female relatives, numerous friends, and the midwife, who carried the baby in her arms. Once at the bathhouse, the mother was washed and bathed. When she had finished the mother's bath, the midwife began to work on the child. Then she soaped and rinsed the baby.

During various intervals gypsies danced, and sweetmeats, sherbets, and coffee were served. At times, the celebrations and festivities at the bathhouse took up an entire day. As the members of the ruling class built homes, which included private bathhouses, the women of the upper classes invited their relatives and friends to their home to celebrate the 40th-day bath.

ROYAL BIRTHS

At the imperial palace, the ceremonies surrounding the birth of a prince or a princess followed many of the same customs and ceremonies that were organized among the ordinary subjects of the sultan. The women of the royal family had their own trusted midwives who were called in when a pregnant wife of the sultan went into labor. As with the women outside the palace, the mother was seated on a couch that, unlike the couch of lower classes, "was draped in red satin embroidered in rubies, emeralds, and pearls."[60]

Three cradles were presented to the mother and her newly born child as gifts. The first came from the mother of the sultan, the second from the grand vizier, and the third was presented by the chamberlain of the imperial treasury. A procession delivered each cradle to the royal harem. With each cradle, the sender attached numerous gifts. For example, the cradle sent by the mother of the sultan was accompanied by "a handsome quilt and an embroidered coverlet," while the cradle presented by the grand vizier carried jewels and, "if the child was a boy," "an aigrette."[61] The cradles and the gifts were presented to the *ağa* of the house of felicity who presented them to the sultan before carrying them into the imperial harem. The men who carried the cradles and gifts in each procession received robes of honor, and even gifts if they were deemed to be appropriate.

The day the child was born, an imperial notice was issued for the public to celebrate the arrival of a new member of the house of Osman. The next day, the grand vizier and other high dignitaries, such as the *şeyhülislam* and the chief of scribes, arrived at the imperial palace to congratulate the sultan. They were all rewarded with robes of honor by their royal master. Meanwhile, the women of the royal palace and the wives of high government officials were invited to the harem. The first group lived in the palace and had no need for transportation. The second group of invitees, who did not reside in the imperial harem, assembled at the home of the grand vizier and from there were taken to the palace by horse-drawn carriages. Once in the harem, the women greeted the lady who had given birth to a new member of the royal family and kissed the coverlet on her bed. They also presented her and the baby, who was held by a wet nurse, with gifts. Sumptuous meals, including sweetmeats and coffee, were served, while musicians played and singers performed to entertain the guests, who sometimes stayed at the harem for several days.

CHILD REARING

A distinguishing trait of the Ottoman popular culture was strong paternal affection and love for children. As one European visitor observed, nothing could be more beautiful than the tenderness of a Turkish father; he hailed "every demonstration of dawning intellect, every proof of infant affection, with a delight that must be witnessed to be thoroughly understood."[62] The father anticipated "every want," he gratified "every wish," and he sacrificed "his own personal comfort to ensure that of his child."[63]

There were many different child-rearing traditions across the Ottoman Empire. After wrapping and swaddling the newborn, and without allowing it to drink the mother's milk, the Abkhazians sent their children to foster mothers, and their parents could not visit them until they were 10 or 15 years old.[64] They believed that if the child suffered homelessness he would become a man.[65] Turkish women, however, generally suckled their own infants and refused to hand them over to a wet nurse; they believed that the attention, care, and love of the child's own mother was the best nourishment for an infant. Children were not merely brought up by their parents. They were the joint responsibility of both sides of the family. Children spent as much time with their grandmothers, aunts, and cousins as with their mothers. Women exchanged babysitting responsibilities with their mothers and sisters, as well as with their in-laws.

Among the Ottomans, children, and particularly male offspring, were greatly prized. The preservation and survival of the family required its reproduction; any family that did not reproduce disappeared and vanished. Among peasant farmers, economic productivity increased when more hands were available, particularly during the harvest season. Children also were needed to provide security and care for their parents when they grew old. In the absence of children, a family would come to the brink of extinction if its sole male member, the husband, were recruited by the army and taken away to a far-away war.[66] A child, and particularly a son, could guard the land and ensure its cultivation in the absence of his father. Additional sons were even better because if one son was taken to a military campaign, his brother or brothers could assume responsibility for his family and his land. Indeed, the idea of a unified family staying together, and protecting and defending its collective interests, was central to Ottoman society and culture. In the rural communities of the empire, children began to work very young and generally developed "into hardy and handsome men and women."[67]

A central feature of Ottoman family culture was the reverence displayed by children toward their parents. Special love and adoration was reserved for the mother of the family. Husbands and wives could advise and reprimand, but the mother was "an oracle"; she was "consulted, confided in, listened to with respect and deference, honored to her latest hour, and remembered with affection and regret beyond the grave."[68]

Among both rich and poor, children were taught to show the utmost respect for parents. When a young boy entered the presence of his parents and other older members of the family, he stood still and, after making proper salutations, proceeded to kiss their hands. He sat down only after he had received permission from his father. When a family decided to leave, the father stood up first, then the mother, and only lastly the children, who allowed their parents to leave first before they followed. Often, the children kissed the hem of their mother's gown and their father's robe. This sensitivity and politeness, remarked upon by numerous Western observers, continued in the relationship between a student and his teacher when he entered school. Pupils regarded their teachers as superior beings, almost as second fathers, who deserved unwavering respect and obedience. Though highly cultured and extremely polite, from the humblest to the most powerful, men and women maintained a strong sense of dignity.

CIRCUMCISION

One of the most important dates in the life of a young Muslim boy was the day he was circumcised. One European observer who lived in Istanbul at the beginning of the 17th century described the Muslim circumcision as a ceremony of the greatest significance, one which was always held with pomp and solemnity among the Ottomans.[69]

The age of a boy at circumcision varied considerably. Regardless of the boy's age, families allowed a lock of hair to grow on the crown of the boy's head until the very day of circumcision.[70] The hair hanging down the middle of the boy's back, over his uppermost jacket, was displayed in such a way as to make it visible to everyone. It served as a sign that the boy had not been circumcised and therefore could not pray with the congregation at a mosque.

On the day of circumcision, a large contingent of male relatives and family friends, on foot or horseback, accompanied the boy to a mosque where he was catechized by an imam, who asked him questions on his faith: Was he a Muslim? Did he believe in Muhammad the prophet of God? Was he willing to defend Islam? And so on. The boy then swore to defend the "true faith," be a friend of Islam and Muslims, and an enemy to the foes and enemies of religion.[71] He then returned home to be circumcised by a local barber.

While the boy was catechized in the mosque, his home was turned upside down as the family prepared a feast to follow the circumcision ceremony. They were obliged by custom and tradition to dispense unbounded hospitality in celebration of their son's coming-of-age. Parents kept an open house and entertained not only neighbors and relatives but also nearby residents. Festivities could last anywhere from one to three days, depending on the social status and the financial means of the family. Refreshments and sweetmeats were served and gifts were offered. Magicians and dancers performed, theatrical productions, such as the popular Karagöz, amused and entertained the head of the household and his guests at the *selamlik* and the women at the harem.

In sharp contrast to the general populace, who celebrated the event for a few days, the festivities surrounding the circumcision of the male members of the Ottoman royal family could last as long as several weeks. Royal circumcisions were always followed by tournaments and entertainments by a host of singers, musicians, theater groups, clowns, fire-eaters, dancers, and artists of all kinds.[72] Clothing, gold coins, underwear, and toys were given as gifts. The significance of these royal circumcisions is best demonstrated by the large number of miniature paintings that depict the circumcision of the sons of various sultans, as well as *surnames* (imperial festival books) that recorded the important events of a sultan's reign.

CLOTHING, VEILING, AND SEGREGATION

No other subject aroused more controversy and discussion among Western visitors to the Ottoman Empire than the status of women, particularly the concept of the harem and the custom of veiling. European diplomats and businessmen lamented the miserable and oppressive confinement of Ottoman women, despite having never visited a harem. The few European ladies who were invited to a Turkish harem did not find the lives of Ottoman women confined and praised their Muslim counterparts for their beauty, power, and sophistication.

As soon as a young girl had reached puberty, she donned the veil and no man could see her face and body unless it was her father, immediate male kin, and, later, her husband. She even covered her hands with gloves. To preserve her privacy and veiled status, the windows of the women's apartment opened to an inner courtyard. If there were any windows facing the street, they were barred so tightly that no outsider could see the inside of the room.

In the first half of the 18th century, ladies of the court and women of upper classes wore a pair of very full pants that reached their shoes and concealed their legs. These pants came in a variety of bright colors and were brocaded with silver flowers. Over this hung their smock with wide sleeves hanging half way down the arm and closed at the neck with a diamond button. The smock was made of fine silk edged with embroidery. The wealthy women wore

Ottoman women in the traditional clothes. Dames Turques (1863–1869). (Picture Collection, The New York Public Library, Astor, Lenox and Tilden Foundations)

a relatively tight waistcoat with very long sleeves falling back and fringed with deep gold fringe and diamond or pearl buttons. Over this they wore a caftan or a robe, exactly fitted to the shape of the body, reaching the feet "with very long straight-falling sleeves and usually made of the same stuff as the pants."[73] Over the robe was the girdle, which for the rich was made of diamonds or other precious stones, and for others was of exquisite embroidery on satin. Regardless of the material it was made of, the girdle had to be fastened "with a clasp of diamonds."[74] Over the caftan and girdle, women wore a loose robe called *cebe*, made of rich brocade and lined either with ermine or sable, was put on according to the weather. The headdress for women from wealthy families "composed of a cap called *kalpak*," which in winter was of "fine velvet embroidered with pearls or diamonds and in summer of a light shining silver stuff."[75] The cap was "fixed on one side of the head hanging a little way down with a gold tassel, and bound on either with a circle of diamonds or a rich embroidered handkerchief."[76] On "the other side of the head," the hair was laid "flat and here the ladies" were "at liberty to show their fancies, some putting flowers, others a plume of heron's feathers," but "the most general fashion" was "a large bouquet of jewels made like natural flowers; that is, the buds of pearl, the roses of different coloured rubies, the jessamines of diamonds, the jonquils of topazes, etc, so well set and enamelled 'tis hard to imagine anything of that kind so beautiful."[77] Finally for their footwear, women wore "white kid leather embroidered with gold."[78]

Women did not leave their homes before sunrise or after sunset, except during the holy month of *Ramazan,* and even then, ladies from wealthy families did not appear on the street unless they were accompanied and attended by several servants, who walked at some distance behind them. Segregation between the sexes was observed at all times. Men did not walk on the street next to their wives or mothers, and inside the house women had their meals apart from the men. Even among poor families, a curtain separated the men's quarters from the women's. On everything from steamers and ferries to streetcars, which were introduced in the 19th century, curtains designated separate compartments for women. Until the

A woman of Istanbul (1667). (Picture Collection, The New York Public Library, Astor, Lenox and Tilden Foundations)

second half of the 19th century, even Christian churches observed and respected the segregation of sexes in a house of worship.

Piety was the hallmark of a woman's life. Muslim women prayed five times a day and fasted during the month of *Ramazan*. On Fridays, many attended prayers at a mosque where they had their own section, separate from men, and, during *Ramazan,* those living in Istanbul went en masse to evening service at the majestic *Şehzade* mosque. Many women of power and prominence had their own personal prayer leaders (imams) and spiritual guides.

Going to a bathhouse was another important occasion for the women of the household. Once a week for at least four to five hours, the women of rich and powerful families set out for a nearby bathhouse, followed by a retinue of servants carrying on their heads bathing robes and towels, as well as baskets full of fruit, pastry, and perfumes their mistress was to consume during her long visit away from her home. Once inside the bathhouse, women relaxed, took off their clothes, drank coffee or sherbet, shared the latest scandal or gossip, and lay down on cushions as their slaves braided their hair. With the introduction of private baths, public hammams lost their popularity, but they never disappeared completely.

Before the arrival of capitalism and modern factories in the 19th century, a woman living in a village or a tribe played a far more important role in the economic life of her community than a wealthy woman living in a city. From working on the land and caring for animals, to spinning wool and cotton, and producing rugs and carpets, the economic function and the social role of a village woman was critical to the survival of her family and community. She was also responsible, by custom and tradition, for keeping the house tidy, preparing meals, and taking care of children.

In sharp contrast, the rich urban woman was far less critical to the economic life and survival of her husband and family. Among the rich, cooks prepared the meals, while nurses, nannies, and tutors took care of the children and their daily basic needs. This level of support provided wealthy women with ample time to enjoy themselves by going to parks for picnics, inviting female friends and relatives for coffee and sweets, and entertaining their guests with dancers and musicians. In the second half of the 19th century, a new middle class educated in European languages and Western ideas emerged. Women from these middle-class families began to attend schools where they studied foreign languages, European history, modern ideas, and philosophies. It was from the ranks of this new class of educated women that a new generation of female business leaders, parliamentarians, and scholars emerged.[79]

DIVORCE

Divorces were prevalent in Ottoman society, and men could divorce their wives without any explanation or justification.[80] In numerous instances, women also filed for divorce. There were three types of divorce. The first was *talaq*, which allowed a man to "divorce his wife unilaterally and without going to court simply by pronouncing a formula of divorce."[81] The Muslim women in the Ottoman Empire could not use *talaq* to divorce their husband, but they had the right "to obtain a court-ordered divorce (*tafriq*)."[82] A "woman could also negotiate a divorce known as *khul* with her husband by agreeing to forego payment of balance of her dower or by absolving him of other financial responsibilities."[83] Affluent women seeking divorce paid an additional sum of money to secure their husband's consent to divorce. Unless "the *khul* divorce specified otherwise, a woman gained certain entitlements upon divorce."[84] She could "receive any balance owed on her dower, and material support for three months following the divorce."[85] Payment of alimony was "decided by the court on the woman's application, not only in cases of formal divorce but also in instances of abandonment or if the husband failed to provide for his family."[86] Additionally, "any underage children born of the marriage were entitled to full financial support from their father."[87] At the time of divorce, it was unlawful for husbands to take from their wives anything they had given them, including gifts before marriage and during the wedding ceremony.

The wife was entitled to divorce her husband and seek another man if she was not satisfied with the house to which her husband had taken her. She could also file for divorce if the marriage remained unconsummated, if the husband was impotent or mentally unstable, or if he had committed sodomy or intended intercourse in ways that were viewed as abnormal, or if he had forced her to drink wine against her wishes. Other legitimate causes for divorce were "incompatibility, ill treatment, including physical abuse by the husband, financial problems that led to altercations between spouses, adultery, failure of one or both parties to keep to the basic expectations of marriage, especially not doing the work the family needed from either husband or wife," and the inability of the wife to produce sons who "were greatly desired and needed for financial security, to carry on the family and support the old folks."[88] Women were often blamed for not producing sons, and divorce "caused by a lack of sons was not uncommon."[89] A man without a son was justified by custom and tradition to marry another wife who would produce a son for him.

Though divorces were common in the Ottoman Empire, there were many factors that worked against them.[90] Because marriages were arranged between families and not individuals, divorces would not only impact the husband and the wife but two large and extended families, which had established personal, familial, and at times, social and financial ties. Both families had invested a great deal, both in expenses and goods, not to mention time and emotions. Poor and struggling families, who had spent a great deal to purchase household goods and build a house, could not afford losing their investment. Outside financial concerns, the impact on children and "public shame" were also important factors in preventing divorces.[91] If "a man or a woman caused a marriage to dissolve for what fellow villagers thought was a bad reason, the entire village would censure him or her, and public shame was not easy to live with in a closed society."[92]

After divorce, both men and women were free to marry again. In the Quran, divorced women were commanded to wait "three menstrual courses" before they could marry again.[93] Very few divorced individuals remained unmarried, and though women were required to wait 100 days before remarrying, this rule "was routinely broken" and remarriage came shortly after divorce.[94] If a man divorced his wife, he could not remarry her until she had wedded another man and been divorced by him. In case of a second marriage between the same individuals, the husband was obligated to promise the payment of *mehr*.

NOTES

1. Judith E. Tucker, "Law and Gender," in *Encyclopedia of the Ottoman Empire*, eds. Gábor Ágoston and Bruce Masters (New York: Facts On File, 2009), 325.

2. Ibid.

3. Madeline C. Zilfi, "Muslim Women in the Early Modern Era," in *The Cambridge History of Turkey: Byzantium to Turkey 1071–1453*, 4 vols. (Cambridge: Cambridge University Press, 2009), 227.

4. Ibid.

5. Ibid.

6. Ibid., 227–28.

7. Dror Zéevi, *Producing Desire: Changing Sexual Discourse in the Ottoman Middle East, 1500–1900* (Berkeley: University of California Press, 2006), 4.

8. Abdelwahab Bouhdiba, *Sexuality in Islam* (London: Routledge and Kegan Paul, 1986), 30, as quoted in Zéevi, *Producing Desire,* 4.

9. Ibid.

10. Ibid.

11. Dror Zéevi, "Sex and Sexuality," in *Encyclopedia of the Ottoman Empire,* eds. Gábor Ágoston and Bruce Masters (New York: Facts On File, 2009), 523.

12. Ibid.

13. Ibid.

14. Ibid.

15. Ibid.

16. Ibid.

17. Ibid.

18. Ibid.

19. Ibid.

20. Ibid.

21. Mark Mazower, *Salonica: City of Ghosts, Christians, Muslims, and Jews* (New York: Random House, 2006), 364; Zéevi, *Producing Desire,* 147.

22. Zéevi, *Producing Desire,* 147.

23. Ibid.

24. Çelebi, *The Intimate Life of an Ottoman Statesman,* trans., Robert Dankoff (Albany: State University of New York Press, 1991), 99.

25. Ibid.

26. Ibid.

27. Zéevi, *Producing Desire,* 147.

28. Ibid.

29. Ibid.

30. Mazower, *Salonica,* 268.

31. Ibid.

32. Godfrey Goodwin, *The Private World of Ottoman Women* (London: Saqi Books, 2006), 98.

33. Ibid.

34. Zéevi, *Producing Desire,* 148.

35. Ibid.

36. Ibid.

37. Ilber Ortayli, "Family," in *Encyclopedia of the Ottoman Empire,* eds. Gábor Ágoston and Bruce Masters (New York: Facts On File, 2009), 213–14.

38. Ibid., 214.

39. Ibid.

40. Ibid.

41. Ibid.

42. Davis, *The Ottoman Lady,* 33.

43. Ibid.

44. Ibid.

45. Ibid., 34.

46. Ibid.

47. Çelebi, *The Intimate Life of an Ottoman Statesman*, 231.

48. Ibid.

49. Ibid.

50. Ibid.

51. Ibid.

52. Ibid.

53. Ibid.

54. Davis, *The Ottoman Lady*, 35.

55. Ibid.

56. Ibid., 36.

57. Halidé Adivar Edib, *Memoirs of Halidé Edib* (New York: Gorgias Press, 2004), 42.

58. Ibid.

59. Ibid.

60. Davis, *The Ottoman Lady*, 35, 38.

61. Ibid., 38–39.

62. Julia Pardoe, *The City of the Sultan and Domestic Manners of the Turks in 1836*, 3 vols. (London: Henry Colburn Publisher, 1838), 1:92.

63. Ibid.

64. Çelebi, *The Intimate Life of an Ottoman Statesman*, 273.

65. Ibid., 272.

66. Justin McCarthy, *The Ottoman Turks: An Introductory History to 1923* (London, New York: Wesley Longman Limited, 1997), 261.

67. Richard Davey, *The Sultan and His Subjects*, 2 vols. (London: Chapman and Hall LD., 1897), 1:238.

68. Pardoe, *The City of the Sultan*, 1:93.

69. Ottaviano Bon, *The Sultan's Seraglio: An Intimate Portrait of Life at the Ottoman Court* (London: Saqi Books, 1996), 138.

70. Ibid.

71. Metin And, "The Social Life of the Ottomans, in the Sixteenth Century," in *Ottoman Civilization*, ed. Halil Inalcik and Günsel Renda, 2 vols. (Istanbul: Republic of Turkey Ministry of Culture Publications, 2003), 1:425.

72. Ibid.

73. Lady Mary Wortley Montagu, *The Turkish Embassy Letters* (London: Virago Press, 2007), 69.

74. Ibid., 70.

75. Ibid.

76. Ibid.

77. Ibid.

78. Ibid.

79. McCarthy, *The Ottoman Turks*, 274.

80. Suraiya Faroqhi, *Subjects of the Sultan: Culture and Daily Life in the Ottoman Empire* (New York: I. B. Tauris, 2007), 103.

81. Tucker, "Law and Gender," 326.

82. Ibid.

83. Ibid.

84. Ibid.

85. Ibid.

86. Ortayli, "Family," 213.

87. Tucker, "Law and Gender," 326.

88. McCarthy, *The Ottoman Turks*, 267.

89. Ibid.

90. Ibid.

91. Ibid

92. Ibid.

93. Quran, Cow, 2:228.

94. McCarthy, *The Ottoman Turks*, 267.

11

EATING, DRINKING, SMOKING, AND CELEBRATING

Preparing, serving, and eating food was of the utmost importance to the social life of every urban and rural community in the Ottoman Empire. Around "this basic element of life revolved numerous rituals of socialization, leisure and politics."[1] Consuming food "in this world was most closely associated with the family and home, for there was no such thing as a culture of restaurants and dining out was rare."[2] When a person ate outside his/her home, "it was usually in the home of a friend or family member."[3]

Ottoman cuisine synthesized a wealth of cooking traditions. The ancestor of the Turks who "migrated from the Altay mountains in Central Asia towards Anatolia encountered different culinary traditions and assimilated many of their features into their own cuisine."[4] As they conquered and settled in Asia Minor and the Balkans, they left a marked impact on the cuisine of the peoples and societies they conquered. Their own daily diet, in turn, was greatly influenced by the culinary traditions of the peoples they came to rule, such as the Greeks, Armenians, Arabs, and Kurds. Indeed, the wide and diverse variety of Ottoman cuisine can be traced back "to the extraordinary melting pot of nationalities that peopled the Ottoman Empire."[5]

Strong elements of Persian cuisine had already influenced Turkish culinary practices during the reign of the Seljuk state.[6] Dishes

Eating house, 1809. Anonymous. (V&A Images, London / Art Resource, NY)

"based on wheat and mutton" were introduced after the Turks settled in Anatolia and seafood dishes were adopted as part of the daily meal after they reached the Aegean and Mediterranean littoral.[7] Anatolia's own ancient culinary heritage "had been built up by scores of civilizations over a period of thousands of years, ranging from the Hittites to the Roman and Byzantine empires. The region was also "blessed with an exceptionally rich fauna and flora, of which many spices found their way into the kitchen."[8] Given this rich diversity of culinary influences, it is not surprising that many words used in Ottoman cooking and cuisine were borrowed from cultures with whom the Turks had come into contact. Thus, *meze, çorba, hoşaf, reçel*, and *pilaf* came "from Persian," while *barbunya pilakisi* from Italian, "*fasulye* from Greek," "*manti* from Chinese or Korean and *muhallebi* from Arabic."[9] Starting in the 19th century, as the Ottoman society "sought renewal in westernization," west European culinary practices and traditions, particularly French cuisine, "made their own impact on the Turkish kitchen."[10] This "unequalled diversity," should not, however, distract us from the rich culinary contributions and creativity of the Ottomans.[11] The Ottomans introduced rice, sesame seeds, and maize to the Middle East and the Balkans in the 15th and 16th centuries. New plants from the New World, such as tomatoes, peppers, and maize, were also introduced to southeastern Europe and the Middle East through the Ottomans.

The diverse climate zones of the Ottoman Empire "resulted in the development of regional specialties."[12] Thus, "the damp climate on the eastern Black Sea coast meant that wheat could not be cultivated there," and so maize "became the principal grain crop," while in "south Anatolia the specialty was cattle-breeding, and the meat was cooked in the form of mouth-watering kebabs," and "on the Aegean coast, the main influence was Mediterranean cooking, and even today the menu there is dominated by vegetables, fish and olive oil."[13]

As with their political and administrative practices, the Ottomans managed to assimilate the best of the culinary traditions they encountered and merge them with their own cooking customs and practices in such a way as to bring about the enrichment of their own cuisine. In this fashion, Albanian liver (*Arnavut cigeri*), Circassian chicken (*Çerkes tavuğu*), Kurdish meatballs (*Kürt köftesi*), and Arab meatballs (*Arap köftesi*), were assimilated into the Ottoman Turkish cuisine, while kebabs, pilafs, *böreks, dolmas* (stuffed grape leaves), yogurt meals, biscuits, meals with olive oil, and syrupy desserts were introduced by the Turks to the countries they conquered.[14] It is not surprising, therefore, that the rich culinary legacy of the Ottomans still appears in Mediterranean cuisine from the Balkans to the Arab world.[15] Indeed, six centuries of Ottoman rule left a profound influence on the culinary culture of all countries of southeast Europe, the Middle East, and North Africa. Even today, "many of the dishes produced in the different nations that once composed the empire have the same name, usually a local variation of a Turkish word."[16] The "pastry known as baklava, for instance, is made in Serbia with apples and layered thin sheets of pastry dough, while that of Greece is made with honey and walnuts and that of Syria, pronounced locally as *baqlava*, is made with sugar-water syrup and pistachios."[17] These "similarities point to the existence of a court cuisine that emanated from the capital in Istanbul, and was carried to the provincial centers by the officials assigned there who wished to represent the imperial style in their own localities."[18]

DAILY COOKING AT THE PALACE

Beginning in the reign of Murad II (1421–1444, 1446–1451), the Ottoman sultans "laid increasing emphasis on culinary creativity."[19]

By the second half of the 15th century, Ottoman cuisine in all its intricacy was revealed in the dishes served at the imperial palace and in the great banquets that the grand vizier organized in honor of foreign ambassadors, dignitaries, and vassal princes. Cooking the food of the sultan was one of the most important daily responsibilities of the palace and the imperial kitchen, which served over 12,000 members of the harem, the court, and the imperial council. Every day "200 sheep, 100 kids, 10 calves, 50 geese, 200 hens, 100 chickens, and 200 pigeons were slaughtered" to feed the sultan, his harem, palace eunuchs, servants and pages, as well as army officers and government officials who worked at the palace.[20] The entire process was of such importance that "the titles of the *janissary* officers were drawn from the camp kitchen such as 'first maker of soup' and 'first cook,'" and "the sacred object of the regiment was the stew pot around which the soldiers gathered to eat and take counsel."[21] The large area designated for the palace kitchen at Topkapi indicated the central importance of food to Ottoman rulers and officials. The "large building in which the kitchens were housed boasted no less than ten domes, beneath which meals were prepared for the occupants of the palace; those for the sultan and his mother, however, were cooked in a separate kitchen."[22]

Starting with the reign of Mehmed II, the conqueror of Constantinople, the sultan "laid down the rules for food preparation," and the royal kitchen was divided into four main sections: the sultan's kitchen; "the sovereign kitchen (responsible for the food of his mother, the princes, and privileged members of the harem); the harem kitchen; and a kitchen for the palace household."[23] Soon, an army of bakers, pastry makers, yogurt makers, and pickle makers joined the staff of the imperial kitchen to bake high-quality breads and specialized desserts. By the beginning of the 17th century, "more than 1,300 cooks and kitchen hands were employed at the palace" with each having developed "his own specialty, inspired by the recipes from his home region—the Balkans, Greece, Arabia," and other regions of the empire.[24] The palace chefs excelled themselves on all important celebrations and festivals. One chronicler in the mid-16th century recorded the list of ingredients for the 13-day feast celebrating the circumcision of a prince: "1,100 chickens, 900 lambs, 2,600 sheep, almost 8,000 kg of honey, and 18,000 eggs."[25]

Food items for the imperial kitchen came from the four corners of the empire. As late as the 18th century, the Black Sea served as "the Nursing Mother" of Istanbul, providing the Ottoman capital "with all necessities and food stuffs such as Grain, Barley, Millet, Salt, cattle, Sheep on the hoof, Lambs, Hens, Eggs, fresh Apples and other Fruits, Butter, . . . Caviar, Fish, and Honey," which the Turks used "as sugar."[26] Egypt sent dates, prunes, rice, lentils, spices, sugar, and pickled meats. Honey, sherbets, and meat stews arrived from Wallachia, Moldavia, and Transylvania, while Greece provided olive oil. In contrast, coffee and rice "were forbidden to leave so that abundance shall reign in Constantinople."[27]

Palace chefs, who were distinguished from other attendants by their white caps, began their work at daybreak with support from 200 under-cooks and scullions, as well as an army of servers and caterers.[28] Ottaviano Bon (1552–1623), who served as the ambassador of Venice to the Ottoman capital from 1603 to 1609, provided a detailed account of the imperial kitchen and the eating habits of the Ottoman sultan Ahmed I, who dined three or four times a day, starting with a meal at 10:00 A.M. and ending with a dinner at 6:00 P.M.[29] Snacks were often served between the two main meals.

When he felt hungry, the sultan informed the chief white eunuch of his desire to eat. The chief eunuch sent a notice to the chief server through one of the eunuchs who worked under him, and, shortly after, the attendants began to serve the sultan dish by dish. Any food that was placed in front of the sultan "had to be tasted by a taster, and the meals were served on celadon dishes, a type of glazed pottery that was believed to change color on contact with poison."[30] The monarch sat with his legs crossed and ate with an expensive and beautiful towel on his knees to keep his garments clean and another hanging on his left arm, which he used as "his napkin to wipe his mouth and fingers."[31] The food dishes were placed on the *sofra,* or a flat leather spread. Three or four kinds of warm and freshly baked white bread and two wooden spoons were placed before him, since he did not use either knife or a fork. One spoon was used "to eat his pottage," and the other to dish up "delicate syrups, made of diverse fruits, compounded with the juice of lemons and sugar to quench his thirst."[32] The meat they served him was so tender "and so delicately dressed" that he did not have any need to use a knife; he simply "pulled the flesh from the bones with his fingers."[33] The sultan tasted the dishes brought to him one by one, and as he was finished with one, another would be brought in.

The sultan's ordinary diet consisted of roasted pigeons, geese, lamb, hens, chickens, mutton, and sometimes, wild fowl. He would eat fish only when he was at the seaside, where he could sit with his women and watch it being caught. The sultan did not use any salt. Broths of all sorts as well as preserves and syrup served in porcelain dishes were always on the *sofra* though pies (*böreks*) were "after their fashion, made of flesh covered with paste."[34] The meal usually ended with the sultan feasting on sweetmeats.[35] Throughout the meal, the sultan drank a variety of sherbets, or "pure fresh fruit juice, iced with snow in summer."[36]

As a Muslim, the sultan was prohibited from eating pork and drinking wine or any other alcoholic beverage. Throughout the long history of the Ottoman dynasty, however, some sultans drank heavily, and at least one, Selim II (1566–1574), was so infatuated with wine that his subjects bestowed the title of Drunkard (*Sarhoş*) upon him. The "prohibition of wine in the Quran" was "held to exclude all things, which have an intoxicating tendency, such as opium, chars, bhang, and tobacco."[37]

While the sultan did not speak to anyone during the meal, "mutes and buffoons" were allowed to entertain him by playing tricks and making fun of one another through "deaf and dumb language."[38] In exceptional cases, the monarch honored one of the court officials in attendance by handing him a loaf of bread. Once the sultan had finished his meal, the leftovers were sent to high officials as a sign of royal generosity and kindness. To express his gratitude for the talents of the mimics, he threw them money from his pockets, which were always filled with coins.

A different kitchen served the harem, and yet another provided food for the grand vizier and other high officials, who served as members of the imperial council; still another provided food for the clerks, scribes, and even the janissaries and other men of sword who were stationed in the palace. Their food was of poorer quality and content, and included fewer dishes. There was even a hierarchy when it came to the quality of bread that each individual ate with his meal. The bread for the sultan was baked with flour from Bursa, whereas high government officials ate lower-quality bread, and the palace servants were served a black and coarse loaf. The female members of the royal household, such as the mother of the sultan and his concubines, though served by a different kitchen, ate the same food as their monarch.

Lady Mary Montagu, who visited the harems of several Ottoman officials, met with a widow of Mustafa II. On this occasion, the Ottoman host served her foreign guest 50 dishes of meat that were placed on the table one at a time, after the Ottoman fashion. The knives at the table "were of gold," and the handles of the knives were set with a diamond.[39] But "the piece of luxury, which grieved" the English visitor was "the table-cloth and napkins," which were all tiffany, "embroidered with silk and gold, in the finest manner, in natural flowers," and it was with "utmost regret" that she "made use of these costly napkins," which "were entirely spoiled before dinner was over."[40] The sherbet used by the Ottomans as the main drink during meals "was served in china bowls, but the covers and salvers were of massy gold."[41] After dinner, "water was brought in gold basins, and towels of the same kind" as the napkins, with which, once again, the English lady "very unwillingly" wiped her hands.[42] Finally, to conclude the dinner, coffee was brought in china with gold saucers and served by young girls who kneeled in front of their royal mistress.[43]

COOKING FOR THE ELITE

Since the palace served as a model for the entire empire, the culinary practices of the sultan and his household had a profound impact on the cooking practices and habits of the elite, which were, in turn, mimicked and replicated by the ordinary subjects of the sultan both in Istanbul and in the provinces. Thus, the meals prepared for the imperial council played an important role in introducing the Ottoman culinary traditions to the outside world.[44]

The grand vizier and his cabinet sat for lunch after they had attended to the affairs of the state. Their meal comprised six separate dishes. The starter was always a rice dish called *dane* (Persian for grain) in the palace, and *pilaf* elsewhere. There were a variety of rice dishes such as plain rice, Persian rice, rice mixed with minced meat, vegetables, raisins, currants, or even rice with pepper alone. The second course was usually the chicken soup, which contained onions, peppers, chickpeas, lemon juice, and parsley. The third course was normally *börek*, a baked or fried pastry made of thin flaky dough filled with chicken, cheese, minced meat, potatoes, and vegetables, such as parsley, spinach, leek, and eggplant. Another popular third or fourth course was *çömlek aşi*, "made from clarified butter, onions, sesame, sumac, chickpeas, and meat."[45] At times *börek* and *çömlek aşi* were replaced by a variety of soups or bullion (*şurba-i sade* or *tarbana* soup), or even vegetable dishes such as *burani*, which consisted of spinach or another vegetable with rice and yogurt.[46] Besides "*burani* and *dolma*, the old-fashioned Turkish pasta dish, *titmaç*, along with yogurt and a kind of wheat gruel with meat," were also served as one of the main courses.[47] The fourth course was usually a sweet dish such as baklava, *palude, zerde, me'muniye*, or *muhallebi*. At times, before serving the sweet dishes, a substantial course, such as sheep's trotters with vinegar, cow's tripe, sausage made of gut, or meat ragout, or poached eggs with yogurt, were served.[48] The last and the sixth course was always a meat dish, most often a variety of kebabs made of lamb, chicken, pigeon, or meatballs, either grilled or fried as *köfte*.

The sumptuous meal was always accompanied by a variety of breads and sherbets. Stewed and sugared fruits, as well as dried fruits, "especially raisins, currants, apricots, and figs, at times together with the fresh varieties," were also served.[49] Dried fruits were also heavily used in various dishes. Sometimes the *böreks* were filled "not only with minced meat and onions, but also with dried apricots, currants, dates, chestnuts, and apples."[50] Raisins, currants, chestnuts, and almonds were also used as ingredients in rice dishes.[51]

The meals for the secretaries, scribes, and servants of the imperial council were not only of lower quality, but they were limited to two dishes, consisting mostly of rice or wheat soup, or plain rice, or a wheat dish that contained eggs, and a yogurt soup called *mastabe*, which was made of "clarified butter, meat, onions, chickpeas, yogurt, and probably, parsley."[52] The simplicity of the menu for the lower-rank members of the imperial divan was also reflected by the absence of sweet dishes.

The diversity and richness of the Ottoman culinary culture was best demonstrated when the palace organized large banquets in honor of a visiting foreign dignitary or celebrated the circumcision of a prince of the royal family or the arrival of the Festival of Sacrifice. Many of the same dishes that appeared on the normal menu for the divan remained, but the order of serving changed, and at times, the quantity of meat and sweets increased. Meat dishes such as chicken ragouts, sheep's rump ragout, roasted pigeons, chickens, ducks, and geese were added, while sweet dishes and pastries were also increased significantly. In the banquets that were held in the palace, the quantity of leftovers was so large that after the guests had finished their meal, the janissaries were invited to practice the custom of "plundering" the food (*yağma*). If the banquet was held outside the palace, servants and attendants, as well as the ordinary subjects of the sultan, were encouraged to participate in the "plunder."

FOOD FOR THE RICH AND POWERFUL

Outside the palace, the diet of the rich and powerful Ottoman differed significantly from that of the lower classes. Wealthy families imitated the manners of the sultan, his harem, and high government officials. Their meals included egg or *börek,* meat, cold and hot vegetables with butter, rice, and pastry or pudding. The main meal was taken in the evening, with the rich eating "soup, spiced dishes of rice and meat, white cheese, fruit, bread, and jam, all washed down with glasses of coffee or tea."[53]

Wealthy Turks relied heavily on lamb as the principal meat in their daily diet. They "preferred mutton to any other meat, and it was served at nearly every meal for those who could afford it."[54] Sheep heads and trotters were a favorite dish.[55] At times, "zucchini and eggplant were stuffed with finely chopped mutton mixed with garlic, spices, and salt and cooked in plain water."[56] Sometimes carrots were stuffed in the same manner or "vine leaves were rolled round a similar mixture of chopped meat and stewed with sour plums placed under them in the water."[57] Yogurt was often used as a sauce, and it was spread on the stuffed eggplant, zucchini, and vine leaves before they were served.

Aside from lamb, goat and deer meat were also consumed in the Anatolian provinces of the empire. Beef was not popular among the Ottomans, and it was difficult to buy, particularly in Istanbul. According to the Turkish scholar Metin And, the Turks did not know "how to cook rabbits, hares, deer, and other game with spices," but they had several specialized techniques for preparing chicken.[58] Stewed chicken "was cut up and put into rice soup, and parsley or cinnamon was sprinkled on top just before it was served."[59] Roasted chicken was usually stuffed with spices and onions. The popularity of chicken was such that many shops sold chickens roasted in big ovens. These ovens, which resembled limekilns, "had either one or two shelves, and the heat from red-hot embers came up through holes in the bottom."[60] The chicken, and at times other meat, was placed in "a covered earthenware pot so it cooked in its own steam."[61] Most meat dishes were cooked in sauces flavored with spices such as pepper and saffron. Bread dough was often "placed on the tray beside the pot so it was baked at the same time."[62] A variety of rice dishes, ranging from *chilau* (white rice without any ingredients) or pilaf (rice with different roasted meats such as chicken, duck, partridge), and kebabs of lamb were mainstays of the diet. Vegetables such as carrots, green beans, and lentils, together with dried or cooked fruits and nuts, such as barberries, raisins, almonds, pine nuts, pistachios, orange peels, mulberries, and dates, were also central to the daily meals.

Islam prohibited eating "all quadrupeds" that seized "their prey with their teeth, and all birds" that seized their kill "with their talons."[63] "Hyenas, foxes, elephants, weasels, pelicans, kites, carrion, crows, ravens, crocodiles, otters, asses, mules, wasps, and in general all insects," as well as dogs, cats, and "fish dying of themselves," were forbidden to Muslims.[64]

FOOD AND EATING AMONG THE POOR

As "in all pre-modern empires, there was a major difference between the cuisine of the palace and that of the countryside."[65] Rice, for example, "was the mainstay of the imperial kitchen, while peasants in Anatolia and Syria ate boiled cracked wheat (bulgur)."[66] Olive oil "was used by the elite while peasants inland from the Mediterranean coast used animal fats; butter in the Balkans, [and] sheep fat in Anatolia and the Arab provinces."[67]

In sharp contrast to the rich, the poor of the Ottoman Empire ate a simple diet based entirely on cereals, locally grown vegetables, beans, lentils, peas, pumpkins, and radishes. Here the food was usually cooked in a little stove. At times, their diet included black bread and rice, "which they ate off wooden platters using three fingers" followed by "inexpensive yogurt" and accompanied by "water to drink."[68] Among the poor, dairy products, such as sour milk, were accompanied, "depending on the season, by cucumbers or melons, an onion, or leek, or stewed dried fruit."[69] *Kaymak*, "a slightly salted boiled cream, and cheeses preserved in leather bottles (*tulum*), in wheels (*tekerlek*), or in balls, such as the famous *cascaval*," a "cheese made of ewes' milk subjected to repeated boiling," were also popular among the poor.[70]

On special occasions, the family might share a chicken stew or "chicken and mutton cooked together in one pot with rice" without adding "any liquid so the rice soaked up all the juices of the meat."[71] The shortage of refrigeration in rural communities caused most perishable foods to be produced and consumed locally. Peasants both in Anatolia and the Balkans consumed a variety of fresh and dried fruits. The most popular fresh fruits were apples, cherries, pears, figs, grapes, apricots, melons, pomegranates, and plums that were grown in gardens and orchards. The inhabitants of these regions did not originally have access to tomatoes, potatoes, corn, peanuts, red and green (bell) peppers, and turkey, which arrived later from Central or North America in the 16th century. Honey was the universal sweetener.

Though the food might not be as sumptuous among the poor as that found in the palace and the private homes of the rich and powerful, "hygiene was nevertheless strictly observed during the preparation and consumption of food."[72] These strict rules also applied to stall owners who were warned in an imperial edict issued by the government that "owners of hot food stalls, sellers of cooked sheep's heads, makers of filo pastries—in short, all makers and sellers of food—must prepare it cleanly and thoroughly," and "they must wash the dishes with clean water, and dry them with clean cloths."[73] The offenders were warned that the market supervisor with the sanction and approval of a religious judge would punish them.[74] Everyone had to also respect the rules relating to spoons: "only the right half of spoon—the landing side—was to be dipped into the communal bowl, the left side being used to raise the food to the lips."[75] For "all other dishes," the Ottomans "used the right hand, as the left was for wiping the body and was therefore considered unclean," and "between courses, they always washed their hands and dried them with fresh towels."[76] Like the wealthy, the poor did not use tables and chairs. Instead, "a special mat was often placed on the floor to serve as a table."[77]

Rich or poor, young or old, women or men, the people of the Ottoman Empire loved Turkish sweetmeats. The very popular custard known as *muhallebi* "was made with rice, milk, flour, sugar, and butter, and flavored with rosewater or other scents."[78] Another sweetmeat was prepared by dropping a spoonful of egg-and-flour batter on a hot metal plate and allowing it to cook and spread like a pancake. Once the pancake had been shaped, it was then "covered with a very thick layer of sugar flavored with rose-water and chopped almonds or walnuts, and folded over and over to make several layers."[79]

Regardless of class and social background, Ottoman Turks ate their meals without pomp and ceremony. They sat cross-legged on carpets and rugs preferably in a flower garden or on the grass by a river or a creek "set with rows of trees" where the shade was "very thick."[80] The food was either served on a *sofra*, a large piece of cloth or leather, or on a very low table that could easily be reached from the ground. Travelers usually carried with them a *sofra* "made of red or yellow leather with a string threaded round it so that it could be opened or shut like a purse."[81] Among the poor who could afford only one dish, the members of the family sat around the cooking pot or a large plate or tray, prayed, and then ate together as a group, using their fingers since they did not use knives or forks. Even the rich and the powerful sometimes ate directly from the cooking-pot.[82] The food was always eaten in silence.

PLEASURES OF DRINKING AND SMOKING

Coffee

It is generally believed that coffee originated in Ethiopia or Yemen and emerged as a popular beverage in the Ottoman Empire sometime in the 16th century. According to one author, "there is no mention of coffee in any source before the 16th century."[83] There is some disagreement on exactly when coffee arrived in Istanbul. The French historian Fernand Braudel wrote that coffee had been introduced to Cairo as early as 1510 and Istanbul as early as 1517.[84] The Ottoman traveler Evliya Çelebi stated that the new black beverage was first brought to the Ottoman capital in 1543.[85] The historian Mustafa Ali, however, wrote that the first coffeehouses of Istanbul opened for business in 1552 or 1553, while another historian, Ibrahim Peçevi, maintained that coffee and coffeehouses appeared in Istanbul in 1554–1555.[86] Coffee was most probably introduced from Yemen to Mecca by the first decade of the 16th century. Coffeehouses in the holy city were bustling with customers before the Ottoman armies defeated the Mamluks in 1516 and 1517, and imposed their rule over the Arab Middle East. From Yemen and Arabia, coffee was brought to Egypt and Syria, and from there to Istanbul and other urban centers of the empire. It is not surprising, therefore, that the Turkish word for coffee, *kahve*, originated from the Arabic word, *qahwa*, and it was through the Ottomans that it was then introduced to Europe, where it was adopted as *kaffe, caffe, café*, and coffee, all originating in the Turkish pronunciation of the original Arabic word.

As the popularity of the new black drink spread, coffeehouses sprang up in Istanbul and other urban centers of Anatolia and the Arab Middle East. They soon emerged "as the very center of male public life" in the Ottoman Empire.[87] The historian Mustafa Ali, who was writing at the end of the 16th century, observed that in Cairo, there were "thousands of coffeehouses."[88] The spread of coffee and coffeehouses was not without major controversy. Acting as the guardians of public morals, the conservative ulema denounced the new drink as the work of the devil. The Ottoman historian and chronicler Ibrahim Peçevi, who stood with the conservatives in opposition to coffee and later tobacco, wrote in 1635 that:

> Until the year 962 (1555), in the high, God-guarded city of Constantinople, as well as in the Ottoman lands generally, coffee and coffeehouses did not exist. About that year, a fellow called Hakam from

Aleppo, and a wag called Shems from Damascus, came to the city: they each opened a large shop in the district called *Tahtalkale*, and began to purvey coffee. These shops became meeting-places of a circle of pleasure-seekers and idlers, and also of some wits from among the men of letters and literati, and they used to meet in groups of about twenty or thirty. Some read books and fine writings, some were busy with backgammon and chess, some brought new poems and talked of literature. Those who used to spend a good deal of money on giving dinners for the sake of convivial entertainment, found that they could attain the joys of conviviality merely by spending an asper or two on the price of coffee. It reached such a point that all kinds of unemployed officers, judges and professors all seeking preferment, and corner-sitters with nothing to do proclaimed that there was no place like it for pleasure and relaxation, and filled it until there was no room to sit or stand. It became so famous that, besides the holders of high offices, even great men could not refrain from coming there. The Imams and muezzins and pious hypocrites said: "People have become addicts of the coffeehouse; nobody comes to the mosques!" The ulema said: "It is a house of evil deeds; it is better to go to the wine-tavern than there." The preachers in particular made great efforts to forbid it. The muftis, arguing that anything which is heated to the point of carbonization, that is, becomes charcoal, is unlawful, issued fetvas against it. In the time of Sultan Murad III, may God pardon him and have mercy on him, there were great interdictions and prohibitions, but certain persons made approaches to the chief of police and the captain of the watch about selling coffee from back-doors in side-alleys, in small and unobtrusive shops, and were allowed to do this . . . After this time, it became so prevalent, that the ban was abandoned. The preachers and muftis now said that it does not get completely carbonized, and to drink it is therefore lawful. Among the ulema, the sheikhs, the viziers and the great, there was nobody left who did not drink it. It even reached such a point that the grand viziers built great coffeehouses as investments, and began to rent them out at one or two gold pieces a day.[89]

The report from Ibrahim Peçevi demonstrates that from the very beginning, the introduction of coffee and coffeehouses ignited controversy and stirred heated and bitter public debate. Many among the conservative ulema condemned the new beverage as "an intoxicant fully comparable to wine," consumption of which the holy Quran banned.[90] The palace and the ulema used coffee as the scapegoat for the decline in public morality and the rise in loose, immoral, and rebellious behavior. The advocates and supporters of the black drink, however, refused to be intimidated. They struck back and used their own interpretation of the Quran and the Islamic law to dismiss the comparison with wine, emphasizing the benefits of drinking coffee and arguing that, as long as it did not interfere with the daily religious obligation, there could not be anything wrong with enjoying several cups of the black beverage.[91]

In spite of vehement and organized opposition from the conservatives, the popularity and consumption of coffee spread like wildfire. By the closing decades of the 16th century, the consumption of the black stimulant had become common enough that even remote towns in Anatolia possessed coffeehouses.[92] After the Syrian merchant Shems, who had introduced coffee to Istanbul, returned home with a handsome profit of five thousand gold pieces, many more coffeehouses were built in the city and the new black drink emerged as the beverage of chess players and thinkers.[93] Elaborate ceremonies were organized around the brewing and serving of coffee at the imperial palace, where the sultan's coffee maker received support from 40 assistants. The women of the harem also received special training in preparing coffee for their royal master, while outside the palace, prospective suitors judged the merits of

Coffee kiosk (house), on the port (Istanbul). William H. Bartlett. From Julie Pardoe, *The Beauties of the Bosphorus* (London: 1839). (Library of Congress)

their intended brides in accordance with the taste of the coffee they prepared.

Coffee was taken at hot temperatures from a special coffee pot called *cezve* and served with Turkish delight. In some areas of the empire, pistachio grains were added into the coffee. By the last decade of the 16th century, the popularity of the black drink had forced the conservatives to back down and concede defeat, albeit grudgingly. Bostanzade Mehmed Effendi, who served as the chief mufti from 1589 to 1592 and again from 1593 to 1598, finally delivered a *fetva* granting his approval to the black drink, which had been denounced by an Arab poet as "the negro enemy of sleep and love."[94] This did not, however, end the controversy and the debate.

During the reign of Murad IV (1623–1640), the authorities cracked down on coffeehouses, denouncing them as centers of unlawful and seditious activities. Many coffeehouses were closed down, and several coffee drinkers and smokers were executed. For the sultan and his ministers, the prevailing social chaos and political anarchy were partially caused by the rapid increase in the number of coffeehouses—where storytellers, poets, and shadow puppeteers ridiculed the mighty and powerful for their corruption and hypocrisy. When, in September 1633, a devastating fire burned thousands of shops in the capital, the sultan interpreted it as a sign of God's wrath and demanded the restoration of the moral order. The use of coffee and tobacco was outlawed, and coffeehouses, which had been used as centers of political and social mobilization, were closed.[95] While the small traders were badly hit by the prohibition, the wealthy merchants survived because they possessed a substantial amount of capital and they could make a profit on the black market.[96]

Despite these repressive measures, the state could not enforce the ban. Moreover, the government gradually recognized that the importation, distribution, and sale of coffee could significantly increase state revenue. Its import was taxed for the first time during the reign of Süleyman II (1687–1698), and "to provide still greater income for the treasury, a further tax was levied on its sale."[97] The central government also increased its profit from the sale of coffee by "farming out the right of coffee-roasting to the highest bidder."[98]

In the second half of the 16th century, European travelers who visited the Ottoman Empire became the first Westerners to discover coffee. The physician Prospero Alpini, who lived in Egypt in 1590, and Pietro della Valle, who visited Istanbul in 1615, wrote of it:

> The Turks also have another beverage, black in colour, which is very refreshing in summer and very warming in winter, without however changing its nature and always remaining the same drink, which is swallowed hot . . . They drink it in long draughts, not during the meal but afterwards, as a sort of delicacy and to converse in comfort in the company of friends. One hardly sees a gathering where it is not drunk. A large fire is kept going for this purpose and little porcelain bowls were kept by it ready-filled with the mixture; when it is hot enough there are men entrusted with the office who do nothing else but carry these little bowls to all the company, as hot as possible, also giving each person a few melon seeds to chew to pass the time. And with the seeds and this beverage, which they call kafoue, they amuse themselves while conversing sometimes for a period of seven or eight hours.[99]

The European merchants purchased Yemeni coffee in Cairo, where the trade reached its zenith in the late 17th and early 18th centuries, "although even between 1624 and 1630 there were some very wealthy Cairo wholesalers dealing in coffee."[100] By 1700, coffee had replaced spices as the mainstay of a large and flourishing trade between "the Orient" and Africa on the one hand, and the Mediterranean on the other.[101] European traders tried to dislodge the Muslims from the coffee trade by force, "as they had done earlier with pepper and spice but they failed."[102] Ottoman control over Aden, which lasted until 1830, allowed Muslim merchants to maintain their control over the lucrative trade, particularly in the Red Sea region, western Arabia, Syria, and Anatolia. This forced the Europeans to establish their own coffee plantations in the Caribbean. The emergence of "plantation colonies" weakened the dominant economic position of Egypt.[103] West Indian coffee first arrived in Marseilles around 1730 and was soon introduced to the bazaars of the eastern Mediterranean. By 1786–1789, 21 percent of the French coffee was sold in the Levant at a price "roughly 25 percent lower than that of Yemeni coffee."[104] The threat posed by the cheaper West Indian coffee was sufficiently serious that "its importation into Egypt was prohibited."[105]

In 18th- and 19th-century Istanbul, splendid coffeehouses were built in the ornate Rococo style—"timber framed with the interiors carved and painted," often equipped with a stove for heating the coffee and charcoal for the pipes, rows of *nargiles,* or glass-bottomed water pipes for smoking, and "small decorative fountains to cool the air in summer" so that "the customers could drink their coffee while listening to music, have a shave, smoke their *çubuks* (long cornel-wood pipes), listen to story-tellers, meet their friends or just relax."[106] Since "these structures were made of wood, they were particularly vulnerable to the terrible fires that broke out frequently in Istanbul."[107]

The popularity of coffee was not confined to the urban centers of the empire. In the distant provinces of the empire, and in the most remote tribal areas of the Middle East, drinking the bitter black liquid brought members of various Arab tribes together. As one foreign traveler observed, the Arab nomadic groups ate very little, particularly when there were no guests, relying primarily on bread and a bowl of camel's milk for their daily nutrition. This may explain why they remained lean and thin, but also why, when a sickness befell a tribe, it carried off a large proportion of the clan's members. In sharp contrast, when guests visited the tribe, a sheep was killed in honor of the occasion and a sumptuous meal of mutton, curds, and flaps of bread was prepared and eaten with fingers.[108] Although the flora of the desert regions of Syria and Jordan were scanty in quantity, it was of many varieties and "almost every kind was put to some useful end."[109] The leaf of *uturfan* was used to scent butter, while a salad was made of the prickly *kursa'aneh*. On these special occasions, preparing, serving, and drinking coffee played a central role in demonstrating the hospitality of the host toward his guest.

Arab nomads lit a bonfire of tamarisk, willow, and other desert scrubs in the earthen fireplace dug into the center of the tent. The guest of honor was motioned to the spot on the carpet between the hearth and the partition that separated the women's quarters from the men's. Sometimes the ceremony of preparing the coffee took a full hour, during which the host and his guest sat in dignified silence. Preparations began by roasting the beans and then crushing them in the mortar—a music dear to the ears of desert Arabs. The coffee pots essential to desert hospitality were then placed in the ashes of the bonfire to simmer. It was an indignity among the Arabs if the coffee served to a visitor was made by women. Often the son of the sheikh (the chief of the clan or tribe) prepared the coffee as a sign of respect for the visitor. When the coffee was ready, an empty cup was handed to the guest, who returned it declaring: "May you live." The coffee was then poured into the cup by the host and handed to the guest. As the guest began to drink, a voice would declare, "double health," and the guest would reply, "Upon your heart." Only after the cups had been passed around once or twice, and all the necessary phrases of politeness had been exchanged, could the business of the evening be discussed.[110] Smoking a pipe went hand in hand with drinking coffee.

Aside from coffee, the other popular drink among the Turks, as well as many residents of the empire in the Balkans, was *boza*, a type of malt drink, which was most probably brought by the Turks from Central Asia.[111] The popular drink differed slightly according to region, depending on crops available and local customs. It was made from corn and wheat in Anatolia, and wheat or millet in Wallachia, Moldavia, and Bulgaria. From Anatolia and the Balkans, *boza* spread to other Ottoman provinces, such as Egypt, where it was prepared from barley and drunk by boatmen of the Nile and many among the lower classes.[112] *Boza* had a thick consistency and a low alcohol content with an acidic sweet flavor. The Ottoman army units consumed *boza* because it was rich in carbohydrates and vitamins. Numerous *boza* makers accompanied the janissaries.

Boza production was an important component of the Ottoman urban economy. During the reign of Selim II (1566–1574), *boza* consumption ran into government restriction when a new brand of the drink, laced with opium, was introduced to the market. The Ottoman government once again imposed restrictions on alcoholic beverages, including *boza*, during the reign of Mehmed IV (1648–1687), but consumption of the drink continued. By the 19th century, the sweet and non-alcoholic Albanian *boza* that was consumed in the imperial palace had triumphed among the masses.

Other drinks and beverages unique to a particular region or district were produced locally. As with food, drinks varied from one region and district of the empire to another, depending on ingredients available. The people of Vlorë (Vlora), in southwestern Albania, produced a white honey with an aroma of musk and ambergris that they mixed with 20 cups of water to make a delicious sherbet or pudding,[113] while the people of Gjirokastër in central Albania drank red wine, *reyhania*, and Polish arrack.[114] In Albania, where fruits such as grapes, pears, apples, cherries, pomegranates, and chestnuts were abundant, the popular drinks consisted of red wine, grape juice flavored with mustard, *reyhania*, sour-cherry juice, honey mead, and *boza*. In the Kurdish-populated eastern Anatolia, "the renowned beverages and stimulants were poppy sherbet, pomegranate sherbet, rice water sherbet, rhubarb sherbet, wine boiled to a third and canonically lawful, apricot julep, and hemlock sherbet."[115]

Wine

Though wine was prohibited in Islam, Ottomans of all ranks and social standing deviated from the precepts of the *şeriat* (Islamic legal code) and drank wine regularly at various parties and gatherings. A European diplomat who lived in the Ottoman Empire in the second half of the 17th century wrote that although it was forbidden and banned by Islamic law, "wine was commonly used" and "publicly drunk" without any "caution or fear" of causing any scandal. He admitted, however, that high government officials were often worried about their image as wine drinkers.[116] He also observed that drinking was often judged in connection to the age of the drinker; thus its use by young men was often tolerated and excused, but it was a scandal and a crime for an old man to drink an alcoholic drink.[117] Less than half a century later, the wife of an English ambassador who visited Istanbul from 1717 to 1718 was shocked when one of her Ottoman hosts, a man of power and status, drank wine in her presence with the same ease and freedom as the Europeans did.[118] When she asked her host how he could allow himself the liberty to enjoy a drink that had been denounced by his religion, the Ottoman dignitary fired back that all of God's creations were good and designed for the use of man. In his interpretation of Islam, "the prohibition of wine was a very wise maxim," but it was meant for the common people and the prophet Muhammad had never designed to confine those who knew how to consume it with moderation.[119]

Outside the ruling elite, the Bektaşi *dervişes*, who believed that their spiritual status absolved them from the prohibitions of Islamic law, consumed wine and *arak*.[120] At some of their convents in the 19th century, they had their own vineyards and produced their own wine.[121] The traveler Evliya Çelebi also mentioned the consumption of wine and *arak*, a clear, colorless, unsweetened, aniseed-flavored distilled alcoholic drink, known as "lion's milk," in the port city of Izmir, which had a large Greek population. *Arak* was used not only in various parts of Anatolia but also throughout the Balkans and the Arab provinces of the empire. Katib Çelebi also made note of wine consumption when he visited a Christian monastery on the island of Chios, where an annual fair and a popular festival organized by the local church allowed the Christian population to enjoy a variety of local wines.

Though allowed to drink at home or private parties, non-Muslims were prohibited from consuming wine in public. Periodically, the central government imposed severe restrictions on consumption of wine as a means of displaying its power and authority and as a preemptive measure against social disorder. The severity of restrictive measures seems to have also been affected by the degree of pressure from hard-line religious groups, and the level of willingness on the part of the reigning sultan to appease them. Thus, during the reign of Süleyman the Magnificent, and yet again under Murad IV, the Ottoman authorities imposed rigid restrictions on the consumption of wine.

Besides wine and *arak,* another popular beverage among the Ottomans was a drink called Arab sherbet, made from a mixture of pounded raisins and hot water that were left in a wooden tub to ferment for several days.[122] If the "process of fermentation was too slow, lees of wine were added."[123] In the beginning, "the liquid tasted excessively sweet, but then it became more acid and for three or four days was delicious, especially if cooled with ice, which was always obtainable" in Istanbul; "but it did not keep well for longer as it quickly became too sour."[124] In its later state, the effects of the Arab sherbet "were as strong as those of wine," so it is not surprising that "it came under the religious ban on alcoholic drinks."[125]

Tobacco

The consumption of coffee, tea, and even *boza* went hand in hand with smoking tobacco, which was introduced to the Ottoman Empire in the early 17th century. Some have attributed the introduction of tobacco to Dutch merchants, while others have blamed the English. Yet others have maintained that because it had originated in the New World, tobacco "must have reached the Ottoman Empire via Europe, either from Italy or over the Habsburg-Ottoman border," where janissaries "who often fought in that area" came into contact with the new product and contributed to its spread and popular use.[126] Regardless of the route it took to enter the Ottoman domains, the introduction of tobacco was immediately denounced by religious classes. The *şeyhülislam* issued a strongly worded *fetva* that denounced smoking as "a hideous and abominable practice" contrary to the precepts of the Quran.[127] The proponents, however, refused to back down and argued that smoking was not mentioned in the Quran, and there was, therefore, no legal ground for its prohibition.

The historian Peçevi, who had expressed his vehement opposition to coffee, joined the conservatives in attacking "the fetid and nauseating smoke of tobacco." He wrote that the English infidels had brought tobacco:

> in the year 1009 (1600–01), and sold it as a remedy for certain diseases of humidity. Some companions from among the pleasure seekers and sensualists said: "Here is an occasion for pleasure" and they became addicted. Soon those who were not mere pleasure-seekers also began to use it. Many even of the great ulema and the mighty fell into this addiction. From the ceaseless smoking of the coffeehouse riff-raff the coffeehouses were filled with blue smoke, to such a point that those who were in them could not see one another. In the markets and the bazaars too their pipes never left their hands. Puff-puffing in each other's faces and eyes, they made the streets and markets stink. In its honour they composed silly verses, and declaimed them without occasion.[128]

Peçevi admitted that he had "arguments with friends" about tobacco and smoking; "I said: Its abominable smell taints a man's beard and turban, the garment on his back and the room where it is used; sometimes it sets fire to carpets and felts and bedding, and soils them from end to end with ash and cinders; after sleep its vapour rises to the brain; and not content with this, its ceaseless use withholds men from toil and gain and keeps hands from work. In view of this and other similar harmful and abominable effects, what pleasure or profit can there be in it?"[129] To these questions, his friends responded that smoking was "an amusement" and "a pleasure of aesthetic taste," to which he fired back that there was "no possibility of spiritual pleasure" from smoking, and his friends' answer was "no answer" but "pure pretension."[130] He further argued that tobacco had been on several occasions "the cause of great fires" in Istanbul, and "several hundred thousand people" had suffered from these fires.[131] Peçevi conceded that tobacco could have limited benefits such as keeping the night guards on various ships awake during the night, but "to perpetuate such great damage for such small benefits" was neither rational nor justifiable.[132]

The government imposed a ban on smoking during the reign of Murad IV, but the authorities could not enforce it. The sultan's prohibition "served only to drive smokers underground."[133] As in the case of coffee, the conservatives were forced to accept defeat. After numerous arguments and reversals, tobacco was finally declared legal in a *fetva* issued by the chief mufti Mehmed Baha'i Effendi, "himself a heavy smoker who had been dismissed and exiled for smoking in 1634."[134] Evliya Çelebi, who was a contemporary of the mufti, rushed to his defense and argued that the ruling was not prompted by the religious leader's own addiction, but "by a concern for what was best suited to the condition of the people, and a belief in the legal principle that all that is not explicitly forbidden is permitted."[135]

Production of tobacco was legalized in 1646, and in a few years the crop was cultivated on large scale across the empire, where climatic conditions permitted. The introduction of tobacco contributed to diversification in agricultural production.[136] It also reinforced family farming, since it required a large concentration of manual labor and individual care.[137] Unlike wine, both production and export of tobacco were taxed.[138] Once legalized, "the combination of coffee and tobacco" became "the hallmarks of Ottoman culture, inseparable from hospitality and socialization," and the two quickly emerged as the first "truly mass consumption commodities in the Ottoman world."[139]

During the second half of the 19th century, Ottoman tobacco exports from most production centers increased dramatically. With the invention of mechanically rolled cigarettes, Ottoman tobacco became highly prized for blending, especially by American manufacturers.[140] With the rise of nationalist revolts among the sultan's Christian subjects, however, the empire began to lose the best tobacco growing lands in the Balkans.[141] The newly independent states, particularly Bulgaria, profited from the acquisition of these profitable lands that increased significantly during the Balkan Wars of 1912–1913.[142] Regardless, by the beginning of the First World War in 1914, tobacco had emerged as the leading export item from Anatolia.[143]

Opium

In sharp contrast to the harsh and repressive measures adopted against wine, coffee, and tobacco, the Ottoman state was unusually tolerant of opium consumption, which was produced "in the form of pastes" that contained the drug.[144] Several European visitors to the Ottoman Empire observed that consumption of drugs "was widespread among the Turks," and at least one attributed the love and fascination for opium and other drugs to the fact that the Ottomans "did not drink wine, or at least not in public, and the punishments for being found drunk were very severe."[145] Many Ottoman sultans were fond of the popular narcotic, and we know that it was also frequently used by members of various Sufi orders in their rituals and ceremonies.[146] This may explain why the opium produced in Anatolia and Arabia was widely available in Istanbul and other major urban centers of the empire.[147]

The 17th-century traveler Evliya Çelebi wrote that in the town of Afyon-Karahisar, in southwestern Anatolia, where poppy was cultivated, many artisans and their wives took opium.[148] He also claimed that in some places, males spent much of their time in coffeehouses because the use of narcotics by both men and women caused frequent "domestic disputes."[149] Another observer living in 19th-century Egypt reported that though the use of opium and other narcotics was not very common in the country, some took it in the dose of three or four grains.[150] Many Egyptians also made "several conserves composed of hellebore, hemp, and opium, and several aromatic drugs," which were "more commonly taken than the simple opium."[151] By 1878–1880, opium was listed as one of the eight most important export commodities next to wheat, barley, raisins, figs, raw silk, raw wool, and tobacco.[152] The state regularly drew revenue from taxing the sale of opium pastes.

Aside from opium, Ottoman Turks "smoked a green powder made from the dried leaves of wild hemp," which "was sold freely everywhere in Istanbul," and the "noisier and rougher types of men found pleasure in meeting together and smoking" it "in hookahs, the Turkish pipe with the smoke inhaled through water."[153] Another popular narcotic was *tatula*, or "Satan's herb," a "yellow seed resembling Spanish pepper and about as big as a lentil."[154] Since it was a highly potent and dangerous drug, *tatula*, which was smuggled in to Istanbul and other large urban centers of the empire by Jewish merchants, was usually bought from a trusted pharmacist. Ottomans believed that the most dangerous form of drug use was "to smoke a mixture of opium and *tatula*."[155]

NOTES

1. Alan Mikhail, "The Heart's Desire: Gender, Urban Space and the Ottoman Coffee House," in *Ottoman Tulips, Ottoman Coffee Leisure and Lifestyle in the Eighteenth Century*, ed. Dana Sajdi (London: Tauris Academic Studies, 2007), 140.

2. Ibid.

3. Ibid.

4. Bozkurt Güvenç, "Food, Culture, and the Culture of Eating," in Semhet Arsel, *Timeless Tastes: Turkish Culinary Culture* (Istanbul: 2003), 16.

5. Isabel Böcking, Laura Salm-Reifferscheidt, and Moritz Stipsicz, *The Bazaars of Istanbul* (New York: Thames & Hudson, 2009), 191.

6. Güvenç, "Food, Culture, and the Culture of Eating," 16.

7. Ibid.

8. Ibid.

9. Ibid., 17.

10. Ibid.

11. Ibid., 16–17.

12. Böcking, Salm-Reifferscheidt, and Stipsicz, *The Bazaars of Istanbul,* 191.

13. Ibid.

14. Nevin Halici, "Ottoman Cuisine," in *The Great Ottoman Turkish Civilization,* 4 vol., ed. Kemal Cicek (Ankara: 2000), 4:94–95.

15. Kenneth F. Kiple and Kriemhild Conee Ornelas, eds. *The Cambridge World History of Food* (Cambridge: Cambridge University Press, 2000) 2 vols., 1:357.

16. Bruce Masters, "Cuisine," in *Encyclopedia of the Ottoman Empire,* eds. Gábor Ágoston and Bruce Masters (New York: Facts On File, 2009), 165.

17. Ibid.

18. Ibid.

19. Böcking, Salm-Reifferscheidt, and Stipsicz, *The Bazaars of Istanbul,* 191.

20. *The Cambridge World History of Food,* 2:1148.

21. Ibid.

22. Böcking, Salm-Reifferscheidt, and Stipsicz, *The Bazaars of Istanbul,* 191.

23. *The Cambridge World History of Food,* 2:1148.

24. Böcking, Salm-Reifferscheidt, and Stipsicz, *The Bazaars of Istanbul,* 191.

25. Ibid.

26. Fernand Braudel, *The Perspective of the World,* 3 vols., trans. Sian Reynolds (New York: Harper & Row Publishers, 1979), 3:477.

27. Ibid.

28. Ottaviano Bon, *The Sultan's Seraglio: An Intimate Portrait of Life at the Ottoman Court* (London: Saqi Books, 1996), 93.

29. Ibid.

30. Böcking, Salm-Reifferscheidt, and Stipsicz, *The Bazaars of Istanbul,* 191.

31. Bon, *The Sultan's Seraglio,* 94.

32. Ibid.

33. Ibid.

34. Ottaviano Bon as quoted in *The Cambridge World History of Food,* 2:1148.

35. Bon, *The Sultan's Seraglio*, 93, 151.

36. Ibid., 95, 151.

37. Thomas Patrick Hughes, *Dictionary of Islam* (New Delhi: Munshiram Manoharlal Publishers, 1999), 130.

38. Bon, *The Sultan's Seraglio*, 95, 151.

39. Lady Mary Wortley Montagu, *The Turkish Embassy Letters* (London: Virago Press, 2007), 116.

40. Ibid.

41. Ibid.

42. Ibid.

43. Ibid.

44. Hedda Reindl-Kiel, "The Chickens of Paradise, Official Meals in the Mid-Seventeenth Century Ottoman Palace," in *The Illuminated Table, the Prosperous House: Food and Shelter in Ottoman Material Culture,* ed. Suraiya Faroqhi and Christoph K. Neumann (Würzburg: Ergon in Kommission, 2003), 60.

45. Ibid., 62.

46. Ibid., 63.

47. Ibid.

48. Ibid., 64.

49. Ibid., 84.

50. Ibid.

51. Ibid.

52. Ibid., 65.

53. Michael Worth Davison, ed., *Everyday Life Through the Ages* (London: Reader's Digest Association Far East Limited, 1992), 175.

54. Metin And, "The Social Life of the Ottomans, in the Sixteenth Century," in *Ottoman Civilization,* ed. Halil Inalcik and Günsel Renda, 2 vols. (Istanbul: Republic of Turkey Ministry of Culture Publications, 2003), 1:427.

55. Çelebi, *The Intimate Life of an Ottoman Statesman,* trans., Robert Dankoff (Albany: State University of New York Press, 1991), 219.

56. And, "The Social Life of the Ottomans," 427.

57. Ibid., 428.

58. Ibid., 427.

59. Ibid.

60. Ibid.

61. Ibid.

62. Ibid.

63. Hughes, *Dictionary of Islam,* 130.

64. Ibid.

65. Masters, "Cuisine," 165.

66. Ibid.

67. Ibid.

68. Davison, *Everyday Life Through the Ages,* 175.

69. Fernand Braudel, *The Structure of Everyday Life,* 2 vols. (New York: Harper & Row, 1979), 1:211.

70. Ibid.

71. And, "The Social Life of the Ottomans," 429.

72. Böcking, Salm-Reifferscheidt, and Stipsicz, *The Bazaars of Istanbul,* 193.

73. Ibid.

74. Ibid.

75. Ibid.

76. Ibid.

77. Masters, "Cuisine," 165.

78. And, "The Social Life of the Ottomans," 427.

79. Ibid.

80. Montagu, *The Turkish Embassy Letters,* 73.

81. And, "The Social Life of the Ottomans," 428.

82. Ibid., 429.

83. Mikhail, "The Heart's Desire," 137.

84. Braudel, *The Structure of Everyday Life,* 1:256.

85. Mikhail, "The Heart's Desire," 138.

86. Ibid.

87. Donald Quataert, *The Ottoman Empire, 1700–1922* (Cambridge: Cambridge University Press, 2005), 160.

88. Mikhail, "The Heart's Desire," 138.

89. Bernard Lewis, *Istanbul and the Civilization of the Ottoman Empire* (Norman: University of Oklahoma Press, 1963), 132–33. See also Cemal Kafadar, *A History of Coffee, Economic History,* Congress XIII (Buenos Aires: 2002).

90. James Grehan, "Smoking and 'Early Modern' Sociability: The Great Tobacco Debate in the Ottoman Middle East (Seventeenth to Eighteenth Centuries)," *American Historical Review* 3, no. 5 (December 2006).

91. Ibid.

92. Suraiya Faroqhi, "Crisis and Change, 1590–1699," in *An Economic and Social History of the Ottoman Empire,* ed. Halil Inalcik, 2 vols. (Cambridge: Cambridge University Press, 1994), 2:508–9.

93. Lewis, *Istanbul,* 135.

94. Ibid.

95. Stanford J. Shaw, *History of the Ottoman Empire and Modern Turkey,* 2 vols. (Cambridge: Cambridge University Press, 1976), 1:198; Colin Imber, *The Ottoman Empire, 1300–1650: The Structure of Power* (New York: Palgrave Macmillan, 2002), 81.

96. Faroqhi, "Crisis and Change," 508.

97. Caroline Finkel, *Osman's Dream: The History of the Ottoman Empire* (New York: Basic Books, 2005), 309.

98. Faroqhi, "Crisis and Change," 508.

99. Braudel, *The Structure of Everyday Life,* 1:256.

100. Faroqhi, "Crisis and Change," 508.

101. Peter Gan, "Late-Eighteenth Early-Nineteenth Century Egypt: Merchant Capitalism or Modern Capitalism," in *The Ottoman Empire and the World Economy,* ed. Huri Islamoğlu-Inan (Cambridge: Cambridge University Press, 2004), 207.

102. Ibid.

103. Ibid.

104. Ibid.

105. Ibid.

106. Charles Newton, *Images of the Ottoman Empire* (London: Victoria and Albert Museum Publications, 2007), 107.

107. Ibid.

108. Gertrude Bell, *The Desert & the Sown: Travels in Palestine and Syria* (London: 1907), 55–56.

109. Ibid., 55.

110. Ibid., 20.

111. Çelebi, *The Intimate Life of an Ottoman Statesman,* 218, 220.

112. Edward William Lane, *An Account of the Manners and Customs of the Modern Egyptians* (New York: Dover Publications, 1973), 335.

113. Evliya Çelebi, *Evliya Çelebi in Albania,* trans. Robert Dankoff and Robert Elsie (Leiden: Brill, 2000), 143.

114. Ibid., 87.

115. Evliya Çelebi, *Evliya Çelebi in Bitlis: The Relevant Sections of the Seyahatnameh,* ed. Robert Dankoff (Leiden: E. J. Brill, 1990), 145.

116. Paul Rycaut, *The Present State of the Ottoman Empire* (New York: Arno Press, 1971), 165.

117. Ibid., 166.

118. Montagu, *The Turkish Embassy Letters,* 62.

119. Ibid.

120. Suraiya Faroqhi, *Subjects of the Sultan: Culture and Daily Life in the Ottoman Empire* (New York: I. B. Tauris, 2007),216.

121. Ibid.

122. And, "The Social Life of the Ottomans," 437.

123. Ibid.

124. Ibid.

125. Ibid.

126. Faroqhi, *Subjects of the Sultan,* 217.

127. Richard Davey, *The Sultan and His Subjects,* 2 vols. (London: Chapman and Hall LD., 1897), 1:140.

128. Lewis, *Istanbul,* 133–34.

129. Ibid., 134.

130. Ibid.

131. Ibid.

132. Ibid., 135.

133. Faroqhi, *Subjects of the Sultan*, 218.

134. Lewis, *Istanbul*, 136.

135. Ibid.

136. Wolf-Dieter Hütteroth, "Ecology of the Ottoman Lands," in *The Cambridge History of Turkey* (Cambridge: Cambridge University of Press, 2006), 4 volumes, 3:39.

137. Ibid., 40.

138. Finkel, *Osman's Dream*, 309.

139. Quataert, *The Ottoman Empire*, 158.

140. Donald Quataert, "The Age of Reforms, 1812–1914," in *An Economic and Social History of the Ottoman Empire*, 2:852.

141. Ibid.

142. Ibid.

143. Ibid.

144. Faroqhi, *Subjects of the Sultan*, 217.

145. And, "The Social Life of the Ottomans," 436.

146. Rycaut, *The Present State of the Ottoman Empire*, 139.

147. And, "The Social Life of the Ottomans," 436.

148. Faroqhi, *Subjects of the Sultan*, 217.

149. Ibid.

150. Lane, *An Account of the Manners*, 335.

151. Ibid.

152. Şevket Pamuk, "Commodity Production for World Markets and Relations of Production in Ottoman Agriculture, 1840–1913," in *The Ottoman Empire and the World Economy*, ed. Huri Islamoğlu-Inan, 182. See also Quataert, *The Ottoman Empire*, 126.

153. And, "The Social Life of the Ottomans," 436.

154. Ibid., 436–37.

155. Ibid., 437.

12

GAMES AND POPULAR SPORTS

Ottoman Turks were fond of various games and sports. As warriors who migrated from the steppes of Central Asia, they brought their ancient sporting tradition to Anatolia, the Balkans, and the Middle East. They were superb riders, archers, and javelin throwers. Hunting and wrestling also numbered among their favorite pastimes.[1] In addition to learning how to read and write and studying various sciences, the *iç oğlans,* or the pages of the palace, and particularly the *acemi oğlans,* or those novices who were trained as janissaries, received physical training and gained skills in horseback riding, weightlifting, wrestling, archery, sword training, *tomak* (a game played with wooden swords), and javelin throwing, or *cereed* (*cirit/ jerid*).[2]

CEREED

One of the most popular sports among the Turkic peoples of Central Asia was polo, which had originated in ancient Iran as a form of training for Persian cavalry units. The game took the form of a miniature battle, and both men and women of the Persian nobility participated in it. From Iran, polo travelled to India, Central Asia, China, and Japan. Among the Turks, polo gradually transformed itself into a new game. Also played on horseback, *cereed* was a javelin chase and an outdoor equestrian team sport. The objective of the game was to score points by throwing a blunt wooden javelin at an opposing team's horseman.[3] In the Arabic of Egypt, where it was popular among the Mamluk ruling elite and Ottoman military units stationed in the main urban centers of the country, the game was called *"La'b al-Djerid."*[4] The actual form of the *cereed*, and the length of the wooden javelin that was used during the game, varied from one region of the empire to another. In Egypt, the *cereed* "consisted of a palm branch stripped bare of its leaves."[5]

Two teams of horsemen—numbering 6, 8, 12, 20, or even 30, on each side—faced each other across an open field perhaps 50 yards wide, the flag of their team flying above them. Dressed in traditional costumes, they armed themselves with long, heavy wooden sticks. The game began with the youngest rider galloping towards the opposing team, calling the name of a player, and tossing a *cereed* at him, challenging the man to enter the game. As he trotted back to his side, the challenged rider pursued him and threw a *cereed* in his direction. Another player from the first team rode out and met the rider who had just thrown his *cereed* and was retreating, chasing the man and trying to intercept him as he threw a *cereed* at his body. Many could throw the blunt wooden javelin over a great distance, and some caught the *cereed* thrown at them.[6] Chasing, fleeing, and all the while trying to hit an opponent with the long wooden stick and avoiding a hit from a rider on the opposite team, was the essence of this game that required exceptional equestrian skills and afforded opportunities for the display of all the tricks and maneuvers of horsemanship, on which the Ottoman youth prided themselves.[7] At times, a player riding a swift horse created a diversion and, instead of returning to his place, rode off to a distance after making his throw, thus encouraging several horsemen from the other side to pursue and overtake him.[8]

The rules of the game were strictly observed, and unfair or unnecessary moves that were construed as rough and violent were not permitted.[9] To strike the horse, instead of the rider, was regarded as a sign of inexperience and violated the most basic rules of the game. Highly trained players rarely missed hitting an opponent and were skilled at avoiding hits themselves by performing special moves on horseback, such as leaning towards either side of the horse, under the horse's stomach or even its neck. Some players scored more points by hitting an opponent three or four times before he managed to escape and take his place back in his row. All these moves and maneuvers meant that the participants in the game faced a considerable risk of serious injury and even death, since the head was one of the principal targets of attack.[10] Part of the necessary skill lay in training the horses to play a significant role in the outcome of the game. A player won points when he managed to hit his rival with the wooden javelin or rode him out or caught an incoming *cereed* in mid-air. He received negative points for any move that endangered the horse, such as riding out of bounds or striking a horse with the *cereed* intentionally. During the mock battle, *cereed* horsemen tried "to gain possession of the darts thrown earlier in the game and carried for this purpose thin canes curved at one end."[11] Throughout a game of *cereed*, as horsemen galloped on the field, musicians played Ottoman military songs or folk songs performed with bass drum and reed windpipes. At the end of the game, the referees counted the number of hits and announced the victorious team, which received awards and a banquet in its honor.

As intrepid horsemen and skilled archers, the Ottomans, who brought the war game to Anatolia, used *cereed* as a means of improving the equestrian skills of their troops and training their army units for battle. While marching, an Ottoman commander lined up his officers and conscripts against one another to play 40 to 50 rounds of *cereed* in order to prepare them for the next military campaign. The exercise stopped as soon as it was decided that the horses were tiring.[12] Ultimately, a specialized cavalry unit was organized from those who excelled in the sport.

Numerous *cereed* grounds sprang up throughout Istanbul and the surrounding suburbs. The best known among these were the Archery Field, where the sultan himself played both polo and *cereed*; the field at the Imperial Arsenal; and the field in Cindi Meydan, where the monarch and the court played every Friday. One European observer wrote that near "the Hippodrome" (At Meydani), there was a large sports ground surrounded by walls where horsemen met on Friday afternoons, holidays, and every day during the summer to play *cereed*.[13] The game allowed the ruler and the palace pages to show off their physical prowess and dexterity.[14] In Istanbul, large numbers of court officials, dignitaries, and palace employees played the game regularly, and "rival factions existed under the name of Lahanadjil (cabbage men) and Bamyadil (gumbo men)."[15]

Cereed was not, however, confined to Istanbul. In every province where Ottoman troops were stationed, the game was played with great intensity and enthusiasm. During the *Ramazan Bayrami*, which celebrated the end of the month of fasting, *cereed* and wrestling were the most popular spectator sports. In villages across Anatolia,

The Atmeidan (At Meydan) or Hippodrome. William H. Bartlett. From Julie Pardoe, *The Beauties of the Bosphorus* (London: 1839). (Library of Congress)

teams of horsemen and javelin throwers contested, as spectators peered through the dust of the flying hooves and cheered the men on horseback.[16]

In Egypt, *cereed* was played initially by the local Mamluk elite and the Ottoman soldiers and officers who were stationed in the country. The Egyptian peasants, however, soon learned the game and played it regularly during the wedding ceremonies of an important person, such as the sheikh of a tribe or village, or when a boy was circumcised, or when "a votive calf, or ox or bull" was "to be sacrificed at the tomb of a saint and a public feast."[17] On these occasions, the *cereed* players, usually representing rival villages or tribes, gathered and were immediately divided into two contending teams. Each team comprised 12 to 20 combatants with each individual mounted on a horse.[18]

ARCHERY

Besides *cereed*, archery was viewed as the most important sport in the Ottoman domains. The Turks were master archers from the time they emerged as a distinct people in Central Asia. While the sword was used as the close-range weapon, a bow and arrow remained the standard long-range weapon. The use of the bow and arrow continued in the Ottoman Empire until the introduction of firearms. Long-distance and target-shooting competitions, as well as archery on horseback, took place under early Ottoman rulers, but not until the reign of Mehmed II, the conqueror of Constantinople, was an archery field designed in Istanbul. During the reign of Mehmed II's successor, Bayezid II, the archery field was expanded and additional ones designed and developed. Bayezid II also offered special privileges to prominent archers and the craftsmen who manufactured archery equipments. These artisans were provided with shops in a designated section of the bazaar. During the 15th and 16th centuries, there were roughly five hundred bow and arrow manufacturers in Istanbul.[19]

During the *Ramazan Bayrami,* crowds of spectators assembled on the plain above Beyoğlu—a district located on the European side of Istanbul, separated from the old city by the Golden Horn—to watch archery competitions.[20] First, the archers sat cross-legged in a long line and chanted the prayers with which Ottomans began all competitions and games. Then the competition began in complete silence as men used short stiff bows and special arrows to shoot a target in the fastest possible time. The prize for this competition was an embroidered towel, which the champion could use for cleaning and wiping his face. The distance competition then followed, and the spot where the longest shot had landed was marked by a stone. If a record was broken, a marble monument with the name of the archer inscribed on it in golden letters was erected.[21] Archers who set a new record were recognized as champions and received special gifts and awards from the sultan. During the competition, the archers also exhibited their skills by targeting small objects such as apples, bottles, and lanterns. The diplomat and author Ogier Ghiselin de Busbecq (1521–1592), who served as the ambassador to the Ottoman Empire for the Habsburg ruler Ferdinand I (and later the future Holy Roman emperor), "marveled at the length of shots he witnessed, but he noticed that the marking-stones from former times lay far beyond those of his day, and the Turks told him that they could not equal their forefathers' strength and skill."[22]

Prominent archers of the day met regularly at designated locations to offer free lessons and display their extraordinary talent and brilliance. Several Ottoman sultans, such as Murad IV, practiced archery a few times a week and went so far as to compete in various archery competitions, in which they set new records that were celebrated by the construction of a marble column.[23] The targets set up in numerous streets of the capital where young and old came to practice archery demonstrated the great enthusiasm of ordinary people for this sport.[24]

Archery remained a passion of Ottoman sultans down to the 19th century. Sultan Mahmud II, who was an avid archer, competed regularly with his favorite officials. After the sultan had shot his arrows, imperial pages and attendants ran to the field to collect the arrows and measure the distances. Once the boys had completed their task, court officials, who had been standing and waiting in a line, took their turn and shot their arrows, "taking special care to keep within bounds" and not to outdo and outshine their royal master.[25] The court-sponsored archery competitions were so frequent that "a long stretch of hilly country immediately in the rear" of Istanbul's Military College had become "dotted over with marble pillars fancifully carved, and carefully inscribed, erected on the spots where the arrows shot" by the sultan "from a terrace on the crest of the height had fallen."[26]

Archery and *cereed* went hand in hand with other war-related games, such as horseback riding, hunting, swordplay, fencing, spear throwing, putting the stone or throwing the boulder, and the game of wielding a mace (*gurz*), a heavy spiked club whose handling required strong arms.[27] All these activities were directly connected to military training and battlefield performance.

WRESTLING

One sport not directly related to warfare was wrestling, which was enormously popular among most ethnic groups in the Ottoman Empire, particularly the Turks, Tatars, Greeks, Bulgarians, Armenians, Kurds, and Gypsies. Every village and town had its own wrestling champion, or *pehlivan*. Matches were organized on Fridays, or during *bayrams,* between the champions of neighboring villages. Large crowds of cheering spectators watched the wrestlers for hours, cheering both the victors and the vanquished. During major festivals in Istanbul, thousands of spectators, including the sultan and the court, attended the wrestling matches between the city's best-known wrestlers. Süleyman the Magnificent greatly enjoyed the sport and sponsored his own strongly built wrestlers, who received a daily wage. These wrestlers were mostly Moors, Indians, and Tatars, and they wore a pair of leather breeches, gathered tightly below the knee. They often oiled their bodies to make it extremely difficult for the opponent to get a grip. After the end of each bout, "the wrestlers wrapped their sweaty bodies in a blue-checked cotton cloth, but away from the ring they wore long gowns girdled with silk and a bonnet of black velvet or astrakhan, which hung down over one shoulder similar to the bonnets of Polish and Georgian gentlemen."[28]

Some sultans, such as Murad IV, were wrestlers themselves. In his *Book of Travels*, Evliya Çelebi wrote that Murad IV frequently stripped and wrestled his court officials, including the sword bearer, Melek Ahmed Paşa; the calligrapher, Deli Husayin Paşa; and the champion, Pehlivan Dişlenk Süleyman, who were all very athletic and fond of wrestling. These royal bouts were held inside the palace, and before each match a prescribed prayer was recited: "Allah! Allah! For the sake of the Lord of all Created beings Muhammad Mustafa; for the sake of Muhammad Bukhara Sari-Saltuk; for the sake of our Sheikh Muhammad who laid hold of the garments and limbs—let there be a laying of hand upon hand, back upon back, chest upon chest! For the Love of Ali, the Lion of God, grant assistance, O Lord!"[29] After this prayer the challengers began to wrestle. When the sultan grew angry, he knelt down upon one knee and tried to lift his opponent from beneath.

Murad IV was so infatuated with wrestling and displaying his strength that, at times, he boasted of his strength by lifting the pages of his court over his head and swinging them in the air:

> One day he came out covered with perspiration from the hammam (bath) in the Khas-oda, saluted those present, and said "Now I have had a bath." . . . I said, "My emperor, you are now clean and comfortable, do not therefore oil yourself for wrestling today, especially as you have already exerted yourself with others, and your strength must be considerably reduced." "Have I no strength left?" Said he, "let us see;" upon which he seized me as an eagle, by my belt, raised me over his head, and whirled me about as children do a top. I exclaimed, "Do not let me fall, my emperor, hold me fast!" He said, "Hold fast yourself," and continued to swing me round, until I cried out, "For God's sake, my emperor, cease, for I am quite giddy." He then began to laugh, released me, and gave me forty eight pieces of gold for the amusement I had afforded him.[30]

To become a wrestler, one had to attend special schools called *tekkes*, which combined athletic and spiritual training under one roof. The *tekkes* were modeled after *zurkhanehs* (houses of strength), a traditional Iranian gymnasium. Here, athletes, who exercised to build a strong body, also learned the philosophical and spiritual principles of mysticism (Sufism), such as purity of heart, selflessness, compassion, humility, and respect toward fellow human beings. They were also taught that abstinence from sex and bodily indulgence preserved their physical strength. A true *pehlivan* was not only a man of muscles and physical strength, but also a spiritual being with unique and distinct personal and ethical qualities. These included grace and humility, particularly when he defeated a challenger. If a younger athlete defeated an older wrestler, for example, he kissed the hand of the defeated man as a sign of respect and humility.

Kirkpinar, on the outskirts of Edirne, was the first site of Ottoman wrestling competition. The area also served as a hunting ground for Ottoman sultans. The first Kirkpinar wrestling tournament was probably held in 1360/1361, during the reigns of the Ottoman sultans Orhan and Murad I. Today, *yagli güresh,* or oil wrestling—where young men compete in leather shorts, their bodies shiny and slippery with oil—remains one of Turkey's most popular national sports. As in Anatolia and parts of the Balkans, in Egypt too, men stripped themselves of all their clothing except their drawers and oiled their bodies before they entangled in a wrestling match. These matches were particularly popular after important processions and during various festivals.

Another nonmilitary sport was the game of *matrak,* in which balls were struck with wooden clubs/sticks that were covered with leather and looked like bowling ten-pins. The tops of the clubs were rounded and slightly wider than the body. The game was a kind of battle animation, and it was considered a lawn game. Throwing heavy stones or boulders was another popular sport that survived until the end of the empire. The sport involved throwing in a pushing motion a heavy stone or rock as far as possible. The game was alluded to in various Greek folk songs, "which recounted the exploits of brigand bands."[31]

Among the more sedentary and less physically demanding games that remained popular throughout the history of the Ottoman Empire were chess, backgammon, checkers (draughts), and cards. All these games were popular among men who spent much of their time in coffeehouses. With the increasing Westernization of the empire in the 19th century, a host of new and competing European sports such as soccer (football), tennis, rugby, cycling, swimming, gymnastics, croquet, boxing, and cricket were introduced.[32] In Izmir in 1890, a soccer and rugby club was organized, and in the win-

Wrestling match, 19th century. Anonymous. (V&A Images, London/Art Resource, NY)

ter of 1908–1909, an Ottoman army officer, who had studied the impact of sports on the youth, embarked on a campaign to educate the urban population on the benefits of physical exercise. He organized several modern sport clubs. In Izmir, an athletic club began to hold Pannonian Games, which included aquatic sports as well as soccer, cricket, tennis, and fencing.[33] Horseracing and hunting clubs also appealed to the Ottoman love for traditional sports, and they sprang up in Istanbul where race courses, mimicking those of France and England, were built by the government.[34] Among the imported sports to catch on, soccer was the most successful, while games such as tennis remained confined to the four walls of the imperial palace.[35]

NOTES

1. Alexander Pallis, *In the Days of the Janissaries: Old Turkish Life As Depicted in the "Travel Book" of Evliya' Chelebi* (London: Hutchinson & Co., 1951), 200.

2. Halil Inalcik, "The Ottoman Civilization and Palace Patronage," in *Ottoman Civilization*, eds. Halil Inalcik and Günsel Renda, 2 vols. (Istanbul: Republic of Turkey Ministry of Culture Publications, 2003), 1:141.

3. Pallis, *In the Days of the Janissaries*, 200.

4. V. J. Parry, "Djerid," in *The Encyclopaedia of Islam*, eds. B. Lewis, Ch. Pellat, and, J. Schacht (Leiden: E. J. Brill, 1963), 2:532.

5. Ibid.

6. Metin And, "The Social Life of the Ottomans, in the Sixteenth Century," in *Ottoman Civilization*, eds. Halil Inalcik and Günsel Renda, 2 vols. (Istanbul: Republic of Turkey Ministry of Culture Publications, 2003), 1:439.

7. Lucy Mary Jane Garnett, *Turkey of the Ottomans* (New York: Charles Scribner's Sons, 1915), 293.

8. Ibid.

9. Ibid.

10. Parry, *Djerid*, 532.

11. Ibid.

12. Çelebi, *The Intimate Life of an Ottoman Statesman*, trans. Robert Dankoff (Albany: State University of New York Press, 1991), 280.

13. And, "The Social Life of the Ottomans," 439.

14. Parry, "Djerid," 532.

15. Ibid.

16. Raphaela Lewis, *Everyday Life in Ottoman Turkey* (London: B. T. Batsford Ltd., 1971), 131–32.

17. Edward William Lane, *An Account of the Manners and Customs of the Modern Egyptians* (New York: Dover Publications, 1973), 351.

18. Ibid.

19. Lewis, *Everyday Life in Ottoman Turkey*, 131–2.

20. And, "The Social Life of the Ottomans," 439.

21. Pallis, *In the Days of the Janissaries*, 204.

22. And, "The Social Life of the Ottomans," 439.

23. Pallis, *In the Days of the Janissaries*, 205.

24. And, "The Social Life of the Ottomans," 439.

25. Julia Pardoe, *The City of the Sultan and Domestic Manners of the Turks in 1836*, 3 vols. (London: Henry Colburn Publisher, 1838), 1:306.

26. Ibid., 1:305.

27. Pallis, *In the Days of the Janissaries*, 205.

28. And, "The Social Life of the Ottomans," 437.

29. Evliya Efendi (Çelebi), *Narratives of Travels in Europe, Asia, and Africa in the Seventeenth Century*, trans. Ritter Joseph Von Hammer (London: Parbury, Allen, & Co., 1834), 1:139.

30. Ibid.

31. Garnett, *Turkey of the Ottomans*, 293.

32. Donald Quataert, *The Ottoman Empire, 1700–1922* (Cambridge: Cambridge University Press, 2005), 160.

33. Garnett, *Turkey of the Ottomans*, 294.

34. Ibid., 295.

35. Quataert, *The Ottoman Empire*, 162.

13

SICKNESS, DEATH, AND DYING

Death was a common occurrence throughout the Ottoman Empire. As in other pre-industrial societies, most deaths in the cities, towns, and villages of the Ottoman Empire "were deaths of children."[1] Children "were particularly susceptible to the intestinal diseases, such as dysentery and giardia," and the "most common killers of young children, from birth to age five, were diseases of the intestines and the pulmonary system."[2] "Measles and smallpox" were also "common causes of death among children."[3] Among the young adults living in the urban centers of the empire, "the most common cause of death" was tuberculosis.[4] According to one source, "one-third to one-half of the recorded deaths of young adults in Istanbul at the end of the 19th century were from tuberculosis and its complications."[5] Typhoid also "killed as many as did smallpox, approximately 5 per cent of the young adult deaths were caused by each."[6]

In the rural regions of the empire, the principal causes of death were malnutrition and lack of access to clean water. A population whose diet was "primarily made up of carbohydrates, with few vegetables, fewer fruits, and limited protein, were naturally susceptible to disease."[7] Water was the principal carrier of many diseases, and "ignorance of the nature of the disease was in itself" one of the most important "causes of death."[8]

Plagues frequently killed thousands of people in a short span of time. Until the second half of the 19th century, plague was endemic and virulent in Istanbul and other urban centers of the empire. Called "*veba* in Turkish, the Arabic *waba*, 'to be contaminated,' the lethal illness known simply as 'plague' usually" referred to "bubonic plague, also known in the West as the Black Plague or the Black Death."[9] Pandemic "throughout the empire from the beginning of the 16th century to the middle of the 19th century, plague was caused by the bacillus *Yersinia pestis* and was usually transmitted by means of rodents infested with infected fleas."[10] Although "the disease was endemic, meaning that it was both geographically widespread and constantly present at some level in the population, periodic epidemic outbreaks of great virulence frequently resulted in a 75 percent mortality rate among those affected."[11] For "this reason, plague was greatly feared by Ottoman subjects and by the foreign travelers who frequented the empire."[12] The disease "spread along trade routes and the paths of pilgrims to and from Mecca."[13] As the majority of pilgrims came from Anatolia and the Arab provinces, regions such as "Western Anatolia, Egypt, and northern Syria reported plague epidemics most often."[14] When a plague struck, people fled from the cities and towns to the countryside.[15]

In "its most serious outbreaks, the plague disrupted the Ottoman economy by interrupting harvests in the countryside and commercial activities and handicrafts in the cities."[16] In many urban communities a plague-stricken person was shunned and abandoned. In the southern Albanian town of Gjirokastër, when a person developed a pimple or a boil, people immediately concluded that he had the plague and fled from him. He was also prohibited from entering homes. For two years afterward, people avoided entering the home of a person who had suffered from the plague. Even after two years, they insisted on cleansing the house with vinegar and disinfecting it with aromatic herbs. At times, people went as far as tearing down and rebuilding various parts of the house and whitewashing "all the rooms with lime before entering."[17] Without "any modern understanding of germ theory, Ottoman doctors, like those in the West, hypothesized that plague was an airborne infection caused by miasmas (unpleasant or unhealthy air), carried by the wind."[18] An "alternative theory attributed the spread of plague to demons, or jinni."[19]

Hardly less terrible "were the variations of cholera," which "once introduced spread with terrible rapidity."[20] The great 19th-century "cholera epidemics struck the Middle East and Balkans with ferocity, each epidemic killing hundreds of thousands."[21] Cholera spread primarily through Muslim pilgrims from India who brought the disease to Mecca where pilgrims from the Ottoman Empire contracted the disease. From Mecca, the pilgrims who had come from all parts of Anatolia, Syria, Egypt, and so forth, brought the disease home. Not surprisingly, Anatolia was devastated by the great cholera epidemics of 1847 and 1865.[22]

Another devastating epidemic that generally struck the Ottoman Empire in times of wars and mass migrations was typhus. In the second half of the 19th century, particularly from 1864 to 1880, Muslim refugees from Russian conquests in the Balkans and the Caucasus died in large numbers from typhus, which they spread in those regions of Anatolia and Syria where they settled.[23]

Borrowing from the practices of European states, during the reign of Abdülhamid II, the Ottoman government introduced major improvements in the area of public health. An international sanitary board was established and quickly organized a quarantine system to prevent the entry of epidemic diseases. Filth and garbage, as well as stray dogs, were removed from the streets of the capital. The main streets of Istanbul and other urban centers were paved "with basalt blocks," which allowed rain water to wash them and "lessen the accumulations of filth."[24] A well-organized medical school was established in the capital to train students in medicine and modern sciences.[25]

TRADITIONAL REMEDIES

Until the introduction of modern medicine, the people of the Ottoman Empire relied on traditional remedies that had been passed down from one generation to the next. In the 17th century, to cleanse their bodies or as a remedy for various ailments such as yellow and black bile, phlegm, and parasites, the people of Vlorë (Vlora), a major seaport and commercial center in southwestern Albania, poured boiling pitch into a new cup, then rinsed it thoroughly and drank water from the cleaned cup.[26] Throughout the empire, popular belief held that certain foods alleviated certain ailments and assisted with certain deficiencies. For instance, according to popular belief, the eels of Ohrid, the deepest lake in the Balkans, if caught fresh and wrapped in leaves and roasted, not only made "a very nutritious meal" but also helped a man "have intercourse with his wife five or six times" a day.[27] Anyone "with consumption" [pulmonary tuberculosis] who put "a salted eel head on his own head" was said to be cured "of his ailments."[28]

At the Egyptian or Spice Bazaar (Misir Çarşi) in Istanbul, gunpowder was prescribed as a remedy for hemorrhoids, and patients were told to boil it with the juice of a whole lemon, strain off the liquid, dry the powder and swallow it the next morning with a little water on an empty stomach.[29] Gunpowder was also "supposed to be a good cure for pimples when mixed with a little crushed garlic."[30] Whatever its value as a pharmaceutical remedy, gunpowder "was finally banned from the market because the shops in which it was sold kept blowing up."[31]

The Ottoman traveler Evliya Çelebi writing in the 17th century, reported that there were 2,000 men producing "ointments, pills, and tinctures" and "selling around 3,000 different medicinal herbs and spices" in and around the Egyptian Bazaar.[32] Healers and men of medicine "made effective pills from ambergris, a secretion from the alimentary tract of the sperm whale," which was believed "to strengthen the nerves and stimulate the senses."[33] Thus, the spices, herbs, scented oils, and remedies sold in the form of paste, cream, and syrup or powder traded in the Egyptian Bazaar were used not only to flavor Ottoman foods and dishes but also as remedies for a wide variety of deficiencies and ailments. From the sultans and members of the ruling family to the humblest subject of the state, everyone relied on potions, thick syrups, herbs, and spices as miracle cures.

In 1520, when Ayşe Hafsa Sultan, the mother of Süleyman the Magnificent, became ill, the sultan sent a letter to a well-known physician and healer who lived and worked at a mosque in the town of Manisa (Magnesia) in western Anatolia, pleading with him to offer a cure for his ailing mother who had fallen ill after mourning the loss of her husband, the deceased sultan Selim I. Mixing 41 herbs and spices, the physician "concocted a thick syrup" that saved the sick and dying widow.[34] The queen mother expressed her gratitude for this miracle by ordering that the syrup responsible for her cure be distributed once a year among the people, a tradition that has persisted to the present day.[35] Every year, during the so-called Mesir Festival, Mesir Paste (*Mesir Macunu*) is thrown to the crowds who gather in the grounds of a mosque at Manisa named after the queen mother Ayşe Hafsa Sultan.[36] Also known as Turkish Viagra or Sultan's Aphrodisiac, Mesir Paste, which is a spiced paste in the form of a candy, is believed to restore health, youth, and potency.

Ottomans also relied on prayers, charms, and spells as potential cures, especially after the remedies of a physician failed to produce positive results. At times, suras from the Quran were recited with gentle breaths over the face and limbs of the ailing patient. Spells read in Arabic and Persian were also considered effective, provided certain conditions were met. Unfortunately, such prerequisites could create embarrassing situations. Reciting a spell to an ailing and dying high government official, Evliya Çelebi complained that the efficacy of his spell required the reciter to "strike the palsied man's face three times with his own shoe, holding it in the left hand."[37] The ailing man in this particular instance, however, was a grand vizier, and Evliya could not strike him with a shoe.

Some holy men used their breath to treat physical, mental, or nervous disorders. The patient was placed in front of the healer, who went "into a kind of trance, at intervals blowing in the direction" of the patient who was being treated.[38] The breath, "thought of as the essence of one's self, was believed to carry healing virtue to the patient."[39] Rich and poor, young and old, women and men were convinced that when doctors failed to cure a patient, puffs of breath from holy men could remedy their illness.

Upon recovery from a severe illness, as was also done upon the birth of a child and a safe return from pilgrimage to Mecca, a sheep was sacrificed as an expression of thankfulness and gratitude to God for restored health.[40] If wealthy, the sick person who had recovered showered gifts and favors among the members of his extended household, including his officers, doorkeepers, irregulars, conscripts, cooks, tasters, muleteers, grooms, torchbearers, as well as the homeless and destitute.[41] He also distributed money among the poor; had several orphan boys circumcised; gave each of the boys into the custody of a master craftsman, or a teacher; and dressed them in a nice suit. The same gratefully recovered man could also find homes for orphaned girls and provide them with new clothing. He could also construct stone pavement over a road; dig gutters to relieve a town from flooding and mud; build shops, coffeehouses, and homes; and establish his property as an endowment for the establishment or upkeep of a charitable foundation.

If the illness worsened and the sick person became convinced of his death, he made his will in favor of his son, or any other individual, in the presence of two or more witnesses. If the ailing man was a person of status, wealth, and power, he summoned the ulema, notables, and his subordinates to compose his last will and testament. These declarations would include a request for where he should be buried, how much of his money could be distributed among those who had served him, and whether any of his money could be used to erect a monument or even a fountain at his tombstone. Many people bequeathed some of their money to the holy cities of Mecca and Medina. In some cases, the dying man freed his slaves, bestowing on them and his servants gifts and gold pieces. He also appointed his executor.

As the hour of death arrived, the family sent for a man who could recite the Quran. He was asked to read in a loud voice the Ya Seen (Ya Sin), or the 36th chapter of the Quran, which has been branded by some as the heart of the holy book. It was believed that hearing the Ya Seen allowed the departing spirit to calm itself and focus on the coming journey. Others present also read prayers in an audible voice. At times, the sick person was encouraged to recite the words of remembrance and forgiveness. Men of religion always recommended, if at all possible, that a Muslim's last words be the declaration of faith: "I bear witness that there is no God. I bear witness that Muhammad is the messenger of God." In certain instances, when a person was on the point of death, the people present poured sherbet made of water and sugar down his throat.

As soon as the person died, his eyes and mouth were closed. The dead person's big toes were "brought in contact and fastened together with a thin slip of cloth, to prevent the legs remaining apart."[42] The body was then temporarily covered with a sheet. Perfumes were also burnt near the body of the deceased. The local imam, or any other man of religion who was present, encouraged the family to remain calm and accept a fate that could only be determined by God who gave life and took it away. The imam also encouraged the family to pray for the departed and to begin preparations for the burial. Although Islam discouraged loud wailing and lamentation, an outpouring of grief followed.

Muslim tradition required burial of the deceased as soon as it was humanly possible, because it was not proper to keep a corpse long in the house. If the person had died in the evening, the shrouding and burial had to take place before midnight; if, however, he/she had died at a later hour, the deceased was buried on the following day. Prior to burial, the body was washed with warm water—usually by a member of the family, a close friend, or an acquaintance. Ottoman women were always washed "by their own sex."[43] Professional washers, both men and women, also were available to wash and shroud the body for a fee.[44] Every effort was made not to wash the body on flat ground because the water could spread over a wide surface. Popular belief held that it was a bad omen to walk on such water.[45] Toward the end of the washing ceremony, camphor and water were mixed and put into several pots and poured "three times first from the head to the feet, then from the right shoulder to the feet, lastly from the left shoulder to the feet" of the deceased.[46] Every time the water was poured, the declaration of faith was repeated by the person washing the body or an individual present at the ceremony. If the dead had been killed as a martyr, he could be buried in the very clothes he had died in.

After bathing the body and drying it with a clean piece of cloth, "several balls of cotton wool were covered in calico and soaked in warm water, to be inserted in the seven orifices of the body."[47] Cotton wools were also placed between the fingers and the toes and also in the armpits. The mourners then placed the deceased in a shroud (*kefen*). For men, this consisted of three pieces of clean white sheets, large enough to conceal the entire body, and for women five pieces of white garments.[48] The color of the shroud had to be white.[49] The *kefen* for both men and women was perfumed with scented water or incense. At times, "pepper, spices, and rose-water" were also "put in other crevices."[50] Attendants then laid the body in a coffin with the face of the deceased facing downward. The coffins of men were distinguished by a turban and those of women by a coif. If the deceased had been a girl and a virgin, the rich and powerful families set garlands and boughs of oranges on the coffin as they carried it to the cemetery.[51] The coffin transported the body to the burial site where funeral prayers were read. Sometimes before the funeral procession, the family of the deceased hired a group of mourners who proceeded through the streets at night proclaiming their grief with the cries of mourning.[52]

During the burial ceremony, only the male relations and male community members could accompany the body to the cemetery. While men participated in the funeral procession, women stayed home and mourned in the privacy of the harem. Christians, Jews, and "foreigners were also excluded."[53] An imam or a member of the religious class led the procession to the cemetery by walking in front of the coffin. Other members of the religious establishment walked on either side of the coffin. Mourners walked behind. While escorting the body, the mourners remained silent. Islam discouraged carrying candles, shouting the name of God, weeping loudly, playing music, or even reading the Quran. Thus, "no external signs of mourning" were used by the Ottomans "either for a funeral or subsequently," nor were "periods of seclusion observed by them on the death of a relative."[54] "Excessive sorrow" for dead children was "considered not only sinful, but detrimental to their happiness and rest in Paradise."[55] It was, however, "an act of filial duty to mourn consistently for lost parents, and not to cease praying for their forgiveness and acceptance with Allah."[56] The coffin "was draped with a red or green pall over which were spread blue cloths embroidered with gold thread and silk."[57] When the mourners passed a mosque or a shrine, they set the coffin down and offered prayers for the deceased.

Once the funeral procession had reached the cemetery, family, friends, and acquaintances gathered to pray as the prayer leader or the imam stood in front of the body of the deceased facing away from the mourners. After the prayers had ended, "the lid of the coffin was removed before it was lowered into the earth."[58] The shrouded body was lifted out of the coffin while prayers were recited and was placed in the grave still wrapped in a *kefen.* The body of the deceased had to be positioned in a recumbent posture at right angles to the *kibla* (Arabic: *qibla*) or the direction of prayer towards Mecca. In this way the body would face the holy city of Mecca if it turned to its side. This placement enabled the faithful to have the same physical relationship with Mecca in both life and death.

Cemeteries were located outside cities, towns, or villages, and were not demarcated by walls, fences, and gates. Every attempt was made to bury the dead in a beautiful cemetery amid flowers and cypress. Thus, one of the largest cemeteries in Istanbul stretched along the slope of a hill overlooking the blue waters of the Bosphorus and was densely shaded by old cypress trees. Not surprisingly, the locals used the cemeteries as a park. It was not unusual to find a Turk smoking his pipe or *chubuk* "with his back resting against a turban-crested grave stone," the Greek spreading "his meal upon a tomb," the Armenian sheltering himself "from the sunshine beneath the boughs" that overshadowed "the burial places of his people," "the women" sitting "in groups" and talking "of their homes and of their little ones," and "the children" gathering "the wild flowers" that grew "amid the graves as gaily as though death had never entered there."[59]

Several days after the funeral, women of the household visited the cemetery and uttered lamentations over the grave. Once they had expressed and released their grief and sorrow, the female mourners left food offerings on the grave. There was no prescribed clothing for a mourning ceremony, but men generally wore a coat in a somber color such as black or brown.

Cemetery overlooking the Bosphorus and Istanbul. (Library of Congress)

When an Ottoman dignitary or high official passed away, funeral procedures followed the official Hanafi rite.[60] The body was laid out and an *iskat* prayer was recited. *Iskat* was "alms given on behalf of the dead as compensation for their neglected religious duties."[61] The body was then washed, wrapped in a shroud, and placed in an ornamental coffin for "transport to a mosque for prayers."[62] Viziers, ulema, *şeyhs*, notables, and dignitaries assembled and carried the body to the mosque of Aya Sofya, while muezzins and *dervişes* recited prayers and litanies.[63] At the mosque, a ritual prayer was performed. The funeral procession then continued with the coffin carried to its final resting place at the cemetery.[64] At the cemetery, tents were set up and the holy Quran was recited by men of religion as well as *dervişes* for several days.[65]

Each grave "was marked at the head by a single stone, about fifty centimeters high, either cylindrical or uncut."[66] A person of wealth and power was buried "in a rectangular marble tomb, a round marble column as high as a man at the head, topped by a sculpture of the Turkish headgear appropriate to the rank of the deceased."[67] The column was usually inscribed with Arabic inscriptions from the Quran. Occasionally "instead of a column, the headstone was a marble plaque about a hand span in width and as high as a man and again carved with inscriptions."[68] Women's "gravestones were carved with flowers and verses of hope and if a headstone fell it was considered unlucky to set it up again."[69]

Except as a special privilege, which could apply only to sultans, dead bodies could not be interred in a mosque, church, or synagogue, or even within the town or city, but rather in cemeteries in the suburbs where the Muslims, Christians, and Jews had their own separate graveyards.[70] In unique circumstances, particularly when the body of a slain sultan was involved, the internment could assume a significant political meaning. After Murad I was killed on the battlefield of Kosovo Polje in 1389, his vital organs were removed and buried in a mausoleum on the banks of the river Llap (Serbo-Croatian: Lab; Turkish: Klab). His body meanwhile was carried to Bursa, where it was buried at the courtyard of the city's Great Mosque.[71] Miloš Kobilić or Obilić, the Serbian "hero" who assassinated Murad I, was interred in a grave at a monastery a short distance from the sultan's resting place. Nearly three centuries later, the mausoleum of the assassin was "lit with jeweled lamps and scented with ambergris and musk" and "supported by wealthy endowments and ministered by priests who played host to passing visitors" and pilgrims.[72] In contrast, the mausoleum grave of the Ottoman sultan "was besmirched with filth" and excrement, because the local Serbs used the royal tomb as a privy and defecated on it to insult the Turkish invaders who had occupied their homeland.[73] To protect the royal mausoleum from future assaults, an Ottoman official ordered the construction of a huge wall with a gate around the tomb "so that people on horseback could not get in."[74] Five hundred fruit trees were also planted and a well was dug. A keeper was appointed to live there with his family so that they could care for "the silk carpets, candlesticks, censers, rose-water containers and lamps" that furnished the mausoleum.[75]

For Muslims, a grave was a "halting place" for the soul of the deceased, while it was interrogated by the two angels, Nekir and Munker, who guarded the gates of heaven and appeared as soon as the dead had entered the grave. They asked the dead to sit up and prepare for a harsh interrogation. This explains why, after the mourners had dispersed, the imam remained by the grave to assist with the interrogation of the dead.[76] The two angels questioned the newly deceased on his faith by asking: "Who is your God? What is your religion? And, who is this man?" The man in the third question was the prophet Muhammad who was shown to the dead. If the deceased had been a true believer and a devout Muslim during his life, he answered the first question by stating that his creator was Allah (God), the second by saying that Islam was his religion, and the third by recognizing Muhammad and declaring him to be the true messenger of God.

If the deceased had been "lax" in performing his religious duties, according to Muslim belief, at the time of questioning he would forget the basic tenets of his faith and fail to answer the questions.[77] Failure to provide the two angels with correct answers condemned the dead to eternal torment and torture. The two angels beat the condemned with iron mallets and filled the grave with snakes and scorpions. On the other hand, those who passed the test and convinced the interrogating angels of their faith were allowed to rest until the day of resurrection and enjoy the fragrance of paradise. On the Day of Judgment, all were raised from the dead and judged once again according to their deeds on earth, before being forced to walk over the bridge of Sirat that stood over the fire of hell and led ultimately to paradise. The evildoers slipped and fell into the fires and torments of hell while the innocent crossed the bridge with ease and dignity. Those who were guaranteed a safe passage over the bridge included infants, soldiers who had fought and died in the name of Islam, and all those who had perished during a plague.

The mourning ceremonies of the living varied from one religious community to another, with each practicing its own unique mourning and funeral rites, customs, and traditions. In many Muslim communities, relatives and close friends observed a mourning period during which they received visitors expressing their grief and condolences. Those in grief dressed in black and avoided jewelry or brightly colored and decorative clothing. If "the deceased" was "well-to-do," alms were paid to the poor and "specially prepared dishes, consisting chiefly of pastry and stewed fruits," were sent "to the houses of friends" and distributed among the poor "in return for which their prayers" were "requested for the soul of the departed."[78] On the 7th and the 40th day after the funeral these activities repeated and "ceremonies of commemoration were held."[79] Widows were expected to mourn for a much longer period. During this time, a widow was not allowed to remarry, move from her house, or wear jewelry and colorful dresses.

In some parts of Albania, the natives mourned their dead relatives for many years. Every Sunday, all the relatives of the deceased gathered in a house and paid professional mourners who would weep and wail. When they had finished their lamentation, the host prepared "various pastries, including . . . saffron-flavored sweets to be distributed in town from house to house . . . free of charge to rich and poor alike and to all travelers and sojourners . . . for the sake of spirits."[80] Immediately following the death of a loved one, Albanian families performed many of the same rituals as other families in the empire. After the funeral, the family of the deceased distributed money and gifts among the poor. They also prepared dishes of food as well as pastry that were sent to the homes of relatives, friends, neighbors, and the poor—who were asked to pray for the soul of the dead. Two other memorials were organized on the 7th and 40th day after the funeral.

In the daily life of the Ottoman state, many met a violent death. Those members of the sultan's household who had been condemned to death were first imprisoned before they were strangled in secrecy and neither their heads nor bodies were displayed publicly. Rebels and enemy leaders, however, were beheaded or hanged publicly to cause them disgrace and humiliation.

NOTES

1. Justin McCarthy, *The Ottoman Turks: An Introductory History to 1923* (London, New York: Wesley Longman Limited, 1997), 279.
2. Ibid., 278–79.
3. Ibid., 278.
4. Ibid.
5. Ibid., 278–79.
6. Ibid., 279.
7. Ibid.
8. Ibid.
9. Daniel Panzac, "Plague," in *Encyclopedia of the Ottoman Empire,* eds. Gábor Ágoston and Bruce Masters (New York: Facts On File, 2009), 462.
10. Ibid.
11. Ibid.
12. Ibid.
13. McCarthy, *The Ottoman Turks,* 280.
14. Ibid.
15. Çelebi, *The Intimate Life of an Ottoman Statesman,* trans. Robert Dankoff (Albany: State University of New York Press, 1991), 99–100.
16. Panzac, "Plague," 462.
17. Evliya Çelebi, *Evliya Çelebi in Albania,* trans. Robert Dankoff and Robert Elsie (Leiden: Brill, 2000), 81.
18. Panzac, "Plague," 462.
19. Ibid.
20. Edwin Pears, *Turkey and Its People* (London: Methuen, 1912), 377.

21. McCarthy, *The Ottoman Turks*, 280.

22. Ibid.

23. Ibid.

24. Pears, *Turkey And Its People*, 378.

25. Ibid., 379.

26. Çelebi, *Evliya Çelebi in Albania*, 143.

27. Ibid., 197.

28. Ibid.

29. Tom Brosnahan and Pat Yale, *Turkey* (Hawthorn, Australia: Lonely Planet Publications, 1996), 163.

30. Ibid.

31. Ibid.

32. Isabel Böcking, Laura Salm-Reifferscheidt, and Moritz Stipsicz, *The Bazaars of Istanbul* (New York: Thames & Hudson, 2009), 171.

33. Ibid.

34. Ibid.

35. Ibid.

36. Ibid.

37. Çelebi, *The Intimate Life of an Ottoman Statesman*, 109.

38. John Kingsley Birge, *The Bektashi Order of Dervishes* (London: Luzac and Company, 1937), 84.

39. Ibid.

40. Julia Pardoe, *The City of the Sultan and Domestic Manners of the Turks in 1836*, 3 vols. (London: Henry Colburn Publisher, 1838), 1:168.

41. Çelebi, *The Intimate Life of an Ottoman Statesman*, 104.

42. Thomas Patrick Hughes, *Dictionary of Islam* (New Delhi: Munshiram Manoharlal Publishers, 1999), 80.

43. Godfrey Goodwin, *The Private World of Ottoman Women* (London: Saqi Books, 2006), 115.

44. Hughes, *Dictionary of Islam*, 81.

45. Ibid.

46. Ibid.

47. Goodwin, *The Private World of Ottoman Women*, 115.

48. Hughes, *Dictionary of Islam*, 81.

49. Ibid.

50. Goodwin, *The Private World of Ottoman Women*, 116.

51. Ottaviano Bon, *The Sultan's Seraglio: An Intimate Portrait of Life at the Ottoman Court* (London: Saqi Books, 1996), 141.

52. Metin And, "The Social Life of the Ottomans, in the Sixteenth Century," in *Ottoman Civilization*, ed. Halil Inalcik and Günsel Renda, 2 vols. (Istanbul: Republic of Turkey Ministry of Culture Publications, 2003), 1:425.

53. Goodwin, *The Private World of Ottoman Women*, 116.

54. Lucy Mary Jane Garnett, *Turkey of the Ottomans* (New York: Charles Scribner's Sons, 1915), 111.

55. Ibid.

56. Ibid.

57. And, "The Social Life of the Ottomans," 425–26.

58. Ibid., 426.

59. Pardoe, *The City of the Sultan,* 1:260–61.

60. Jane Hathaway, *Beshir Agha: Chief Eunuch of the Ottoman Imperial Harem.* (Oxford: Oneworld Publications, 2005), 104.

61. Çelebi, *The Intimate Life of an Ottoman Statesman,* 283. See also *New Redhouse Turkish-English Dictionary* (Istanbul: Redhouse Yaynevi, 1968).

62. Hathaway, *Beshir Agha,* 104.

63. Çelebi, *The Intimate Life of an Ottoman Statesman,* 267.

64. Ibid.

65. Ibid., 268.

66. And, "The Social Life of the Ottomans," 426.

67. Ibid.

68. Ibid.

69. Goodwin, *The Private World of Ottoman Women,* 116–17.

70. Pietro Della Valle, *The Pilgrim: The Journeys of Pietro Della Valle,* trans. George Bull (London: The Folio Society, 1989), 105.

71. Çelebi, *Evliya Çelebi in Albania,* 17.

72. Ibid., 19, 21.

73. Ibid., 21.

74. Ibid.

75. Ibid.

76. Garnett, *Turkey of the Ottomans,* 110.

77. Ibid.

78. Ibid.

79. Goodwin, *The Private World of Ottoman Women,* 116; See also Garnett, *Turkey of the Ottomans,* 110.

80. Çelebi, *Evliya Çelebi in Albania,* 83.

SELECTED BIBLIOGRAPHY

Ágoston, Gábor, and Bruce Masters. *Encyclopedia of the Ottoman Empire.* New York: Facts On File, 2009.

Ahmad, Feroz. *The Young Turks: The Committee of Union and Progress in Turkish Politics.* Oxford: Clarendon Press, 1969.

Aksan, Virginia H. *An Ottoman Statesman in War and Peace: Ahmed Resmi Efendi, 1700–1783.* Leiden: E. J. Brill, 1995.

Akşin, Sina. *Turkey From Empire to Revolutionary Republic: The Emergence of the Turkish Nation from 1789 to Present.* Albany: New York University Press, 2007.

Arsel, Semhet, ed. *Timeless Tastes: Turkish Culinary Culture.* Istanbul: Vehbi Koç Vakfi, 2003.

Bayerle, Gustav. *Pashas, Begs and Effendis: A Historical Dictionary of Titles and Terms in the Ottoman Empire.* Istanbul: Isis Press, 1997.

Behar, Cem. *A Neighborhood in Ottoman Istanbul: Fruit Vendors and Civil Servants in the Kasap Ilyas Mahalle.* Albany: State University of New York, 2003.

Bon, Ottaviano. *The Sultan's Seraglio, An Intimate Portrait of Life at the Ottoman Court.* London: Saqi Books, 1996.

Braude, Benjamin, and Bernard Lewis, eds. *Christians and Jews in the Ottoman Empire,* 2 vols. New York: Holmes and Meier, 1982.

Braudel, Fernand. *The Mediterranean and the Mediterranean World in the Age of Philip II.* New York: Harper & Row Publishers 1973.

Braudel, Fernand. *The Perspective of the World: Civilization & Capitalism 15th–18th Century*, trans. Sian Reynolds. New York: Harper & Row Publishers, 1979.

Burton, Richard F. *Personal Narrative of a Pilgrimage to Al-Madinah and Meccah*. 2 vols. New York: Dover Publications, 1964.

Cicek, Kemal, ed. *The Great Ottoman Turkish Civilization*, 4 vols. Ankara: 2000.

Clot, André. *Suleiman the Magnificent*. London: Saqi Books, 2005.

Davey, Richard. *The Sultan and His Subjects*, 2 vols. London: Chapman and Hall LD., 1897.

Davis, Fanny. *The Ottoman Lady: A Social History from 1718 to 1918*. New York: Greenwood Press, 1986.

Davison, Roderic H. *Nineteenth Century Ottoman Diplomacy and Reforms*. Istanbul: Isis Press, 1999.

Davison, Roderic H. *Reform in the Ottoman Empire, 1856–1876*. New York: Gordian Press, 1973.

Della Valle, Pietro. *The Pilgrim*. London: The Folio Society, 1989.

Edib, Halidé. *Memoirs of Halidé Edib*. New York: Gorgias Press, 2004.

Elsie, Robert. *A Dictionary of Albanian Religion, Mythology, and Folk Culture*. New York: New York University Press, 2001.

Evliya Çelebi. *The Intimate Life of an Ottoman Statesman: Melek Ahmed Pasha, 1588–1662*. trans. Robert Dankoff. Albany: State University of New York Press, 1991.

Evliya Çelebi. *Seyahatnameh, Book of Travels*, Vol. II. *Evliya Çelebi in Bitlis*. eds. Robert Dankoff and Robert Elise. Leiden: Brill, 1990.

Evliya Çelebi. *Seyahatnameh, Book of Travels*, Vol. V. *Evliya Çelebi in Albania and Adjacent Regions (Kosovo, Montenegro, Ohrid)*. eds. Robert Dankoff and Robert Elise. Leiden: Brill, 2000.

Evliya Effendi. *Narratives of Travels in Europe, Asia, and Africa in the Seventeenth Century*. 2 vols. trans. Ritter Joseph Von Hammer. New York: Johnson Reprint Corporation, 1968.

Faroqhi, Suraiya. *Crisis and Change, 1590–1699*, in *An Economic and Social History of the Ottoman History*, ed. Halil Inalcik. Cambridge: Cambridge University Press, 1994.

Faroqhi, Suraiya. *Making a Living in the Ottoman Lands 1480 to 1820*. Istanbul: Isis Press, 1995.

Faroqhi, Suraiya. *Subjects of the Sultan: Culture and Daily Life in the Ottoman Empire*. London: I. B. Tauris, 2000.

Faroqhi, Suraiya, and Christoph K. Neumann, eds. *The Illuminated Table, the Prosperous House: Food and Shelter in Ottoman Material Culture*. Würzburg: Ergon in Kommission, 2003.

Faroqhi, Suraiya. *The Ottoman Empire and the World around It*. London: I. B. Tauris, 2006.

Faroqhi, Suraiya. *Artisans of Empire: Crafts and Craftspeople Under the Ottomans*. London: I. B. Tauris, 2009.

Findley, Carter V. *Bureaucratic Reform in the Ottoman Empire: the Sublime Porte, 1789–1922.* Princeton: Princeton University Press, 1980.

Finkel, Caroline. *Osman's Dream: The History of the Ottoman Empire.* New York: Basic Books, 2005.

Finkelstein, Louis, ed. *The Jews: Their History, Culture, and Religion.* New York: Harpers & Brothers Publishers, 1960.

Freely, John. *Inside the Seraglio: Private Lives of the Sultans in Istanbul.* London: Penguin Books, 1999.

Garnett, Lucy Mary Jane. *Turkey of the Ottomans.* New York: Charles Scribner's Sons, 1915.

Gibb, H.A.R., and Harold Bowen. *Islamic Society and the West: A Study of the Impact of Western Civilization on Moslem Culture in the Near East.* London: Oxford University Press, 1957.

Goodwin, Godfrey. *The Private World of Ottoman Women.* London: Saqi Books, 2006.

Hale, William. *Turkish Foreign Policy, 1774–2000.* London: Frank Cass, 2000.

Hathaway, Jane. *The Arab Lands Under Ottoman Rule, 1516–1800.* London: Pearson Longman, 2008.

Hathaway, Jane. *Beshir Agha: Chief Eunuch of the Ottoman Imperial Harem.* Oxford: Oneworld Publications, 2005.

Hathaway, Jane. *The Politics of Households in Ottoman Egypt.* Cambridge: Cambridge University Press, 1997.

Hourani, Albert. *Arabic Thought in the Liberal Age: 1798–1939.* Cambridge: Cambridge University Press, 1983.

Hughes, Thomas Patrick. *Dictionary of Islam.* New Delhi: Munshiram Manoharlal Publishers, 1999.

Hurewitz, J. C. *Diplomacy in the Near and Middle East: A Documentary Record.* 2 vols. Princeton: D. Van Nostrand Company, 1956.

Ibn Battuta. *The Travels of Ibn Battuta,* trans. H.A.R. Gibb. Cambridge: Cambridge University Press, 1962.

Imber, Colin. *The Ottoman Empire, 1300–1650: The Structure of Power.* New York: Palgrave Macmillan, 2002.

Inalcik, Halil. *The Ottoman Empire, The Classical Age 1300–1600.* New York: Praeger Publishers, 1973.

Inalcik, Halil. *The Middle East and the Balkans under the Ottoman Empire Essays on Economy and Society.* Bloomington: Indiana University Turkish Studies, 1993.

Inalcik, Halil, and Günsel Renda, eds. *Ottoman Civilization,* 2 vols. Ankara: Ministry of Culture, 2002.

Islamoğlu-Inan, Huri. *The Ottoman Empire and the World Economy.* Cambridge: Cambridge University Press, 1987.

Islamoğlu-Inan, Huri. *State & Peasant in the Ottoman Empire, Agrarian Power Relations & Regional Economic Development in Ottoman Anatolia During the Sixteenth Century.* Leiden: E. J. Brill, 1994.

Jelavich, Barbara. *History of the Balkans: Eighteenth and Nineteenth Centuries,* Vol. 1. Cambridge: Cambridge University Press, 1983.

Jelavich, Charles and Barbara. *The Establishment of the Balkan National States, 1804–1920.* Seattle: University of Washington Press, 1977.

Karpat, Kemal H. *Ottoman Population 1830–1914: Demographic and Social Characteristics.* Madison: University of Wisconsin Press, 1985.

Karpat, Kemal H., and Robert W. Zens. *Ottoman Borderlands: Issues, Personalities and Political Change.* Madison: University of Wisconsin Press, 2003.

Kasaba, Reşat. *The Ottoman Empire and the World Economy: The Nineteenth Century.* Albany: State University of New York Press, 1988.

Khoury, Dina Rizk. *State and Provincial Society in the Ottoman Empire Mosul, 1540–1834.* Cambridge: Cambridge University Press, 1997.

Kiple, Kenneth F., and Kriemhild Conee, eds. *The Cambridge World History of Food.* 2 vols. Cambridge: Cambridge University Press, 2000.

Lane, Edward William. *An Account of the Manners and Customs of the Modern Egyptians.* New York: Dover Publications, 1973.

Le Gall, Dina. *A Culture of Sufism: Naqshbandis in the Ottoman World, 1450–1700.* Albany: State University of New York Press, 2005.

Lewis, Bernard. *The Emergence of Modern Turkey.* Oxford: Oxford University Press, 1961.

Lewis, Bernard. *Istanbul and the Civilization of the Ottoman Empire.* Norman: University of Oklahoma Press, 1963.

Lewis, Raphaela. *Everyday Life in Ottoman Turkey.* London: B. T. Batsford, 1971.

Lewy, Guenter. *The Armenian Massacres in Ottoman Turkey.* Salt Lake City: University of Utah Press, 2005.

Lovrenovic, Ivan. *Bosnia: A Cultural History.* New York: New York University Press, 2001.

Mango, Andrew. *Atatürk: The Biography of the Founder of Modern Turkey.* New York: Overlook Press, 1999.

Mardin, Şerif. *The Genesis of Young Ottoman Thought: A Study in the Modernization of Turkish Political Ideas.* Princeton: Princeton University Press, 1963.

Mazower, Mark. *Salonica: City of Ghosts, Christians, Muslims and Jews, 1430–1950.* New York: Vintage Books, 2006.

McCarthy, Justin. *The Ottoman Turks: An Introductory History to 1923.* London, New York: Wesley Longman Limited, 1997.

Montagu, Lady Mary Wortley. *The Turkish Embassy Letters.* London: Virago Press, 1994.

Naima, Mustafa (Mustafa Naim). *Annals of the Turkish Empire from 1591 to 1659 of the Christian Era,* trans. Charles Fraser. New York: Arno Press, 1973.

Newton, Charles. *Images of the Ottoman Empire.* London: Victoria and Albert Museum Publications, 2007.

O'Kane, Bernard. *Treasures of Islam: Artistic Glories of the Muslim World.* London: Duncan Baird Publishers, 2007.

Özdemir Nutku, "Sinf," in *The Encyclopaedia of Islam,* eds. C.E.E. Bosworth, E. van Donzel, W. P. Heinrichs, and G. Lecomte. Leiden: Brill, 1997.

Pallis, Alexander. *In the Days of the Janissaries: Old Turkish Life As Depicted in the "Travel Book" of Evliya' Chelebi.* London: Hutchinson & Co. Publishers, 1951.

Pardoe, Julia. *Beauties of the Bosphorus.* London: George Virtue, 1839.

Pardoe, Julia. *The City of the Sultan and Domestic Manners of the Turks in 1836.* 2 vols. London: 1838.

Payaslian, Simon. *The History of Armenia.* New York: Palgrave MacMillan, 2007.

Pears, Edwin. *Turkey and Its People.* London: Methuen, 1912.

Quataert, Donald. *The Ottoman Empire, 1700–1922.* Cambridge: Cambridge University Press, 2005.

Quataert, Donald. *Ottoman Manufacturing in the Age of the Industrial Revolution.* Cambridge: Cambridge University Press, 2002.

Rycaut, Paul. *The Present State of the Ottoman Empire.* New York: Arno Press, 1971.

Sajdi, Dana, ed. *Ottoman Tulips, Ottoman Coffee, Leisure and Lifestyle in the Eighteenth Century.* London: Tauris Academic Studies, 2007.

Shaw, Stanford J. *History of the Ottoman Empire and Modern Turkey.* 2 vols. Cambridge: Cambridge University Press, 1976.

Somel, Selcuk Aksin. *Historical Dictionary of the Ottoman Empire.* Lanham, MD: Scarecrow Press, 2003.

Sugar, Peter. *Southeastern Europe under Ottoman Rule, 1354–1805.* Seattle: University of Washington Press, 1977.

Zéevi, Dror. *Producing Desire: Changing Sexual Discourse in the Ottoman Middle East, 1500–1900.* Berkeley: University of California Press, 2006.

Zürcher, Erik-Jan. *Turkey: A Modern History.* London: I. B. Tauris, 2004.

FILMS, DOCUMENTARIES, AND CD-ROM

Suleyman the Magnificent
National Gallery of Art, Metropolitan Museum of Art, 1987
Format: VHS/NTSC. 57 minutes

The Ottoman Empire
Films Media Group, 1996
Format: VHS/DVD, 47 minutes

Istanbul: Crossroads of Civilizations, Melting Pots of Religions
Mutgan Films, 2004
Format: DVD, NTSC, Subtitled, 142 minutes

Hidden Turkey
PBS Home Video, 2005
Format: DVD, NTSC, 60 minutes

Turkey: Volume 1, Gate to the East-Turkish Coasts & Istanbul
Education 2000, 2005
Format: DVD, NTSC, 57 minutes

Ottoman Empire: The War Machine
The History Channel, 2006
Format: NTSC/DVD, 120 minutes

Cities of the Underworld: Istanbul
The History Channel, 2006
Format: close-captioned, Color, DVD-Video, NTSC, 50 minutes

Lonely Planet Six Degrees Series 3: Istanbul
Beyond Entertainment Limited, 2006
Format: DVD, NTSC, 60 minutes

Global Treasures: Topkapi, Istanbul, Turkey
TravelVideoStore.Com, 2007
Format: DVD, NTSC, 10 minutes

Global Treasures: Hagia Sophia, Istanbul, Turkey
TravelVideoStore.Com, 2007
Format: DVD, NTSC, 10 minutes

Global Treasures: Blue Mosque, Sultan Ahmed Mosque, Istanbul, Turkey
TravelVideoStore.Com, 2007
Format: DVD, NTSC, 10 minutes

Global Treasures: Dolmabahce, Istanbul, Turkey
TravelVideoStore.Com, 2007
Format: DVD, NTSC, 10 minutes

Global Treasures: Istanbul-Old City, Turkey
TravelVideoStore.Com, 2007
Format: DVD, NTSC, 10 minutes

Islamic Mysticism: The Sufi Way
Hartley Film Foundation, 2009
Format: DVD, NTSC, 30 minutes

Cities of the World: Istanbul, Turkey
Shepherd Entertainment, 2009
Format: DVD, NTSC, 60 minutes

WEBSITES

Athanasios Gekas, "A Global History of Ottoman Cotton Textiles, 1600–1850," European University Institute, Max Weber Programme, 2007. http://cadmus.eui.eu/dspace/bitstream/1814/8132/1/MWP-2007-30.pdf

The Bruce Museum of Arts and Science, "Empire of the Sultans," October 2001. http://antiquesandthearts.com/%5CGH0-10-23-2001-13-25-35

Burak Sansal, "All About Turkey," 1996–2010. http://www.allabouttur key.com/index.htm

Elisa Turner, "Topkapi: Ft. Lauderdale Showcases the Opulence of a Powerful Empire," *Miami Herald*, October 22, 2000. http://www2.fiu.edu/~tosun/tsa/topkapi_palace.htm

Gunsel Renda, "The Image of the Turks in European Art," May 2008. http://turkishimage.blogspot.com/2008_05_01_archive.html

Kevin Kenjar, "Balkan Culinary Nationalism and Ottoman Heritage," March 5, 2007. http://classics.uc.edu/~campbell/Kenjar/Culinary-Nationalism.pdf

Michael Palomino, "Encyclopedia Judaica: Jews in the Ottoman Empire 13: Cultural Life," 2008. http://www.geschichteinchronologie.ch/ottoman/EncJud_juden-ottoman13-kulturleben-ENGL.html

Naim Güleryüz, "A History of Turkish Jews," 2006. http://www.mersina.com/lib/turkish_jews/history/index.html

Nejat Muallimoglu, "From the Turkish Delights, A Treasury of Proverbs and Folk Saying," New York, 1988. http://www.ottomansouvenir.com/Turkish_Proverbs/Turkish_Proverbs_3.htm

The Textile Museum, Washington, DC, "The Carron Collection Ltd.," February–July, 2000. http://www.caron-net.com/may00files/may 00fea.html

The Textile Museum, "Flowers of Silk and Gold: Four Centuries of Ottoman Embroidery," Washington, DC, 2000. http://www.textilemu seum.org/fsg/teachers/index.html

Turkish Cultural Foundation, "The Tradition of Coffee and Coffeehouses Among Turks," 2010. http://www.turkishculture.org/pages.php?ChildID=204&ParentID=12&ID=56&ChildID1=204

INDEX

About the Author

MEHRDAD KIA is the associate provost for international programs and the director of the Central and Southwest Asian Studies Center at the University of Montana.